In Pursuit of Silence

Also by George Prochnik

Putnam Camp: Sigmund Freud, James Jackson Putnam,
and the Purpose of American Psychology

George Prochnik

DOUBLEDAY

New York   London   Toronto   Sydney   Auckland

IN
PURSUIT
OF
SILENCE

Listening for Meaning
in a World of Noise

ⅅⅅ
DOUBLEDAY

www.doubleday.com

DOUBLEDAY and the DD colophon are registered trademarks of Random House, Inc.

Book design by Maria Carella

Library of Congress Cataloging-in-Publication Data
Prochnik, George.
In pursuit of silence : listening for meaning in a world of noise / by
George Prochnik.—1st ed.
p. cm.
Includes bibliographical references.
1. Noise—Psychological aspects. 2. Silence. I. Title.
BF353.5.N65P76 2010
155.9'115—dc22   2009041991

ISBN 978-0-385-52888-7

PRINTED IN THE UNITED STATES OF AMERICA

1 3 5 7 9 10 8 6 4 2

First Edition

For Rebecca,

who knew when to speak and when to fall silent

Contents

In Pursuit of Silence

Introduction

One spring day I went in pursuit of silence in downtown Brooklyn. I live not far away from the place where I began my search, on a leafy street that is, relatively speaking, a haven of quiet in a relentless city. I have a small garden, and the rooms where I sleep, work, and spend time with loved ones are surrounded by old, thick walls. Even so, I'm woken by traffic helicopters; I'm aggravated by sirens and construction (often these days by music played on the sites rather than by sounds of actual building). And then there are screeching bus brakes, rumbling trucks unsettling manhole lids, and the unpredictable eruptions of my neighbors' sound systems. I'm scared of becoming a noise crank, but I've just always loved quiet. I love to have conversations without straining to hear. I love, frankly, staring up from my book into space and following my thoughts without having any sound crashing down, demanding attention. I love playing a game with my child while he floats on his back in the bath in which I have him name all the different sounds he can hear at a given moment, from water burbling in the pipes, to the electricity zizzing behind the lights, to a cat thumping off the couch below, to the skirmishing of squirrels on a heavy branch outside. I like there to be an abundance of noises for us to listen to—not just one blast overwhelming the rest. When I start worrying that I'm making too big a fuss about conserving silence, I try to remember lofty examples from history of people who defended quiet. There's a lovely quote from Supreme Court justice Felix Frankfurter that I come back to: "The men whose labors brought forth the Constitution of the United States had the street outside Independence Hall covered with earth so that their deliberations might not be disturbed by passing traffic. Our democracy presupposed the deliberative process as a condition of thought and of responsible choice by the electorate."

The idea that quiet and the democratic process go together is an inspiring one. But I can't say it completely assuages the anxiety associated with sensitivity to sound. And I've had my passion for quiet as long as I can remember. I've snitched on contractors who started work early. I've battled neighbors who hold large parties—and befriended them to get into their parties as a way of trying to befriend the noise itself. I've worn so many earplugs (powerful, swimming-pool-blue Hearos from the Xtreme Protection Series) that if they were laid end to end they'd probably manage to extend all the way around a New York City block. My yearning for quiet has inspired family jokes, rolled eyes, and long sighs. My most notorious moment occurred when I called our cable company to come check out the volume of sound that the DVR made when it was turned off. I wasn't home when the cable man showed up, and my wife was forced to try and help him make out the faint clicking projecting from deep inside the machine. ("There, can you—there, no—wait, I think that's it. Isn't that it? Maybe if you bend a little closer . . .") It's an incident I will never live down. But how could I explain that it wasn't so much the noise the recorder made as the silence it took away from what had been an otherwise remarkably quiet room that made the sound so painful?

I reached a point a couple of years ago when I'd had it. I was as tired of hearing myself complain about noise as I was about the noise itself. It was time to *do* something. I wanted to understand whether my sensitivity to sound and longing for silence was ridiculous—or maybe worse, like the state of the narrator at the start of Edgar Allan Poe's "The Tell-Tale Heart," who observes, "Above all was the sense of hearing acute. I heard all things in the heaven and in the earth. I heard many things in hell. How, then, am I mad?" If, on the other hand, there was something of real value in silence that was being placed at risk by all the noise of our society, what was it exactly? And was there anything we could do to cultivate more of it? Instead of just grumbling and weeping (or at least whimpering quietly to myself) about all the noise, what about trying to find something positive in silence to aspire to? Instead of being against noise, what about searching out reasons *for* silence? That was where my search began. And that search became this book.

※

My first sortie into silence was to the Quakers. Large numbers of people from almost every faith harbor associations between God, the state of godliness, and silence. Indeed, if one were to look for shared theological (as opposed to ethical) ground between religions, a good starting point would be silence. We all might be able to come up with a list of reasons for why silence evokes the holy, such as a kinship with peace and contemplation. But if we scratch the surface a little, the connection becomes less self-evident. Why should something imagined to be infinite and all-powerful be associated with soundlessness? And what about all the associations between silence and indifference, or even collaboration with evil, which somehow coexist with the positive, sacred notions of silence? I wanted to better understand what led people to think of silence as both a route to God and a reflection of God's nature.

I visited the Brooklyn Friends Meeting, held in a lovely mid-nineteenth-century stone building with tall windows cut into walls the shade of lemon frosting. At first the room seemed almost supernaturally quiet. The shadow of one mullioned window frame slipped in and out of visibility across the light-brown carpet with the passage of clouds across the sky. No one around me was even coughing. Everybody sat very still, usually quite straight against the pews, with their legs together and their hands cupped or folded in their laps. More Friends came into the chamber, eventually forming a racially and generationally diverse congregation. I found the Quaker strain of quiet most appealing for the ways that it did not seem aimed primarily at the individual self. Though many people closed their eyes, not everyone did, and the silence felt less inwardly focused than communally aware. For what felt like a long time, there was no sound except for the door occasionally opening and closing to admit additional Friends, the creaking of the wooden benches as people shuffled their weight into place.

After about twenty minutes, there came a digital trilling, repeated several times before being shut off. A moment later, a heavyset man in his early forties rose to his feet. He had pleasantly fuzzy auburn hair tied back in a ponytail. "I apologize for my cell phone having gone off. I forgot to turn it off when I came into the meeting. But before it went off I was thinking of all sorts of worldly things—all sorts of things I had to do were running through my mind, and I was asking myself whether I really had time for this . . . And then my cell phone went off." Chuckles relayed around the room. "But we can't allow ourselves to become too distracted by worldly things from the things that matter. We have to make time for the meetings." He sat back down.

Over the next half hour, several other people rose abruptly to their feet and began speaking. At one point, I noticed a man of about fifty with a gray, drooping mustache sitting some distance away from me with his hands on his thighs. As I watched, his denim shirt began fluttering out from his chest in the most remarkable manner, as though there really were a turbulent, divine breath "quaking" to get out of him. What was most astonishing was that I couldn't see him move a muscle of his body; there was just that wild billowing of his shirt. Suddenly, he jerked up to his feet, stood rigid for a moment, then parted his lips. "How much we know, and how little we do." And then he launched into a parable about the way the desire to save the whole world can be an impediment to taking even one small action to improve it.

After the meeting, different people gave me their thoughts about Quaker silence. One heavily bearded frontier trading post of a man told me that there were different levels of silence and that while "sometimes you feel everyone sinking into it, sometimes it sings." A gentle female professor of medieval studies spoke of the idea of worshipping in silence as an antidote to the distraction of noise. A short, bald man with very dark eyebrows and very black mod glasses described the silence as "definitely a listening. Because basically Quakers believe there is that of God in all of us."

The first book of Kings declares that God will manifest not in a great tempest or rumbling of the earth but after the cataclysm, in the "thin voice of silence." In its essence, this idea is shared by many faiths. For many people, silence is the way God speaks to us, and when we ourselves are in silence, we are speaking the language of the soul. This was not my experience, exactly. My encounters with the religious life have been ever hopeful, and ever disappointed (if not with the particular faith, with my self; if not with my self, with the particular faith). But later I recalled how after only a few moments of being inside the high-ceilinged meeting room, surrounded by people all sitting in silence, I became more aware of the sun than I'd been while standing outside the building's entrance.

⌗

I had another experience early on in my exploration of silence that pointed to the effect silence can have on appreciation of the natural world.

I got it into my head that it was vital I speak with an astronaut. Astronauts, I imagined, were exposed to the most spectacular juxtaposition of noise and silence conceivable. What could be louder than a rocket launch? And what could be quieter than the depths of space? It seemed to me that the contrast between these two experiences, appearing as it did in so short a span of time, would give astronauts a unique insight into the essence of silence.

After weeks of back and forth with Houston, I got the welcome news that astronaut Suni Williams would grant me a fifteen-minute interview. I read her NASA biography. She had logged more than 2,770 hours in space on 30 different aircraft, and had clocked a spacewalking world record. In addition to serving on helicopter combat squadrons and U.S. Navy diving details, and helping to develop the International Space Station Robotic Arm, she listed her hobbies as including "running, swimming, biking, triathlons, windsurfing, snowboarding and bow hunting." Whatever Williams said about anything was not to be taken lightly.

Quickly and unassumingly Williams shot down 90 percent of my suppositions. The noise of takeoff these days was nothing really to speak of—hardly louder than what you'd hear being on an airplane. In fact, for years NASA had been involved in some of the most advanced noise-abatement work on the planet, and the sleeping area of the space station was now one of the quietest places you could ever hope to find. Ventilation systems had been redesigned. New kinds of formfitting earplugs had been perfected. "Tonal measures" had been built into the walls and doors.

Just as the launch wasn't all that loud, Williams explained, walking in space wasn't all that quiet. Ground control was in constant contact—"and when you have people from the ground telling you 'do this, don't do that' all the time, you don't feel the silence of space so much."

Of course, I thought, the sound from their support team on

Earth was pumped directly into the astronauts' ears, making sure they weren't drifting away or otherwise deviating from the mission assigned them. I felt embarrassed at my ignorance and ready to truncate our interview. But then, after a short pause, Williams began to speak again.

"Reflecting back, there was one time I remember feeling quiet in space. We were out on a spacewalk and were asked to wait for the night pass to go through." (The night pass is the forty-five minutes of its ninety-minute orbit when the spacecraft is on the dark side of the planet.) While they were waiting, the chatter from Houston died down, then cut out altogether. "So we were just hanging out there, quiet, just hearing ourselves breathe out there at the end of the station," Williams continued. "And it was like putting on a pair of glasses . . . Everything, all at once so clear, like after a wonderful rainstorm . . . You could see the stars really bright. You could see the depth of space."

In that brief spell of silence, Williams faced the brilliant, untethered magnitude of our universe.

Henry David Thoreau writes in his account of a voyage he took on the Concord and Merrimack Rivers that all sounds are, ultimately, servants and purveyors of silence. As he rows through the quiet of night, the splash and trickle from his oars lead his gaze upward: "the valleys echoed the sound to the stars." Sounds, he declares, are but a "faint utterance" of silence, "and then only agreeable to our auditory nerves when they contrast themselves with and relieve the former."

This idea of a nourishing contrast works two ways. Just as

certain sounds can throw the silence enfolding us into high relief, silences mold sound. In another expedition I made near the outset of my journey, this time to a laboratory, I saw how the current of silence flowing beneath our utterances enables us to segment what we hear into meaningful speech.

Dr. Mario Svirsky is a professor of hearing science in the Department of Otolaryngology at New York University Langone Medical Center. Given his profession, it's impossible not to notice the handsome Svirsky's enormous Vulcan ears, which he's chosen to highlight by piercing their lobes with gleaming hoops that shine like rings of Saturn. I had asked Svirsky to explain the process of sound filtering. I wanted to understand how we are able to pick out the voice we want to listen to in a room crowded with other speakers.

He turned to his computer screen. "Here, I can show you," he said. "Let's make a sound." He spoke into a microphone attached to the computer. "Hello. Hello. Hello." As he spoke, multicolored jagged lines, representing all the different frequencies and temporal modulations of his speech, danced out across the screen.

"You see how there are lots of little peaks—clusters of activity—and then there are long, almost flat lines," he continued. "Those long lines are the areas where sound has windows— spaces of relative silence; spaces of lower energy. It's when the windows line up that we're able to pick out a single voice if more than one person is speaking."

I stared for a long time at the image of Svirsky's analyzed speech wave. The idea that even when we're talking there is silence embedded in our words seemed marvelous to me. When we make sounds, it's often the silent falls built into those sounds that enable them to function as signals of communication rather than noise. Or at least that's what's supposed to happen. Svirsky indicated one of the bright clumps of sharp points on his screen and resumed talking. "At the places where the energy peaks overlap, it will obviously be hardest to make out what any voice is saying." He shrugged. "It's the windows of silence in our speech that may be in danger today with the rise of ambient noise."

⚎

The roots of our English term "silence" sink down through the language in multiple directions. Among the word's antecedents is the Gothic verb *anasilan*, a word that denotes the wind dying down, and the Latin *dēsinere*, a word meaning "stop." Both of these etymologies suggest the way that silence is bound up with the idea of interrupted action. The pursuit of silence, likewise, is dissimilar from most other pursuits in that it generally begins with a surrender of the chase, the abandonment of efforts to impose our will and vision on the world. Not only is it about standing still; with rare exceptions, the pursuit of silence seems initially to involve a step backward from the tussle of life. The different stories that first drove home to me what the engagement with silence could bring were centered on a kind of listening that only occurs after a break in the circuit of busyness. But it's as though, as a culture, we've learned to "mind the gaps" so well that they've all but disappeared. We live in an age of incessancy, under the banner of the already heard and forgotten.

Part of what makes snowfall in a city magical is the way that muted sound and the sight of buildings and cars draped in whiteness go together. If we're not too worried about missing appointments, we feel the excitement of moving into a new place where none of the old clutter and racket of our lives has yet arrived. We might think of sound, by way of contrast, as a force that stitches us in time and space. We twist when we hear the sound of our name. We wake to the alarm, the baby's cry, the whiny grind of a garbage truck. Bells, gongs, whistles, drums, horns, and guns are "sounded" to announce the hour of the day and to launch significant events. A painter friend of mine once told me that he thought of sound as an usher for the here and now. When he was a small child, Adam suffered an illness that left him profoundly deaf for several months. His memories of that time are vivid and not, he insists, at all negative. Indeed, they opened a world in which the images he saw could be woven together with much greater freedom and originality than he'd ever known. The experience was powerful enough that it helped steer him toward his lifelong immersion in the visual arts. "Sound imposes a narrative on you," he said, "and it's always someone else's narrative. My experience of silence was like being awake inside a dream I could direct."

While the extremity of Adam's experience might appeal to only the most dedicated pursuers of silence, the larger idea of silence as a break, a rest, a road to reflection, renewal, and personal growth is one that resonates with many people. And beyond the many individual stories I heard that testified to this potential of silence, there are increasing hints from the world of neuroscience that support the notion of silence as a fertile pause. Recent studies using fMRI technology have shown that the brains of people who practice silent meditation appear to work more efficiently than the brains of people who do not. This may have something to do with ways in which silence enhances our powers of attention, subtracting auditory distractions that dissipate our mental energy. Neuroscientists at Stanford University have demonstrated that when we listen to music it is the silent intervals in what we hear that trigger the most intense, positive brain activity. In part, this reflects the way our brains are always searching for closure. When we confront silence, the mind reaches outward.

Other intriguing possibilities for how silence might benefit us on a systemic level suggest affinities between certain stages of sleep and silence. With all the lingering mysteries surrounding sleep, we now have abundant clinical evidence that the suspension of our conscious activity brought about by sleep is essential for our health. Silence, which interrupts the general noise of our day-to-day lives, may carry some of the replenishing power we take from the full rest of sleep. If we can't find a place to lie down in the midst of our working days, we may still reap some of sleep's benefits by finding a relatively quiet space in which to take a sound break.

※

There are numerous personal stories and considerable scientific evidence suggesting that silence can exert a positive influence on our individual lives and our relationship to the world. Nearly everyone I raised the subject with went into rhapsodies about how much they loved quiet, while lamenting the fact they did not have more of it to recharge their minds, bodies, and spirits. But if everyone values silence so highly, why is there so little of it? Why,

I wondered, does there appear to be a growing consensus about the benefits of silence at the same time as the world seems, on so many fronts, to be getting noisier?

Many people feel victimized by the loud noises besieging them from all sides. Traffic noise—road, air, and marine—undoubtedly represents a problem that extends beyond individual control. The same could be said about construction noise, heavy industry, and the sound of power generators. The stress of these forms of noise can be deadly, especially in the developing world, where loud generators are everywhere, and where some experts now suggest that 45,000 fatal heart attacks per year may be attributable to noise-related cardiovascular strain. But while much more can and must be done to reduce the impact of these macroscale sound offenders, they are not the whole story. Indeed, the biggest, most obnoxious noisemakers may actually be blocking a subtler, perhaps even deeper noise problem than that presented by our perpetually jammed highways.

When I first began to speak with audiologists, cochlear implant surgeons, and neuroscientists about the benefits of silence, they were, if anything, even more worked up about the risks presented by what they saw as our increasingly loud world than the nonprofessionals had been. A study released by the Johns Hopkins University in July 2008 reported that the incidence of hearing loss in the United States is approaching epidemic proportions. According to this study, a staggering one in three Americans now suffers some degree of hearing impairment— much of it noise induced. However, the doctors and scientists I spoke with did not talk about jackhammers and jets, or about highways and factories. Rather, the experts spoke to me about personal sound devices. Tom Roland, director of NYU Medical Center's Department of Cochlear Implants, told me, "Anytime you can hear someone else's music leaking through their headphones or earbuds, that person is causing themselves hearing damage." Hearing specialists also brought up cell phones and electronic toys. You can buy a Hannah Montana in Concert Collection Doll that reaches 103 decibels, and a Tickle Me Elmo that hits a rocking 100 decibels—acoustically comparable to tickling a snowmobile. Computer games are often cranked higher still. Neuroscientists who work on the problem of hearing loss didn't talk to me about noise in terms of single jolts of sound but rather about duration of exposure to adult and children's gadgetry, like air conditioners and white-noise machines, that were turned on by the same people who were losing their hearing. The professionals brought up the hazards of what might have been considered by an earlier generation to be luxury noise: the sounds we choose to surround ourselves with, the discretionary clamor that shields us from the unsought tumult beyond.

The special character of the new noisiness was driven home to me one summer weekend when I rode around Washington, D.C., with an officer from the Metropolitan Police to find out how the force responds to noise complaints. John Spencer was a large, unassuming, talkative man who'd grown up in high-crime neighborhoods of the city, worked all his life for the District police, and had retained few illusions about human nature or the capacities of the law to muzzle it.

The first noise complaint arrived around one in the morning and took us down a dark, narrow street. Officer Spencer slowed the pace of his cruiser to a crawl. He turned off the blasting air conditioner, since it was impossible to hear anything outside the vehicle with the conditioner on full power the way he liked it. Still, nothing was audible. Officer Spencer pushed a button and cracked the window half an inch. He peered up at the houses, literally cocking his ear at one point and then shaking his head. At the end of the street he shrugged, rolled the window back up, and we continued on our leisurely orbit of the neighborhood. A little while later, we drove down a street full of bars with pounding music and mobs of people whooping on the sidewalk, shoving and spilling onto the streets. I looked at Officer Spencer expectantly. He shrugged again. As far as the police were concerned, if there were no complaints, there was no noise.

When the bars at last shut, we were called to intervene with a disorderly trio of plastered young women hollering outside a closed restaurant. After this, a call alerted us to a boom box set up on a folding lawn chair on a small patch of grass in front of a housing complex. But it wasn't playing very loudly, and there was no one around to tell to turn it down. We drove on. Although it was the Friday before July Fourth—a night that my liaison officer with the force had told me was a night of surefire noise—it seemed that, at least in the ears of the law, this was to be a silent night. Every so often the car radio crackled with the dispatcher reporting a fight somewhere. Officer Spencer would shake his head and tell me that the complaint was not in our precinct. When the dispatcher would repeat the call, he would shake his head again and repeat, with a harassed edge to his voice, that the problem belonged to another patrol.

All of a sudden, at about three in the morning, Officer Spencer turned to me and said, "You know, I'll tell you something. The majority of domestic disputes we get called into these days are actually noise complaints." What did he mean? I asked. "You go into these houses where the couple, or the roommate, or the whole family is fighting and yelling and you've got the television blaring so you can't think, and a radio on top of that, and somebody got home from work who wants to relax or to sleep, and it's just obvious what they're actually fighting about. They're fighting about the noise. They don't know it, but that's the problem. They've just got everything on at once. And so the first thing I'll say to them is, 'You know what, don't even tell me what you think you're fighting about! First, turn down the music. Switch off the game station. Turn down the television.' Then I just let them sit there for a minute, and I say to them, 'Now that feels different, doesn't it? Maybe the real reason you were fighting is how *loud* it was inside your apartment. Do you still have anything to tell me? Do you?' Well, you would be amazed how often that's the end of it."

⚒

It was the recognition of this new noisiness that made me realize my search would have to be twofold. In order to understand the pursuit of silence, it would be necessary, also, to track the pursuit of noise. The two were bound together—each, in its own way, was reactive. Something seems to have made us as a society fall in love with noise. It's a torrid, choppy affair that we are often in denial about, or tend to laugh off as a bass-heavy, summer's night fling. But it seems to have a surprisingly tenacious hold on us, and if we are ever going to begin making a serious investment in the cultivation of silence, we have to understand how we became so entangled with noise. We have to explore what silence has to offer, and the different factors that stimulated us to become so loud, as two halves of a single problem.

The two pursuits took me many places: from neurobiology laboratories to Zen gardens, shopping malls, and conventions of soundproofers; from a Trappist monastery to a manufacturer of noise-measurement instruments, and an extreme car-audio competition. Each place I traveled added another layer to the story, and I came, at the end, to understand the difficulty of pursuing silence—and the reasons why this pursuit has become more vital than ever before. I hope that what I learned opens other lines of thought about what a societal investment in silence might contribute to our lives, and adds a little awareness about ways we may be hurtling forward in flight from the very silence we profess to cherish.

✴

Part of the challenge in this project is that, while the pursuit of noise is one we can undertake with supreme confidence of success, nobody really triumphs in pursuit of silence in the strict sense of the word until they cease to exist. The pursuit of silence in this life is fated to be endless and imperfect. This is one reason why the pursuit of silence often turns us deeper and deeper inward. In this spirit, Gene Lushtak, who leads silent Buddhist retreats in the Bay Area, told me a story about Ajahn Chah, the most prominent leader of twentieth-century Thai Buddhism.

A young monk came to live in the monastery where Ajahn Chah was practicing. The people who lived in the town outside the monastery were holding a series of festivals in which they sang and danced all night long. When the monks would rise at three thirty in the morning to begin their meditation, the parties from the night before would still be going strong. At last, one morning the young monk cried out to Ajahn Chah, "Venerable One, the noise is interrupting my practice—I can't meditate with all this noise!" "The noise isn't bothering you," Ajahn responded. "You are bothering the noise." As Lushtak put it to me, "Silence is not a function of what we think of as silence. It's when my reaction is quiet. What's silent is my protest against the way things are."

This poignant sentiment recurred to me throughout my search. It represents, in fact, the great dilemma behind the advocacy of silence: To effectively promote silence, how does one avoid becoming louder than the sources of noise one is protesting against? If there's a way out of this conundrum, I believe it involves the kind of acute listening I was introduced to at the outset of my own exploration. Throughout the course of writing this book, I found myself asking what it was that people were trying to hear, and what it was that they were trying to block out. The loudest argument for quiet may be a reflection on what otherwise remains in danger of going unheard.

CHAPTER ONE

Listening for the Unknown

On my second night in the monastery, I heard the silence. I was inside the church: a beautiful, vast chamber of limestone blocks that resemble lumpy oatmeal and were quarried from the Iowan earth by the monks themselves in the mid-nineteenth century. The monks had finished compline, the last of the day's seven prayer services, and had filed off into the inner recesses of the monastery, where they would observe the Great Silence, speaking to no one until after mass the next morning. The last of the monks to leave had switched off the lights above the choir, and then the light over the lectern. Though the section of visitors' pews where I sat still had a little illumination, the body of the church was now in total blackness except for the faint flickering of a votive candle suspended high in the distance against the far wall. For the first quarter hour, a few worshippers remained on the benches around me.

Although I sat very quietly, I found my mind busy and loud.

Mostly I was reflecting on the service I had just heard, which Brother Alberic, my gracious liaison to the world of the monastery, had described as a kind of lullaby. Compline is lovely, and I was frustrated that I had not been able to find it more profound. These weren't my prayers. I yearned only for more quiet. My thoughts were noisy enough that I half expected to see them break out of my skull and begin dancing a musical number up and down the wooden benches.

Soon the other worshippers departed and I was left alone. For a moment or two, my experience was of literal silence. Then, all at once, there came a *ting*, a *tic*, another *tic*, a *tap*, and a *clang*. The sounds came from all around the enormous dark church. They ranged from the verge of inaudibility to the violence of hammer blows; discrete chips of sound and reverberatory *gonnngs*. Out of nowhere, I was treated to a concert by the sound of heat in the pipes. It was a grand, slightly menacing sound that I had been oblivious to not only during the prayer service but afterward in the din of my mental dithering. And it was worth that long opening pause. The ever-changing sonic punctuation of this empty space—which had first seemed soundless—gave me a tingling sense of elevation. This is it, I told myself. Silence made everything resonate.

And yet . . . Later that night when I retreated to my room, and my euphoria had subsided, I wondered why I had been affected so powerfully. Objectively, the only thing that had happened, after all, was that I had heard the metal of the pipes expanding and contracting as they heated and cooled. Why should that experience have made me feel that I was "hearing the silence"? Why did I feel at that lonely hour that I had found what I was looking for when I came to the monastery?

❖

What brought me to the New Melleray Abbey in Dubuque, Iowa, was the desire to learn from people who had made a lifelong commitment to devout silence. Trappist monks, a branch of the Cistercian order, do not make a vow of total silence, and today there are times when they engage in conversation; but silence is their mother tongue. Saint Benedict, who is credited with founding Western Christian monasticism in the sixth century, most famously at Monte Cassino, southeast of Rome, wrote a document known as the Rule that remains their guide to this day. In the Rule, monks are defined before all else as disciples, and the defining quality of the disciple is "to be silent and listen." Trappists are among the monks known as "contemplatives." Their interaction with the world outside the monastery is minimal. Much of their worship is silent. They study in silence. They work almost entirely in silence. They eat primarily in silence. They pass each other in the monastery corridors without speaking. They retire at 8 PM to separate cells and rise at 3:15 AM, when they gather in silence to pray. They avoid idle talk at all times. And even after the morning mass, throughout much of their demanding day, they are discouraged from speaking. Almost everything the Trappist does takes place in silence—is pressed close by its weight, or opens out onto that expanse, depending on how you look at it.

Monks have, moreover, been at the pursuit for quite some

time. Alberic remarked at one point that while it is often said that prostitution is the oldest profession, he believes that monks were around before there were prostitutes. This struck me as unlikely, but it still gave me pause.

There was a personal stake in this journey as well: I needed a break. I'd had a hectic, noisy winter in the city—medically harrowing, filled with bills, the hassles of insurance claims, technology fiascos, and preschool worries. Plans to visit friends in the country had fallen through several times. I'd tried to go to a Zen retreat in New England that taught the breath- and silence-based meditation practice of vipassana, only to be told at the last moment that although I could come and sit silently with the retreatants, the guesthouse itself was overbooked and I'd have to stay in a bed-and-breakfast in town. The thought of beginning my daily practice over fussy French toast in a dining room packed with antiquers—where tasteful classical music would be piped in to glaze over the gaps in conversation—didn't conduce to inner quiet. I had to get out of New York. Yet it was hard to arrange anything. Just because we have a nagging sense that silence is good for us doesn't make it any easier to actually commit to.

I didn't think of quiet only as one of those overdue restoratives. Beyond the idea of wanting to learn something about the Trappist path and get away from the noise in my own life, I was hoping to find some truth in the silence of the monastery that I could take back to New York. I'd packed a stack of books and volumes of photocopied pages representing different theological and philosophical traditions—everything from Martin Heidegger and Max Picard to kabbalistic disquisitions, an array of Buddhist tracts, and enough Christian monastic literature to envelop a monk from tonsure to toe. I needed help.

THE DESERT

From the air, the Great Plains in winter look like silence. During Advent week, when I made my trip to the monastery, the freeze of the landscape was so extreme that I couldn't imagine anything down below ever vibrating. On the approach to Dubuque, the snow-covered squares of the farms resembled bathroom tiles painted over with primer that had bubbled and cracked. As we descended, the topographical buckling intensified; clumps of frayed brown trees bristled up through the white; little snow-crusted settlements traced ghostly circuit boards. We flew past clusters of red farm buildings with steep, snow-caked roofs. Then we circled 180 degrees, a seam of pale orange-gold suddenly opened across an endless gray horizon, and the plane touched down.

After we exchanged greetings, the first thing Alberic said was that I was in for some particularly ugly weather, even by Iowa standards. His voice was sad.

Alberic is a solidly built man a little above average height, in his early fifties. He wears round, dark-framed glasses over dark, shadowed eyes. His black hair is cropped close to the skull, and whenever he is at home he wears a full-length white robe beneath a long black apron with a pointy hood. Alberic "entered monastery to stay," as he puts it, in 1984. At the age of tw he was working as a security guard at the Metropoli of Art in New York City, spending his free tir living a kind of bare-bones bohemian existence. Though he'd grown up with some degree of wealth, mostly in the suburbs of Atlanta, he had never liked "stuff" and had always sought out a life of austerity. Raised a Catholic, and always seeking silence— his mother called him "the little Buddha"—Alberic had given up active involvement in the church long before moving to New York. After several years of work at the museum, mostly on the night watch, he began to sink into a spiritual malaise. Then he learned that his sister was dying of cancer. Three weeks after her death, he was diagnosed with the same disease. "That was my wake-up call, and the beginning of my monastic formation," Alberic told me. "It took the cancer for me to look in the mirror and ask myself, 'What am I doing here?' "

For the first year after his diagnosis, he struggled with fear. Then, as his odds for survival began to improve, he started a gradual return to the church that brought him, eventually, to visit a monastery near Atlanta. He got lost on the way and arrived at night, just before compline. The church, when he entered, was quiet and dark. Then the monks walked in, their white cowls falling all the way to the floor. "I was transfixed," Alberic said. "I saw the truth about myself. I saw my monastic soul externalized. There was no sound, just the vague rustling of robes as they came in one or two at a time, to kneel or stand in their stall. All my life I'd met priests who tried to evangelize, but nothing came close to that moment. I had a sense of God walking right up to me." The experience, he said, "hijacked my life. I realized I'd 'ways been a monk, and now I was home."

"Monks live in the desert," Alberic told me, after we'd driven back to the monastery and had a chance to sit down together. "These giant, snow-covered fields are the desert. It's where monks have always been drawn. We come for a radical confrontation with ourselves. Silence is for bumping into yourself. That's why monks pursue it. And that's also why people can't get into a car without turning the radio on, or walk into a room without switching on a television. They seek to avoid that confrontation. I think this may be one reason for the incredible violence of that final surge during the Gulf War." I stared at him in surprise. He lowered his eyes. "You remember there were those long, long delays before the last invasion, with waves of troops going over there and just sitting in the desert, week after week. The soldiers just sat and waited in more silence than many of them had ever experienced. And then, all of a sudden there was that huge, violent surge—the Highway of Death. Americans don't sit in a quiet, solitary place and flourish. They were starting to have a monastic experience. And that doesn't jibe well with the military's goals."

Explaining the carnage on Highway 80 en route to Basra was, at the least, a provocative claim for the transformative power of even short-term exposure to monastic silence. But Alberic is clearly not alone in his belief that a taste of monk's life can wreak meaningful changes on a person's mind and spirit. Like many other monasteries around the world, New Melleray Abbey has something close to an all-time low in terms of permanent resident members—and a constantly overspilling guesthouse. Brother Neal, the monk in charge of bookkeeping at New Melleray, told me that whereas even five or six years ago if someone contacted the abbey during the workweek saying that they wanted to make a retreat or just visit for a night or two there was always room, now it is often booked solid long in advance. "There's much more hunger," he said. "People just looking for quiet."

There are now silent retreats offered in the name of almost every belief system, and at least one interfaith silent retreat, in Virginia, in which a swami, a Catholic priest, a rabbi, and a sheikh work together to guide retreatants, as the description reads, to "their own unique experience of inner peace, joy and spiritual unity at the heart of all the faiths." Spas are increasingly promoted as a retreat from the overstimulation of everyday life, as much as for their treatments and aesthetic services. ("Our philosophy . . . is simple," begins one advertisement. "Soothe the spirit and beauty will follow. We intend to be a quiet refuge.") The same longing for respite is driving people into the jungles of Thailand to visit Buddhist monasteries, sometimes for months at a time. The numbers of ten-day silent vipassana retreats offered in Southern California are multiplying, and there has been a recent surge in shorter "McRetreats" for teenagers—along with meditation classes for children as young as eight years old. Gene Lushtak and some of his fellow silent-meditation guides in the Bay Area are now being enlisted by the public school systems to provide sessions in "mindfulness and concentration," a stealth way of introducing silent meditation in the classroom. "Teachers are scared," Lushtak told me. "They can't get the kids to settle down, and silent meditation is one of the only things that helps."

At one point, Lushtak put me in touch with a woman named Kris, whom he described as having great insights into silence— someone who had spent considerable time living as a monastic and many years practicing silent meditation. When I called her, Kris spoke to me of how the hunger for silence is "hunger for the thing that silence facilitates or acts as a catalyst of," rather than for the silence itself. "Silence," she continued, "is one experience of getting in touch with that which is. The practitioners and teachers I know who have practiced for many years can walk into a room full of chaos and be as kind and gathered as though they're with a baby, or a lizard." I asked her whether her own experiences with silence had drawn her to devote more and more of her daily life to meditative practices. "You're speaking to me through a speakerphone," she snapped. "I'm a corporate lawyer sitting on the twenty-ninth floor of a downtown skyscraper! But even if I'm not spending as much time with it as when I was wearing little robes in Burma, it's still a key part of my life."

IDENTIFYING WITH SILENCE

When I retired to my plain but pleasant room in the guesthouse of New Melleray, I picked up a few volumes from the mini-library I'd brought with me and sat down in a chair by the window overlooking the courtyard, where a modest stone fountain and a few sprays of black branches thrust up through deep white snow. The room was completely quiet, except for a bar radiator by my feet that made a constant *crickly-crackling*, as though a microphone were being held up to a bowl of Rice Krispies.

When I had told friends that I was going to spend a little time in a Trappist monastery in Iowa, they responded with professions of envy. "You're so lucky! The peace, and *quiet . . .* ," they sighed. Yet the hope of finding a walled-off spa of rest and relaxation was not what drove people to visit monasteries in the past. In earlier ages, when people sought out the ascetic monks they did so to be enlightened as to why we live and die. Just as Benedict thought of the monk as a disciple commanded, above all, to be silent and listen, worldly sorts have always sought out those who cut themselves off from the rest of humanity to hear what they had to say. There is an abiding popular sympathy with the notion expressed by contemplative monks to a synod of bishops after Vatican II, that the monk withdraws from the world not to indulge a lust for ascetic martyrdom but rather "to place himself more intensely at the divine source from which the forces that drive the world onward originate, and to understand in this light the great designs of mankind."

The precursors of the contemplative monks were the men of Egypt who left home in the fourth century to dwell in the desert. This was the great era of perching in silence on top of poles under the burning eye of the North African sun, and fasting sleepless in Tora Bora–style caves while assailed by noisy visions of jeering demons, inviting maidens, and various upsetting combinations of the two. Since the withdrawal from the world that gave the Desert Fathers their name was intended to promote self-transformation, the type of silence with which they were most concerned was that which came when they shut their own lips. As Abbas Diadochus, fifth-century bishop of Photiki, remarked, "Just as, if you leave open the door of the public baths the steam escapes and their virtue is lost, so the virtue of the person who talks a lot escapes the open doors of the voice." One hermit spent three years with a stone in his mouth to help him learn to stay quiet. How he managed to eat enough to survive without swallowing the rock is a matter about which the chronicles remain silent.

When people managed to track down a Desert Father in his desolate lair, they would stand before him to beg, "Abba, a word!" ("Abba" is the Hebrew and Aramaic term for "father," from which the words abbot and abbey derive.) After one anonymous fourth-century truth-seeker had traveled deep into the desert of Scetes to plead for a word from Abbot Moses, the old man dismissed him with a single sentence: "Go and sit in thy cell, and thy cell shall teach thee all things." The parable suggests some of the great questions surrounding silence: How much does our pursuit of silence require us to withdraw from the world? To what extent is silence experiential in a manner that can be neither explained nor conveyed? To what degree must we remain literally still in order to experience the truths of silence?

All of us have intuitive formulas for gauging the point at which silence has been attained. The study of the human reception of sound moves quickly from the realm of physics and physiology to that of psychology and psychoacoustics. Mental associations that we bring to sounds along with intricacies of how the brain maps sound waves define our experience of what we hear.

A sniper named Robert who served with the U.S. military in Iraq described for me the experience of silence in battle. One listens, he said, "for anything that will keep you alive, orienting to any sound that may be a threat, just like an animal." It is in those moments of silence, he explained, when he is maximally focused, before the "fireworks begin and while the silence is everywhere, that the weight of the silence is almost too much." He compared this to an animal trying to orient itself to a threat when there is nothing visible, and nothing to be heard—yet the threat is certain and everywhere. It's in those states, he believes, that we fall within ourselves, our vision narrowing, our hearing becoming fainter. "The more we hear nothing, the more nothing we hear," he went on, "while we wait for . . . for death really. And, maybe, like the animals on the plains in Africa when they are rolled on their backs by the lion and enter some trance-like state before being eaten, I would, in these still moments, feel the weight of silence pulling me into myself, and I would fight against it for a chance to live."

⚎

Theologians push the origins of the pursuit of silence far back in time. The doctrine of *tsimtsum*, developed by Isaac Luria, a sixteenth-century Jewish mystic, makes the pursuit of silence nothing less than the foundational act of the universe.

Luria began his own pursuit as a young man in a series of solitary retreats to islands in the Nile, where he gained renown for being able to interpret the language of birds, swishing palm-tree fronds, and burning embers. (Certain kabbalists thought that after the destruction of the temple, guardian angels used birds as a kind of remote storage for some of the deepest secrets of the Torah, hence their chirping was full of wisdom. Luria kept mum about what the leaves and coals had to say.) Eventually he moved to Safed in Palestine, and there developed the body of mystical thought for which he is most remembered. He himself wrote almost nothing, being constrained by the vastness of the truth he wished to articulate. "I can hardly open up my mouth to speak without feeling as though the sea burst its dams and overflowed," he explained. *Tsimtsum* (roughly translated as "contraction") is also premised on a problem of space. If God is everything—infinite and all-filling—how could there be any room for God's creations? Thus, the first act in genesis had to be God's withdrawal of Himself into Himself in order to make space for anything else. This withdrawal—a kind of inner retreat of the Divine—has been described both as a self-limiting and a self-silencing. (The Jewish identification of God with language makes any pullback on His part a retraction of the Divine tongue.) In Luria's vision, God becomes the original monkish pursuer of silence, retreating into the dark, secluded depths of His nature so that creation would one day have the chance to sing in the light. Early commentators on Luria's theories likened this process to a kind of cosmic inhalation: "How did He produce and create His world? Like a man who holds and restricts his breath, in order that the little may contain the many." Each new expression of God's creative force had to be preceded by another withdrawal, another self-emptying.

A humanistic reading of Luria's myth might lead us to reflect that when we shut up and yank ourselves out of the picture, the world rushes vibrantly into the gap we leave behind—springing into fresh visibility and audibility. The eighteenth-century Hasidic master Nahman of Bratslav, however, invested the lesson of *tsimtsum* with a further mystical twist. Nahman argued that mankind had to reproduce the steps the Divine had gone through in His self-silencing so as to make contact with God's essence. A process of emptying and quieting takes the pursuer deep into an inner void that opens onto the emptiness left behind by God.

Yet once inside what Nahman described as the "mazes of silence," the righteous one discovers that in some inexpressible fashion God exists within the void as well.

What I read about Luria and Nahman called to mind several conversations I'd had with people in which silence triggered a kind of exfoliation of the everyday self. An artist friend named Alfonse, who is also a devout Catholic, told me, "Sometimes when I'm silent and alone, I'll have this feeling of layers of my identity just peeling away, emptying, until I'm down to the core. And when I get there, to that silence, I'm meeting other selves I've loved. All of a sudden, I'm back with my mother and father. They're still here and I'm still with them."

A Buddhist friend described her experience of silent meditation as a never-ending process of emptying herself of thoughts. "By the end of the retreat, the process of getting rid of all this stuff in your head becomes physical," she said. "People are crying—they're coughing—they have colds." The experience has changed how she deals with different situations outside the meditation room. "Whereas before, my mind was constantly vibrating and making noise, I'm much more nonreactive now, which means I see the way everything around me is constantly changing and don't take every little decision I make as life or death. It's like a mental cleansing."

What actually happens inside the brain when we concentrate on experiencing silence?

※

The neuroscientific study of the effects of silent meditation is still in the early stages. But fMRI studies (imaging studies that can track blood flow through the brain) of people involved in vipassana and similar practices consistently show that meditation enhances the ability to make discriminations between important and unimportant stimuli. This translates into a reduction in overall brain activity. Lidia Glodzik-Sobanska, a researcher at the New York University Center for Brain Health, described for me the chain reaction that's set in motion when an individual embarks on an unfamiliar task. Neurons start firing. Glutamate receptors get involved, triggering a process that eventually allows calcium to flow into the cell and activate various enzymes, which in turn initiate other reactions. There is, she said, "an enormous downstream range of events, in which new synaptic connections and branches are being formed." When you're first learning a new task, these patches of intense activity are a sign of healthy brain functioning. But gradually, with training, the network should become more refined. When you don't see that refinement, in which less brain network is engaged to perform a familiar activity, the broad range of downstream events becomes a cacophony. "In Alzheimer studies," Glodzik-Sobanska said, "what shows up in imaging is that certain brain regions vulnerable to the disease reveal a complete absence of activity, while elsewhere in the brain the individual might manifest enhanced activity not present in normal people." Though this other activity is considered compensatory, it doesn't actually compensate for anything; it's just a desperate loudening of brain noise. "The goal over time," Glodzik-Sobanska said, "is always reduced activity. You want to see impulses travel more quickly through certain more limited numbers of synapses to make the whole thing more effective."

The drop in brain activity that's been recorded among experienced meditators seems to be one from which they can quickly snap over to high, concentrated activity. It's comparable to an athlete whose regular pulse rate is very low, but who can smoothly get the rate of blood flow up where it needs to be to perform some challenging physical activity; once the activity is over, the rate rapidly drops back to its baseline of minimal exertion. The brains of individuals who've made deep commitments to silence seem to enjoy its very character on a metabolic level, themselves becoming more still and quiet—less likely to amplify neural responses willy-nilly in a purposeless static when some chance stimulus calls out.

⚎

Despite the bitter cold, after my initial conversations with the New Melleray monks and a few hours of reading, I wanted to stretch my legs before night descended. It was absolutely still outside. The wide sky was iron gray; the earth was a white blank. Trappist monasteries are traditionally situated in flat landscapes, where the repetitive monotony is supposed to turn one's thoughts to mortality. Though snow was forecast for later that night, none had fallen for several days and the path was now packed firm. The deep silence was instantly broken by the *squitch, squatch* of boot tread on snow. "Feet, stop making so much noise," I thought.

The frozen road dipped toward a creek. As I neared the water, a great blue heron suddenly lifted off the brown ripple of water, flapping soundlessly as it rose high above bare branches. After the streets of New York, it seemed magical to have that motion without a soundtrack. I remembered a Brazilian friend telling me that in her country, "everything screams," and that when she eventually traveled to Japan she found the sight of the cityscape "like watching a silent film." The streets and the buildings rose before her without the noise she had always attached to those sights.

I walked along the edge of a dark road that unspooled through the white landscape as far as the eye could see. Tiny clusters of gray farm buildings loomed off in the distance, silos like church towers from which the spires had been snapped. I recalled the message written by contemplative monks defending their vocation to a synod of bishops. The monks noted that God had created his people in the desert, and it was to the desert that he had brought them after their sin in order, in the words of Hosea, to "allure her, and speak to her tenderly."

All ascetic practices, silence as much as fasting, can become forms of seduction if entered into deeply enough. But those of us who don't adopt them can never know the possibilities of life revealed to their adherents. In the early twentieth century, Dr. Frazer, an American anthropologist, went off to study the so-called Silent Widows of a tribe of Australian Aborigines. It was the custom of these women to enter a period of silence lasting as long as two years after the death of a spouse to elude and repel the spirit of the dead husband. Because the rule of silence extended to mothers, sisters, daughters, and mothers-in-law of the departed spouse, it happened that the majority of women in the tribe were prohibited from speaking during the period of mourning. To the outsider, this suggested an awfully limited existence. Yet Frazer noted the "odd circumstance" that many of the women, when the time of mourning was complete, chose to remain silent, communicating only by signs.

As I walked along, white feathers began to twirl down from the sky.

✠

The Trappists are technically known as the Cistercian Order of the Strict Observance. The movement developed in the seventeenth century under the guidance of Abbot Rancé at the French monastery La Trappe, for which the order is named. Before becoming a monk, Rancé had been a dazzling polymath, an ardent hunter, and a lover of fancy dress. Then he had the unfortunate experience of walking into the sickroom of the Duchess de Montbazon, his grand passion, to discover that she was missing her head. After the duchess's unexpectedly abrupt death, an impatient undertaker had decapitated her corpse to make it fit inside a mismeasured coffin. That sight marked the end of Rancé's days of gadding about in lace from the Sorbonne to the chase. He sold everything he had, withdrew into La Trappe with his valet, and set about forging the most ascetic monastic order the world had ever seen. Their rule of silence was absolute, with the brethren discoursing between themselves by sign language alone. For half the year, strict fasts were observed. During the remaining six months, the monks subsided primarily on roots. When not praying and silently meditating, they performed field labor, sometimes adding a chastening innersole of thorns to their wooden sandals.

In the tradition of the older Cluniac order that the Trappists sought to renew, silence, as much as celibacy, was seen as a way of copying the angels who parted their lips only to praise God. By observing quiet as a community, the monks blocked off the main highway to frivolity—chatter—and sought to lift themselves onto a plane of rapt attention where God's sacrifice and human mortality became audible to all.

The idea of silence as the quickest route to solemnity is enshrined in countless religious practices and lies at the origins of national moments of silence as well. While we don't know when silence first became part of mourning rituals where the secular and sacred intermingled, we might glimpse traces of the crossover in Carnival observances. An eyewitness of the Venice Carnival in 1868 recounted how, at the final moment, "As the great clock of St. Mark was striking the midnight hour, the band ceased playing and scarcely a sound was heard in all that immense crowd." After the intervention of "a moment of silence and darkness," a small light appeared, followed by a blaze of fiery serpents, Roman candles, and rockets. Eventually the flames ignited "the figure of the doomed Monarch"—King Carnival—who perished in a "deafening explosion." The moment of silence at midnight signaled the end of the rule of the flesh and reminded the crowd that Lent was imminent.

There are competing claims for the first national moment of silence, most of which—like stories of a memorial silence held across the United States the year that the *Titanic* sank—are suspiciously unmentioned by contemporary sources. The first widely observed national moment of silence appears to have been one commemorating Armistice Day in England. It was begun in 1919, the year after the armistice, at the prompting of Sir Percy Fitzpatrick, a former high commissioner in South Africa who'd been deeply affected by a three-minute pause in work and conversation observed daily in that country throughout the First World War. In a letter he wrote advocating for the silent pause, Fitzpatrick declared that it would serve both to preserve the memory of the sacrifices made by the "Glorious and Immortal" war dead and to create solidarity among the living.

When the British adopted the ritual, not only sound but all motion was interrupted, with trains halting, factories shutting down, and telephone exchanges ceasing to connect calls. So powerful did this two minutes of silence prove to be that the BBC began lobbying to broadcast the silence, instead of just switching off during its observance. In 1929 they began doing so, and these transmissions of national silence became a phenomenon in their own right. As a BBC representative explained, "Its impressiveness is intensified by the fact that the silence is not a dead silence, for Big Ben strikes the hour, and then the bickering of sparrows, the crisp rustle of falling leaves, the creasing of pigeon wings as they take flight, uneasy at this strange hush, contrast with the traffic din of London some minutes before." The BBC's role, he concluded, was to allow the silence to be heard for what it really was, "a solvent which destroys personality and gives us leave to be great and universal."

I remember experiencing some of these emotions myself when I once observed the two minutes of silence held in Israel on Holocaust Memorial Day. I had no expectations for the event, but when the sirens began wailing and everything stopped moving—pedestrians freezing in place on the sidewalk, people stepping out of their cars and simply standing, doors left hanging open—I found myself immediately overwhelmed. I remember watching the traffic lights change color over and over—red, green, yellow; red, green, yellow—with no car responding to the signals. Silence seemed to create a hole in the present into which the unspeakable past poured in a flood, swallowing our individual lives. At the end of it, the trivia surrounding those two minutes sounded painfully loud. I wanted somehow to live up to that moment of suspension.

※

The yearning to be great and universal, so often awakened by war and disaster, seems to lie behind the last boom time of novices entering the silence of New Melleray Abbey as well. Since the surge began shortly after the Second World War, one might suspect that mass revulsion at the violent ways of humanity lay behind the increase in applicants. But an oral history of New Melleray that I paged through from the monastery library suggests a more complicated picture. One monk who came to the abbey after his army service explained, "You can't look at a block of houses that's just been blown to pieces and not realize there is more to life than consumerism and having a good time." For this man, it wasn't a repudiation of war and violence that fueled the decision to enter the monastery but disgust with the peaceable, vacuous face of the American consumer society he returned to. The military and the monastery are each, in their own way, dedicated to the watchful preparation for death—often in silence. The interviews with monks that I read suggested that the spike in monks in the late 1940s and early 1950s reflected the desire not to flee but to *perpetuate* certain intensities of life during wartime.

SILENCE AND THE UNSPEAKABLE

When Alberic and I met at the breakfast table the morning of my second day at the abbey, he looked glum. On the following day Brother Jonas was to be ordained as a priest. It had been a long process for him to reach this milestone. He had family and friends coming from all over to witness the ceremony, and now because of the weather many of them were canceling their visits. We also would be unable to set out to Trappist Caskets, where Alberic had intended to show me the quiet of monks at work. Instead of touring the coffin plant, he'd made arrangements for me to speak to several other monks about their pursuits of silence. "Nature is not friendly here," he remarked, nervously eyeing the window, curtained with white snowfall from the outside. "She'll walk over your face. She's a bipolar mother. The monk in me loves this. We live on the edge, at the extreme of human capacities, but my human nature struggles with it."

The local population struggled with it too, and though not upholding vows of silence, they were little given to idle conversation, Alberic said. The farming was relentlessly difficult and unprofitable. It would also, I knew, have been deafening, despite the rural setting: 75 percent of farmworkers are said to have a hearing problem due to their use of heavy machinery.

Indeed, the traditional Midwestern tight-lipped stoicism is now only rarely complemented by a larger environmental quiet. A priest I met at lunch after Brother Jonas's ordination told me that his parishioners simply have no experience of silence. In consequence, Father David and other religious leaders increasingly prescribe very basic, pragmatic experiences of silence as part of

their ministry. "We'll tell people, 'Allow for a period of no television or music each day,' " he told me. " 'Sit alone in quiet for a
while.' And I've had some people—after as little as *half an hour*—
say, 'Father, that was the most profound thing I've ever experienced!' They just have nothing comparable in their life."

But what do they do with that profound experience? I asked.
Father Stephen, an older, retired priest who was seated at our
table, said that in his experience the problem was that without
silence people had no ability to understand one another. He
currently oversees meetings for councils that set policy for different parishes, and he has recently stopped allowing any difficult
decisions to be made by discussion. Doing so, he has found,
means that "the noise makes the decision." Instead, he sends
everyone off to meditate on their own about their place in the
discord. They'll regather much later and as often as not he finds
people's minds have changed. " 'Father, I was out walking the
farm, and I was thinking about how I would feel bad if I were
them and the matter were to be worked out the way I said it
should be.' " Perhaps this was what Saint Bernard, the patron
saint of the Cistercians, meant when, in one of his letters, he
cited Isaiah to the effect that "silence is the work of justice."

As Alberic spoke of life on the Great Plains, much of which
revolved around an extraordinary work ethic, I began thinking
about the laborious rigor of the monks' own lives. It seemed a far
cry from the idyll my friends had envisioned. "Why *do* you get up
so early?" I blurted out. "Why skew the day to begin at 3:15 AM?"

"We're supposed to cultivate wakefulness," Alberic said, and
he described vigil, the first prayer service of the day, as a micro-
cosm of the hyperawareness that a Cistercian monk is called to

uphold at all hours. To him, Alberic said, "the darkness is a very safe space. It's about birth. Christmas night. The night when anything can happen. The quiet, dark places are where the treasure is buried."

"What do you do after you've finished vigil?" I asked.

"We go back to our cells and read. Monks and books just belong together. We study. We pray. We meditate. We have six free hours before our workday begins. How many rich people can say that? We call it 'holy leisure.' Having that time does something to your humanity."

✠

Brother Neal, a tall, slender, slightly stooped man with a face that tends to cock to one side and piercing, pale eyes that crinkle and gleam, had his own perspective. "How do you relate to the fact of God being incomprehensible to us?" he asked me. Citing the twentieth-century German theologian Karl Rahner, Neal answered his rhetorical question: "Ultimately the only adequate response to God is silent adoration." This is another idea that crosses multiple traditions, though it was slow to catch on in ancient religions. For much of antiquity, prayers were said out loud since the ears of the gods were thought to resemble gigantic human ears, requiring worshippers to make actual sound. Silent prayer was also looked on askance because the rationale for praying inaudibly was often the wish to conceal what one was praying for—taboo sex, magical powers, and criminal plunder, for example. As the gods shed their physical sensory apparatus, attitudes began to change. The late Platonists believed that, in order to reach a transcendent being, prayer itself needed to be distilled beyond the world of the senses. "Let us sacrifice in such a manner as is fit, offering different sacrifices to different natures," wrote Porphyry, the third-century Neoplatonist. "For there is nothing material which is not immediately impure to an immaterial nature . . . Hence neither is vocal language nor internal speech adapted to the highest God . . . but we should venerate him in profound silence." Rather than Alberic's notion of silence serving as a reminder of dependence of being, what Neal talked about was the way that silence can represent a dissolving of all our habitual perceptions before some great truth.

This aspect of Neal's faith brushes up against many secular ideals of silence, often in relationship to the natural world. A famous Japanese poem about the islands of Matsushima consists only of the words, "Oh Matsushima!" The poet is so overwhelmed by the place's beauty that he can only speak its name before he falls into silence. Many early-twentieth-century philosophies of silence resonate with this idea of an incommensurability between truth and our powers of expression. Wittgenstein ended his first book of philosophy with the proposition: "Whereof one cannot speak, thereof one must be silent." Heidegger once declared: "Above all, silence about silence." The French philosopher Max Picard wrote that the "silence points to a state where only being is valid." In Picard's view, this is "the state of the Divine." Here Picard, a practicing Catholic, echoes many of the foundational ideas in Zen Buddhism. At one point in our conversations, Lushtak, my meditation-teacher friend, described silent meditation as an effort to "unplug from the mental story" we are constantly telling ourselves, in order to be completely attentive to the wonder of the ever-unfolding present moment.

The Apaches, among other Native American tribes, are famous for their silence, and sociolinguistic research has found that the contexts in which silence dominates the dialogue include courtship and reunions after long separations, in which ambiguities about social roles abound. Silence seems a mark of acknowledgment of these uncertainties; the long pause gives people time to come into a new relationship with one another. The rest of us confront these same ambiguities all the time, but we often pave over them with speech and so deprive ourselves and our interlocutors both of the chance to know what it is *not* to know where we stand with each other—and to find new grounds for meaningful exchange.

In some folklore rituals, silence is invested with the power not just to enrich existing relationships but to conjure up future lovers. The English tradition of the "dumb cake" involves variations on the idea of young women baking and eating a cake in absolute silence. After the women go to bed—sometimes sliding a slice of dumb cake under their pillows beforehand—visions of their husbands-to-be are supposed to appear to them. (In the eighteenth-century *Journal of a Young Lady of Virginia*, we find the young diarist on a visit to the house of Mr. George Washington trying to persuade a friend to join her one night in eating the "dum cake," but her friend is too spooked to take part.) There are also rituals of "Dumb Suppers," comprising midnight meals consumed in total silence. Sometimes these suppers were rites of divination that foretold a woman's fate in marriage; on other occasions they enabled the guests to make contact with a recently deceased loved one.

In many traditions, silence forms a bridge to the unknowable

far side of human experience, whether the searcher is gazing forward or backward in time.

✠

Before I left New Melleray, Alberic told me that he was going to
"bend the rules a little" and take me down to a chapel reserved
for the monks beneath the church that was, in his estimation,
the most silent place in the abbey. He warned me that the silence
in the room was so intense that it was likely to "take me outside
of my comfort zone." He knew of cases where people from the big
city had found themselves physically unable to remain in the
chapel for even five minutes.

We descended lower and lower, and then wound our way
through interminable unlit corridors. Alberic gestured for me to
wait against a stone wall in a low-ceilinged hall and went on
ahead of me to investigate the state of the chapel. After a minute,
he returned, whispering in a low voice that he would not be able
to read me the passage he'd hoped to recite as preparation for the
silence since there was another monk inside the chapel. He led
me forward through another door, and then we passed around a
barrier wall into a small room that was completely dark except for
a tiny candle in a glass at the far end, suspended from the ceiling
by a chain. In the center of a row of chairs directly across from
the candle, I could faintly make out the silhouette of a large man
sitting with his legs wide apart and his hands on his thighs, breathing quite loudly. Alberic and I lowered ourselves into chairs along
the side wall.

Here, in this darkness, I began to feel a real gravity to the
silence of the monastery, an *inescapability* that made me glean

something of the rigor with which these men spend their lives preparing for death. The death of a monk is, in Alberic's words, a "graduation ceremony. You haven't persevered in the monk's calling until you die. Death marks the point at which you've completed your transaction. There's a lightness, even joy to the funeral. The night before a monk is buried, we light an Easter candle. We put two chairs on either side of the body, which has been placed in the center of the church. The candle is placed at the feet of the body. We take turns praying two by two over the body all night. And talk about entering into that silence." Alberic shook his head. "You'd think it would be morbid or scary, but those are some of the lightest, most joyful moments in the monastery. The silence is telling you it's going to be okay. Unless you have real psychological resistance, you know it's going to be okay."

In the chapel, my eyes were drawn to the candle in the glass. Though I couldn't feel a breath of air where I was, the chain was being tugged gently this way and that by an otherwise imperceptible draft; the reflection of fire on the glass doubled the image of its burning orange glow and made it look like two wings fluttering tremulously open and closed, as though the proverbial moth had actually become the flame.

So far from being taken outside my comfort zone, I found myself wanting to remain and sink deeper into it.

The monks at New Melleray each, in one way or another, described themselves listening to silence for self-knowledge. Yet the self-knowledge that the silence of the monastery promotes is, in the end, less about discovering whom one really is, in our conventional use of the term, than about acknowledging the

limitations of our grasp on what lies within and without us. Indeed, the self-knowledge the monks advocate—and which they
believe the quiet of monastic life reveals to them—is the knowledge that there's something beyond the self.

All the time I'd been in the monastery, I'd been searching
for some kind of clear, encapsulated lesson in the silence—
something that I could take home with me. But what I'd received
instead was a powerful reminder of the good that can come from
not knowing, from lingering where the mind keeps reaching
outward. I remembered speaking earlier to Vinod Menon, a neuroscientist who has done extensive fMRI studies of people listening to music. Menon discovered that the peak of positive brain
activity actually occurs in the silent pauses between sounds, when
the brain is striving to anticipate what the next note will be. The
burst of neural firing that takes place in the absence of sound
stimulus enables the mind to perform some of its most vital work
of maintaining attention and encoding memories. I asked Menon
what he took from this finding. His small, dark eyes twinkled.
"Silence is golden," he said. "Silence in the right contexts."

Even brief silence, it seems, can inject us with a fertile
unknown: a space in which to focus and absorb experience—a
reminder that the person we are with may yet surprise us; a reflection that some things we cannot put into words are yet
resoundingly real; a reawakening to our dependency on something greater than ourselves.

※

I wanted to stay in the chapel. But Alberic was already rising to
his feet and beckoning me forward. I resisted his summons a few

moments longer, then stood. I don't know how long we remained in the end. It wasn't long enough, and I felt overcome with sadness as we stepped away—rising back up from the depths of darkness and stillness, into the light and echoing footsteps of the abbey's upper stories.

CHAPTER TWO

Why We Hear

"You hear a snap off in the distance, what do you do?"

The question was put to me—in a gruff voice that made me feel I should be paying better attention—by Rickye Heffner, a professor of psychology at the University of Toledo.

"I turn my head and try to see where the snap is coming from?" I ventured.

"You look for it! You want to know what made the sound and where it is. You want to orient your eyes toward it. Among mammals, the ears are animal detectors and they tell your eyes where to go to hunt for the animals they detect. So the ears have to have sufficient range and be able to hear the right frequencies to locate a sound source. That seems to be what's driving the evolution of hearing."

Heffner and her husband, Henry Heffner, have dedicated the last forty-plus years of their lives to producing a vast profusion of studies with titles like "Hearing in Glires: Domestic Rabbit, Cotton Rat, Feral House Mouse, and Kangaroo Rat."

They seem to have explored the auditory mechanisms and evolution of hearing in every warm-blooded, young-suckling creature in existence. I telephoned Heffner because, after my initial ruminations on silence and noise, I realized that if there was something meaningful in the idea of listening to the unknown, I needed a better sense of what *is* known. It's impossible to understand how noise or silence affects us without getting a handle on why we began to hear in the first place.

After all, on the face of it, the very notion of a pursuit of silence seems a bit of sensory nonsense. Who, by way of comparison, would want to pursue an existence in which there was nothing to touch? We don't go in search of a place without taste or scent (however many fragrances we might prefer not to sniff). Why would so many people have come to believe there was something not just enjoyable but beneficial in pursuing a state where one sense was exercised as little as possible? What is it about the sense of hearing that makes the idea of having next to nothing to hear so appealing?

Heffner broke off our Socratic dialogue to announce that a family of deer had just stepped in front of her window despite the fact that a train was blasting past on the nearby rails (I could faintly hear its roar). She told me that she also regularly saw groundhogs and rabbits, along with the odd fox, the "dreaded muskrat," and "platoons of evil raccoons." They're habituated to trains, she said, "so the animals don't get frightened away—even though the noise is terrible." Almost all of the Heffners' research has been directed toward exploring an overarching, two-part theory: animals hear what they need to hear in order to survive; animals with the same kinds of lifestyles hear the same kinds of things. As it turns out, this amounts to a theory wherein skull size is destiny and sound localization is the raison d'être of the auditory apparatus.

In the 1960s, the Heffners were both students of the evolutionary neuroscientist R. Bruce Masterton. Henry co-authored and Rickye helped with statistical analysis on Masterton's first landmark paper, "The Evolution of Human Hearing," a comparative study of the hearing of eighteen mammals. They discovered that if you could measure the space between an animal's ears, you could predict its high-frequency hearing with tremendous accuracy. This is because we graph the location of a sound source in space on the basis of the differences in the way sound waves strike each of our ears. The amount of inter-ear distance available to an animal will be the main factor determining what cues it can leverage to track which way a beating wing or falling paw is moving.

Since that study, the Heffners have looked at close to seventy additional species, and while the theory has been expanded and tweaked, the correlation remains unchanged: if you've got a big head, your high-frequency hearing is going to be less sensitive than if you have a small head. Most mammals take advantage of both time cues and "spectral differences"—changes in the intensity of the sound striking each ear successively—to identify the position of a sound source.

Temporal signals are straightforward. Given sufficient distance between the ears, a sound on one side is going to hit one ear before the other. Time delay is the strongest, most reliable cue. "But," Heffner noted, "not everybody has that luxury." I found myself patting my hands to the sides of my head as she spoke to try and gauge my own head span. "If you're a mouse, think about how far apart the ears are," she said. "Sound travels from one ear to the next in perhaps thirty microseconds and the nervous system just can't calculate a sound source being off at three o'clock or two o'clock in that interval." So what does the mouse do? "When the chips are down you use what you've got—intensity. There are plenty of good reasons for being a small animal and you want to occupy that niche as effectively as you can. So you hear really high frequencies to make as much use as you can of the intensity signals."

The usefulness of the "sound shadow" cast by the head in localizing sound has been recognized since the mid-1870s. It was then that Lord Rayleigh, the indefatigable English physicist who discovered argon and explained the irregular flight of tennis balls, stood with his eyes shut at the center of a lawn in Cambridge surrounded by a ring of assistants brandishing tuning forks. When one assistant set his tuning fork vibrating at a sufficient intensity, Rayleigh could accurately identify that man's position in the circle. If sound-wave cycles are sufficiently close together, he found, sound is louder in the first ear it hits, since the head blocks out the upper frequencies of the waves en route to the second ear. Rayleigh dubbed this variation in intensity the "binaural ratio," with "binaural" signifying the employment of both ears. In the last century, the extent of this shadowing was calculated electronically. At one thousand cycles, the ear closest to the sound source receives the wave at a level eight decibels more intense than that of the farther ear. At ten thousand cycles this ratio jumps to a thirty-decibel difference.

Spectral difference is vital for creatures with tiny skulls, but time delay doesn't work at low frequencies. When a sound wave is long enough, the whole wave can just "hang ten" around the skull and strike the second ear without being blocked at all. Masterton predicted that the smaller the skull, the higher the upper range of an animal's hearing would be.

Exceptions to the correlation between skull size and high-frequency hearing appear most notably in the case of pea-headed subterranean creatures like pocket gophers, which have poor high-frequency hearing. In these instances, the Heffners argue, having adapted themselves to "the one-dimensional world of an underground habitat," sound localization becomes an empty exercise. Throughout the animal kingdom, the selective pressures on hearing concern the need to detect the nature and location of what's out there snapping the twig. Rickye Heffner argues that much of the time when we try to use noise either to protect or frighten animals, we end up doing so on the basis of human psychology rather than evolutionary realities. Particular bugbears for her in this regard are ultrasonic deer whistles and flea collars. "Like the sound of a deer whistle on a truck is going to scare an animal more than the sound of the truck!" she scoffed. Our awareness that a sound is pitched outside our hearing range triggers in *us* an association with danger, she contends. Flea collars blast eighty decibels directly beneath the cat's ear at a frequency the felines hear perfectly well and quite possibly find agonizing—despite the fact that there's no evidence the fleas themselves even perceive, let alone are affected by the sound. "There's one born every minute," Heffner sighed, "and most of them seem to own cats."

THE EVOLUTIONARY PURSUIT OF SILENCE

A cross-section of the ear suggests an improbable patent application: a bagpipe, several models for the St. Louis Arch, and a couple of snapped rubber bands grafted onto a sea snail. Until recently, the ear was understood to operate on a model that might be abridged to the CBCs of hearing—channel, boost, convert—with those three steps corresponding to the external, middle, and inner ear respectively. The outer-ear channels and condenses sound waves from outside so that those waves strike against the eardrum. The eardrum then sends the mechanical energy of the sound into the middle ear, with its three tiny bones: the hammer, anvil, and stirrup. The wave amplifies as it passes along these vibration-friendly ossicles, the last of which is pressed flush against the oval window of the liquid-filled coil of the cochlea. This entrance to the cochlea marks the threshold of the inner ear. At the point where the stirrup goads the oval window, the pressure of the original force will have multiplied dramatically. The energized vibration now ripples into the fluid in the cochlea, triggering thousands of hair cells into motion. The movement of those cells transduces the vibration into an electrical signal that enters the auditory nerve, which, in turns, sends the sound into the brain. But this is not the whole story.

Complications with the model begin at the innocent-seeming flaps on the sides of our heads. For all the confidence produced by three decades of work demonstrating correlation between skull size and high-frequency hearing, the visible ear throws a spanner into Heffner's work. When she spoke about it, her voice took on a bitterness otherwise reserved for deer whistles and flea collars. "The pinnas," she said, using the technical name for the external ear, "act as independent sound shadowers. They alter the degree of the sound shadow cast by the skull. This is part of their work as directional amplifiers. Animals point their ears at something and then they can hear it better." But the extent of the pinna's impact as a frontline amplification system continues to defy researchers. "The head is basically a lumpy sphere with two big funnels on it," Heffner said. "Those funnels intensify a sound as it drops down toward the eardrums. But we've never tried to measure pinna dimensions because—what do you measure? Ideally, you'd get some of these animals and take several of their pinnas and measure the physical properties of what the pinnas do to sound coming into the sound canal, but it's not remotely practical. Pinnas are very complicated shapes. Some are kind of flat. Some have big openings. There are all kinds of folds. And while animals with big heads generally have big pinnas, that's not always the case. It's known that the external folds help to augment sound and create a difference between what's heard in each ear. So if you have a sound off to the right quadrant somewhere, and you're a little bat with big ears full of fancy convoluted folds, sound coming in is going to have very different features than it does for a cow."

The mysteries of the inner ear are still more pronounced. Jim Hudspeth, who works at Rockefeller University studying the molecular and biological basis of hearing, has shown that the motion of the hair cells not only converts the mechanical wave into an electrical signal that can be read by the auditory nerve in the brain; the various reactions set in motion by the oscillation of the hair cells also serve to magnify the sound. A huge "power gain" takes place, he says, within the inner ear itself. How exactly this happens is still not understood.

Regardless, we now know that all three parts of the ear play a dynamic role in boosting sound. If our auditory mechanism is working normally, Hudspeth told me, by the time we realize we've heard a sound it's a hundred times louder than it was before it began bouncing around inside our ears. When you consider how little energy is released by a pin falling onto the floor, the amplification power of our ears is clear. Indeed, since so much of what the ear accomplishes involves making noise louder, it's unsurprising that a majority of hearing problems represent an inability not to perceive sound but to properly amplify it.

People like to distinguish between the ears and the eyes by saying that the latter have lids. But, in fact, the amplification function of the middle ear is complemented by a series of equivalent mechanisms that mitigate the effects of a loud noise. Our middle-ear bones have small muscles attached to them that are part of a reflex to reduce the vibration of the bones under the impact of a loud sound. One of them jerks on the eardrum itself so that it tightens and vibrates less violently. Another yanks the stirrup back from the oval window. The eustachian tube performs a complicated maneuver to equalize air pressure. But why amplify to begin with if you're only going to end up deadening the noise?

Because in nature, there aren't very many loud sounds.

"Most animals don't announce their presence if they can help it," Heffner told me. "Even the famous roar of the lion is an exceptional event to threaten an intruder." For the most part, animals move through space as quietly as possible. Today people make noise to reassert their importance, but for our predecessors silence was almost always the secret to survival. "That's why kids today are at such risk," Heffner added. "I can guarantee you they're going to have hearing loss, because when you're listening to headphones you don't realize the volume. Continuing loud sounds put a stress on the auditory system because the middle-ear reflexes are constantly trying to protect you from them . . . If you've got a generally noisy environment, you don't hear the twig snap. But really loud sounds are just going to knock you off your perch no matter how preoccupied you are."

⚅

In 1961, Dr. Samuel Rosen, a New York ear specialist, wanted to measure the hearing of a people who had not "become adjusted to the constant bombardment of modern mechanization." Rosen went off to visit the Mabaan tribe, some 650 miles southeast of Khartoum, in what was then one of the most noise-free regions of Africa. The Mabaans were notable among their neighbors for having neither drums nor guns. He went armed with 1,000 bottle caps, which he planned to distribute to tribe members as rewards for their participation in audio tests: Mabaan women, he had heard, liked to fix the caps to their ears and make necklaces from them.

Rosen discovered that the hearing of Mabaan tribe members at the age of seventy was often superior to that of Americans in their twenties. Some 53 percent of Mabaan villagers could discern sounds that only 2 percent of New Yorkers could hear. "Two Mabaans standing 300 feet apart, or the length of a football field, can carry on a conversation in a soft voice with their backs turned," he reported. Rosen attributed the extraordinary preservation of hearing among the Mabaans to both their low-fat diet—which along with eliminating heart disease kept the cochlea well nourished—and the fact that they heard so little noise. The imbalance between noise and silence to which most of us who don't live in remote tribal areas are subject dramatically accelerates the aging process of our hearing.

Without having recourse to the hearing power of the Mabaans, there are still a few groups of people who use their ears in a manner consistent with the evolutionary pursuit of silence.

※

When Jason Everman spearheaded the Third Infantry in the invasion of Iraq, he and his team were fitted with state-of-the-art noise-canceling headphones that had two radios, one internal and one external. He was never comfortable with them because of the auditory isolation they created. He always wanted to be, he said, "totally tuned in to the ambient sound." Every noise a soldier hears on a special operation can be a clue to the situation he's approaching. Everman didn't want to miss a single auditory clue, and so he often just cupped one side of the headphones to his ear as he walked. He was also never comfortable with the modified Toyota trucks he and his team drove around in because, he said, "they were like an enclosed bubble, and if someone wanted to shoot at me, I wanted to hear it."

Everman has a certain sparkle in his light eyes and a beard that flows in great scrolls, making him appear rather like a better-groomed version of Santa Claus, if Santa Claus were given to dying his hair ginger-gold and wearing exotic finger rings. He is listed as second guitarist on *Bleach*, Nirvana's debut album. (Kurt Cobain later said that Everman didn't actually play on the album but was credited as a thank-you gesture for having paid the $606.17 recording-session fee.) While he was in high school, Everman read Benvenuto Cellini's autobiography, and resolved to make a project of developing the artist, warrior, and philosopher facets of his personality, in accordance with the Renaissance ideal. Having completed a stint as a grunge guitarist and service with the U.S. Airborne Rangers, he is now studying philosophy at Columbia University. Everman is not to be monkeyed with. When he met me at a dim SoHo wine bar, the slowness of his movements made me anxious. It was as though a big-game animal had wandered into a petting farm and might accelerate from zero to a throat-ripping sixty at a heartbeat.

Silence, Everman told me, was at the crux of all his work in Iraq and Afghanistan. Most of his special-operations activities involved long walks, since news about the liftoff and progress of helicopters, and even of their reconfigured Toyotas, would often be relayed via cell phone from village to village, far in advance of their movements. Engine noise eliminated the possibility of surprise. And for the same reason that they avoided vehicular transport, he and his unit almost always moved at night. Even with their night-vision goggles, hearing was the primary sense they employed as they closed in on a target. "In an assault on a compound, everyone would be listening as hard as they could—and straining to be as quiet as possible. Without silence, the teeter-totter of success will tilt in the bad guy's favor."

Soldiers are taught the acronym SLLS, which stands for

stop, look, listen, smell. But since operations are normally done at night, Everman continued, "the vision part is impaired. And I think the smell part really comes from Vietnam days, you know—the smell of rice cooking. It wasn't too applicable to my experience. But you're definitely listening. And you're definitely being quiet."

Even when you're being as quiet as you can, Everman said, you still make sounds. He and his team would try to fasten down any loose gear with rubber bands to prevent rattling. But even if they succeeded, their own motion would often be loud enough to mask important warnings. And on top of these "regular sounds," he went on, "you're moving at night, over rough terrain. Everyone's going to fall down. It's not like in the movies. I've taken a lot of diggers." After someone falls, they all freeze, listen, make sure there aren't any new sounds indicating they've been heard.

The other element Everman's unit had to contend with was also an acoustical threat: barking dogs. "That's why nomadic, pastoralist cultures keep dogs," he noted. "They're a good early-warning system. But dogs bark so much," Everman added. "It's like sirens here in New York. Especially in a village, when one dog barks all the other dogs start barking . . ."

There was one aspect of Everman's experience that I figured would ignore silence: the actual assault on a compound; the deafening volleys of bullets released when they took out "the bad guys." But here a mysterious combination of psychology and physiology kicked in to counter my expectations.

Everman reduces the essence of combat to two principles: stress management and problem solving. At their core is yet another dimension of silence. "When a gunfight kicks off, it's fucking *loud*," he told me. "But every time, the real *cracks* are over in the first few seconds. Then it's just"—Everman lifted his hands up by the sides of his head and then suctioned them violently into his ears—"*whooosh*. It's like that scene at the opening of *Saving Private Ryan*. The first thing that goes is your hearing—partly because you're blasting your eardrum or whatever, but there's something else happening as well. The way it goes silent allows me to focus on solving the problem. You're not going to be able to solve any problems if you're not managing stress, and aural exclusion is a key part of stress management. It puts you in a Zen state. I've never been more in the moment than I have in combat situations."

The mind, it seems, can create silence where actual silence is least present. For Everman, the switch to silence, entering what he described as a Zen state, meant the changeover from listening to seeing. "Once the gunfire starts, I'm always cued into muzzle flashes rather than sound," he said.

At the end of our conversation, I asked Everman what his most powerful "sound memory" was of his time as a soldier. At first, he spoke of how, in Afghanistan, if you took away the AK-47s and the cell phones, the noise of the place was "completely biblical. What you heard were goats, donkeys, livestock." But then he told me there was one thing that did stand out above everything. He was stationed for a time in Kandahar, next to a mosque where someone kept pigeons and attached tiny bells to the birds' feet. "Once in a while, they'd take the flocks out, and you'd just hear hundreds of bells up in the sky." It was, Everman said, one of the most transfixing sounds he'd ever heard.

My conversation with Everman underscored the centrality of silence to life in a biosystem based on predation. His experience approaching a gunfight neatly diagrammed two primary effects of silence: enabling us to gather critical information about our environment (where threats and targets are positioned in space) and placing us in a state of calm that maximizes our ability to respond appropriately to the environment. But if the natural world was all about trying to be as quiet as possible, why did it become necessary to evolve the middle-ear noise-abatement function? I called Heffner again.

She sounded testy. I asked whether this was an alright time for her to talk.

"If you want to learn something about sound-pressure levels and evolutionary psychology, you should have been at my house last night," she said. "They're doing repairs on the train tracks." I made a clicking sound with my lips. "But it wasn't the actual work on the tracks that was the problem."

"No?"

"No! It was the guys driving the railroad construction vehicles. They have air horns. They don't get to blow them very often I guess, because they were making a symphony. It's not directional at all. They'll blow their horns as they approach, and sometimes when they're 200 yards past. Do they really need to keep that up at 2 AM?"

After a sympathetic pause, I ventured my question. "Dr. Heffner, since the evolution of hearing seems to be concerned mostly with trying to hear as much as possible as clearly as possible, why did we ever develop the ear shutter in the first place?"

"Because of the loudness of an animal's own voice," Heffner shot back. As an animal gets ready to vocalize, the middle-ear reflex will often kick in to provide protection from the noise made by the beast itself. No wonder the initial theological notion of silence involved closing one's own trap.

※

There's a suggestive symmetry in the idea that our built-in hearing protection exists to block the noise we expel from our own lips. In evolutionary terms, our middle ears and our mouths share a lot of history. Zhe-Xi Luo, a paleontologist at the Carnegie Museum of Natural History, recently led an expedition into the Yan Mountains some three thousand kilometers outside Beijing on which he made a remarkable discovery: the intact skull of a *Yanoconodon*—a hitherto unknown feisty little five-inch-long mammal from the Mesozoic era. The fossil provides a snapshot of a key step in the evolution of hearing.

"What was most revealing for me here," said Luo, "was that the middle-ear bone was still attached to the jawbone, but its shape was already quite similar to that of the modern platypus."

Some people believe that after Beethoven went completely deaf he hacked the legs off his piano so that it rested directly on the floor, then placed his ear against the lid so that he could feel the vibrations of the notes. Thomas Edison, who lost his hearing as a child, enjoyed chomping into the wooden box of his gramophone as a way of listening to music. "I bite my teeth in the wood good and hard, then I get it good and strong," he declared, and even went so far as to claim that his ability to hear "splendidly" through skull and teeth gave him an advantage because the sound waves then traveled "almost direct to my brain," protected by deafness itself "from the millions of noises that dim the hearing of ears that hear everything." Both Beethoven and Edison were resorting to forms of auditory perception that predate the evolution of a middle ear by some 125 million years. The amphibians and reptiles that crawled out of the watery deep with their heads flush to the earth, and the early mammals as well, heard the world largely through their bones.

Luo described for me a process which went something like this: When bone conduction was the primary mode of sound perception, *Yanoconodon*'s ancestors were among those who made much use of the lower jaw in picking up vibrations. Unlike humans today, the bottom jaw of the primitive mammal was itself divided into two parts, the dentary (where the teeth were) and the post-dentary (the back, toothless part of the jaw). Around 250 million years ago, the protomammals had some ability to register sound waves in the back of the jaw, along with limited innovation in the inner ear. If we could see a fast-motion film clip of the next 125 million years, we'd see the post-dentary bone shrinking and becoming more sensitive as its role in feeding diminished and its utility as a hearing apparatus became more pronounced. At the same time, the dentary bone expanded to establish a new, powerful hinge connecting it with the rest of the jaw. Exempted from chewing, the post-dentary bone gets even smaller and more sensitive until, not long before *Yanoconodon* enters the stage, the bone performs an astonishing grand jeté—splitting off from the lower jaw and rising up into the cranium. With *Yanoconodon*, although the bone has soared almost all the

way up into the skull to find its place among the auditory en-
semble in the ear, the attachment to the lower jaw is still visible.
But soon after *Yanoconodon* leaves the stage, the bone will sever
its last ties to the mouth and hover suspended in the cranium
where we find the middle ear today.

When I asked Luo what message the latest discoveries about
the evolution of mammalian hearing suggested to him, he said,
"All that hearing mechanism took 200 million years to build up!
You better take care of it!" He laughed. "Don't listen to too much
rock and roll!"

For Luo, and many other scientists whose work focuses on
the era in which mammals were establishing their viability as a
life form, hearing may in fact be *the* sensory factor determining
evolutionary sustainability. Only by being able to operate effectively at night were the pint-size early mammals able to evade the
depredations of their giant forerunners on dry land.

※

All of this poses a question: If we acquired our extraordinary
auditory sensitivity—a sensitivity so pronounced that it can detect energy levels one hundred times lower than the energy emitted by a solitary photon in the green wavelength—because the
world was striving to be as quiet as possible, what happens now
when almost every day we're exposed to sounds that treat our
eardrums like bass drums? Is it possible that the sublime sensitivity of human hearing has become just a point of vulnerability?
Will our very sensitivity get clobbered down to where we end up
not being able to hear anything at all? Hearing may be the only

one of our five senses that evolved to deal with an ecology, a ratio of sound to silence, the terms of which have been reversed over the course of human history.

The more I learned about hearing, the more unfathomable it seemed that we became loud on purpose.

CHAPTER THREE

Why We Are Noisy

On December 28, 1938, a speaker at the American speech teachers' convention in Cleveland, Ohio, unveiled evidence that their modest profession held the secret to Hitler's rise to power. In an address before a hushed crowd of fellow instructors, Professor M. D. Steer, director of the Purdue Speech Clinic, revealed his analysis of the German leader's speeches. Exhibiting pictures of "Hitler sound waves," with lines "zig-zagging sharply and remaining almost constantly in the higher voice level," Steer showed how Hitler's voice managed to batter his listeners into "a submissive state bordering closely on hypnotism." The secret lay in frequency. Steer claimed the typical frequency at which anger was expressed was 220 vibrations; Hitler's voice clocked in at 228 vibrations. This relentlessly shrill pitch dazed audiences "in much the same fashion as we are stunned by an auto horn."

It was a bold claim for the scientist from Indiana to make, but not altogether groundless. Hitler himself once remarked that without the loudspeaker he could not have conquered Germany, and his loud voice was a treasured property of the rising Nazi Party. So essential was its power to the Reich that he even had a voice double, one Adolf Wagner, whose sole claim to distinction seems to have been that his voice grew raspy and broke in exactly the same cadences as Hitler's. The American National Broadcasting Company charted the volume of Hitler's speech to the Reichstag on October 6, 1939, comparing it with that of the speeches by Prime Minister Chamberlain, Premier Daladier, King George, and President Roosevelt on September 3, when Britain and France declared war on Germany. Though the French leader hit some impressive high notes, nobody could compete with Hitler for consistent loudness. Chamberlain's voice chart looks like a flatlining patient.

If, as the monks believe, we seal our lips in order to draw closer to a higher truth, we shout to acquire earthly clout.

※

Darwin viewed adult animal vocalization as a weapon. In Darwin's schema, males make a lot of noise to threaten other males and to seduce potential mates, while females make a racket to indicate their choice of partner for reproduction. "The sexes of many animals incessantly call for each other during the breeding-season," he wrote; "and in not a few cases the male endeavors thus to charm or excite the female. This, indeed, seems to have been the primeval use and means of development of the voice."

In more recent decades, perhaps in line with our own evolving self-image, the focus of animal research has shifted away from competition toward the use of learned vocalizations in coalition building. In addition to adding nuances to the story of

animal bonding, the expansion of animal-communication studies
has led many evolutionary biologists to enlarge the boundaries of
the unknown. Birds that use their songs to imitate other birds
and animal species are considered especially mysterious. "What
are myna birds doing in the wild?" Heather Williams, a bird expert at Williams College, said when I questioned her about noise
and song production among the feathered flocks. "And parrots?
No one understands the vocalizations of parrots in the wild."

But the dynamic that Darwin focused on more than 125
years ago remains dominant: the intentional emission of sound
helps animals secure their niche in a relentlessly competitive
environment. And coalition building, for the most part, comes
down to finding one's rank in a group, and assuring oneself of a
protective partner in family planning. Perhaps what has changed
most is our understanding of the power of sound. It's now widely
accepted that sounds made by males can supplant the need for
other physical action against a competitor, while sounds made by
females can circumvent the need for making a firm choice
among different potential mates. Males willfully maximize perceptions of their fighting prowess through acoustical displays,
while females purposefully confuse their listeners with sounds
suggesting multiple choices simultaneously. Both of these capacities have been dubbed "diplomacy." They might also be thought
of as a strategic deployment of noise. While silence is often used
by an animal to foster invisibility, noise functions as signage for
the bodily reality behind it.

Since the late 1970s, Eugene Morton, a zoologist and orni-
thologist with the National Zoo, has been constructing sonograms analyzing the sounds made by a wide array of birds and

mammals. Morton has found a near-perfect correlation between the pitch of a vocalization and its social utility. Low-pitched sounds are equated with aggression, while high-pitched sounds are associated with submissiveness and friendliness. (The cat is the singular, confounding exception to this rule.) A vocalized back and forth between two animals consisting of a bellow and a high-pitched whine might mean the difference between retreat and a clash to the death. The duet becomes its own form of duel.

Long before Bruce Masterton's contributions, an intuitive understanding of this dynamic was exploited in the commercial sphere. One of the earliest histories of the telephone, by Herbert Casson, a Canadian journalist, published in 1910, describes how the first telephone exchanges were deafeningly loud because the switchboards were staffed entirely by boys who engaged in more or less constant "cat-and-dog squabble" with the public, "with every one yelling at the top of his voice." Then one day someone thought to replace the boys with girls. "The quiet voice, pitched high, the deft fingers . . . these qualities were precisely what the gentle telephone required in its attendants," Casson wrote. Girls "did not waste time in retaliatory conversation . . . and they were much more likely to give 'the soft answer that turneth away wrath.' A telephone call under the boy regime meant Bedlam and five minutes; afterwards, under the girl regime, it meant silence and twenty seconds."

☒

Behind this phenomenon lies the notion of fundamental frequency. Assuming there are no mitigating factors, the frequency of an animal's vocalization will be inversely related to the size of its vibrating vocal cords. Even when depth of pitch does not indicate an animal's size, low-frequency calls often attest to higher testosterone levels. (Testosterone may cause vocal folds to lengthen independently of the rest of the body.) Whether on account of body mass or hormone rush, the deeper the sound, the more threatening the beast. Animals can thus size each other up and determine the advisability of doing battle on the basis of the frequency struck by their opponent.

Among fallow deer, for example, bucks vocalize only during the mating season, producing a call known as a groan. Researchers from the University of Zurich have recently shown that the higher-ranking male deer in a herd produce the lowest groans—and that this ranking is also the best predictor of their odds for mating success. Female deer are magnetized by the same acoustic cues indicating dominant status that males rear back from. So important is this call to the future of the deer that at the height of the breeding season a buck will groan up to three thousand times per hour—making them sound more hoarse than a hard-smoking heavy-metal singer after sixty. At the peak of the rut, this hoarseness actually raises the pitch of the buck's call (perhaps also signaling to its rivals a drop in testosterone-fueled fighting spirit).

Although this dynamic, wherein lower pitch indicates greater reproductive viability, holds sway throughout most of the animal kingdom, human noise may be starting to throw a wrench into the works. Studies of certain frog species have indicated that in areas with significant traffic noise, male frogs are being forced to raise the pitch of their call in order to make themselves heard. But the calculus for the croakers is tricky since the price of audibility is a commensurate drop in their appeal to females—and a reduction in their ability to threaten other males. Only by sounding littler and weaker than they actually are can these male frogs get the females to recognize they even exist.

John J. Ohala, professor emeritus of linguistics at the University of California at Berkeley, has tied the vulnerable submissiveness associated with higher frequencies to the acoustic origins of the smile. Smiling reduces the resonant cavity of the mouth, thereby raising the vocal pitch of sound emitted. He has also made the case that the larger the vibrating membrane, "the more likely it is that secondary vibrations could arise," giving the voice in question an irregular, rough texture. When a sound includes a number of secondary vibrations, it will be less predictable. Since we are biologically programmed to associate unpredictability with danger, a low and rough voice is the most frightening. (It is not coincidental that one of the oldest, most widespread religious artifacts is an object called a "bull-roarer"—a piece of wood tied to a string which, when swiftly spun around, produces a loud, roaring, eerie noise. Versions of the bull-roarer have been found everywhere from ancient Greece to Mexico, Africa, Australia, and Ceylon, with its use varying between summoning the gods and chasing off evil spirits.) When I spoke with David Huron, head of the Cognitive and Systematic Musicology Laboratory at Ohio State University, on the subject of the male urge to make loud, deep noises, he said, "It's all about pecking order. That's why men don't cry and why the pitch of their voice drops at pubescence." But what about the fact that acoustical bluster is no guarantee that a physical fight will actually be avoided? "It's females who have a low-risk reproductive strategy," he fired back. "Males have a very low likelihood of contributing to the gene pool."

By now I had a few ideas about the roots of the pursuit of silence. Our forebears sought quiet to hear threats and potential meals in motion more clearly, and because silence helped them focus. I also could see the way that making loud sounds might, on occasion, have provided a weapon to ward off enemies and attract erotic partners for whom, when it came to vocal cords, size mattered. But still I wondered, is it really true that all our reactions to sound are dictated by simple equations: loud, low sound equals something powerful, so be scared or be prepared to mate, or both; soft, little sound equals something small, so be calm, be prepared to mate, or both? What about noises that stimulate pleasure, pain, or fury apart from nearby mates and predators? How did these fit in with ideas of evolutionary psychology?

SEARCHING FOR THE FUNDAMENTAL FREQUENCY

"Sound is a brute force," Daniel Gaydos, president of the Museum of Sound Recording, declared. He held a long-fingered hand flat in the air before his face and moved it slowly up and down. "That is a sound disturbance at two times a second," he said. "Though you can't hear it as sound. If you see a suspension bridge moving up and down once every two seconds, its pitch is half a cycle per second. We can see a vibration up to about twenty times a second. After that it starts to blur. When we can no longer track a vibration visually, we begin to hear it. Human hearing falls roughly between the range of twenty and twenty thousand wave cycles per second. Whenever you start thinking about sound, you've got to keep coming back to that idea of a physical force: objects vibrating and shaking off mechanical waves that clench and release the molecules of whatever medium they're moving through."

Gaydos is a tall, bony man with a mellifluous radio-announcer's voice, the limpid eyes of a far-seeing bird, and a somehow predictable devotion to the more mystical later writings of Carl Jung. I visited him at the Institute of Audio Research, in New York City, where he is a professor. I wanted to understand what sound waves are and how they impact us, even when they don't carry specific animal associations.

The institute, which offers a one-year degree to students aspiring to a career in music, occupies most of a narrow town-house off Union Square. On the day I first visited, there was a large group of young men smoking out front of the entrance, almost all of whom were wearing gray hoods over dark hats over white iPods, along with very bright black-and-white sneakers. Under the hoodie of the man nearest the door was a T-shirt emblazoned with an image of a fierce, hairy orange monster wearing headphones and baring its fangs above a turntable on which it was scratching a record album.

Gaydos explained to me that a large part of what the institute offers these days is human contact, since almost all the students have been playing around in their rooms with digital recording technology for years. "Community is gone when it comes to the recording studio," he said. We walked by framed gold and platinum record albums toward his office, passing students on cell phones and rooms filled with animated, mostly male students. They were wearing headphones behind the glass walls of a recording studio and wearing headphones in sound-mixing class while staring at display screens. Students at the institute, Gaydos told me, are "amazingly open" to listening to new sounds, so long as these sounds are coming through headphones. When I later asked Gaydos if he saw commonalities between the students, he thought for a moment and then remarked that attention deficit disorder seemed to serve as a kind of "common language" among his pupils.

In fact, research indicates that music heard through MP3 players or other devices can function as white noise that enables people with attention deficit disorder to concentrate. There are differing explanations for why the brains of many ADD and autistic individuals need noise to focus, but the point is worth bearing in mind when we think about our loudening world. Much professional analysis of noise problems concerns the "signal-to-noise ratio." Simply put, signal-to-noise expresses the ratio of sound carrying significant information to that of the ambient noise surrounding that sound. It could be that when white noise enters an already disordered cognitive system, it resonates with the signal, amplifying it and preventing the signal from being lost amidst competing sounds. Alternately, a steady noise under the individual's control may mask the distraction of other, novel stimuli. Either way, the tendency of more and more people to turn up the sound in more environments may reflect a rise in ADD and autism spectrum conditions across the general population. If this is true, increasing numbers of people whose brains need noise to function optimally may find they have to keep turning up the volume further as the noise made by other people doing the same thing drowns out their personal distraction-of-choice.

As we sat down in an empty classroom, Gaydos began drawing different musical notes and charts on the blackboard. He told me that he wanted to talk about the kinds of relationships between frequencies most likely to trigger serenity, as David's harp soothed the madness of Saul. Pythagoras, whose followers were required to maintain a strict vow of silence for up to five years— during which time, as "auditors," they learned the virtues of listening and "continence of words"—was the most renowned early explorer of the numerical relationships that find expression in the acoustical universe. In a legend passed down through the ages, Pythagoras was passing a blacksmith shop one day when he realized that the notes produced by the hammers were directly proportional to their weights. He rushed back to his workshop, hung four strings to pegs in the wall, fixed hammers of differing weights to these strings, and began discovering the mathematical ratios behind the familiar harmonic intervals of musical expression. In the course of his experimenting, he found that if you snip a vibrating string in half you raise its pitch exactly an octave. When you play two notes an octave apart, so that the frequency of vibration of one note is double the one below, you produce what the Greeks idealized as the most pleasing ratio to the ear. Gaydos calls it "the easiest relationship to feel" and suggests that what may make it so gratifying a sound is our ability to actually hear the two sound waves fit in an octave nestling snug one inside the other. Cutting up more strings to lengths based on divisions of fifteen, Pythagoras was able to reproduce the entire musical scale.

The Pythagorean moment at the blacksmith's has been discredited in modern times by authorities who point out that the sound of hammer blows do not vary based on the weight of the tool, and that Pythagoras wasn't the first to understand the musical relationships he's credited with. His uncontested achievements lie more in the metaphysical line that led him to hypothesize that music, when rightly proportioned, could infuse the harmonic order of the universe into the listener, thereby exerting a benign moral influence. The numerical rules of the sound world operate with a consistency so striking that when he began to grasp their power, Pythagoras compared the entire universe to a musical instrument that brought dissonant elements into harmony. Each planet, Pythagoras believed, produces a note in the course of its orbit based on its distance from the still center of the Earth by the same laws that determine the relative pitch of different-length strings. Apollo, the sun god, conducted the music of the spheres with his lyre.

Augustine added a Christian framework to the ethical resonance of well-ordered sound, writing that through the mathematical ratios governing holy music one could intuit God's harmonious arrangement of the universe, which provided a template for the proper structuring of individual existence. The medieval church drew heavily on the so-called "sacred geometries" that embodied these ratios in all of its this-worldly constructions. Saint Bernard wrote: "What is God? He is length, width, height and depth." The visual grace of Cistercian architecture, which is often referred to as an "architecture of silence," derives from the way it conforms to the ratios of musical harmony. "There must be no decoration, only proportion," remarked Saint Bernard. And the ideas of sacred order, in turn, found their way back into the modes and cadences of Gregorian chant.

These ratios still carry power. In the summer of 2008, Universal Records released a recording of monks chanting in one of the oldest Cistercian monasteries in the world, Stift Heiligenkreuz, near Vienna. The album soared in popularity, for a time eclipsing sales of superstars like Madonna. Coincident with the release of *Chant: Music for the Soul*, Alan Watkins, senior lecturer in neuroscience at Imperial College, London, released a report on research conducted by his team that found "the regular breathing and musical structure of chanting" could have positive physiological effects. Watkins's findings followed on earlier studies that showed how chanting reduced blood pressure and upped the levels of the performance hormone DHEA. The beneficial physical and mental effects of Cistercian chanting described by Watkins looked a lot like the ones I'd seen associated with silent meditation.

Indeed, Gaydos told me that the sacred geometries are part of the acoustical "bible" that professionals like him make use of all the time. "Anyone who builds a recording studio is aware, on some level, of the golden proportions, and the mathematical ratios and sequences that were subsequently developed from these equations," he said. They have to be, Gaydos believes, because for sound purposes those proportions have rarely been improved upon. "Traditional churches sound beautiful," he remarked. Some of the most successful recording studios in the world have, in fact, been churches—both the celebrated Columbia and Decca studios in New York City were converted church buildings, the former an Armenian church with a hundred-foot-high ceiling. It's only in very recent times, Gaydos believes, that church architects have abandoned Pythagorean conventions to create spaces that are, he said, "completely fucked up acoustically."

In a cosmos composed with such attention to harmonic order, issuing so awesome an invitation to unity and coherence, a note that does not play its rightful role in the larger pattern can be as disruptive as a conforming sound is gratifying. Thinking of this call to synchronize with the measure of the world, the medieval philosopher Boethius declared, "We love similarity, but hate and resent dissimilarity." (A contemporary sound designer I spoke with, who produces CDs to help children fall asleep, described his process of combining sounds like chimes, bubbles blowing, waves, harps, and a heartbeat as one of "minimizing change and harmonic tension" in order to "reach habituation.") Along these lines, Gaydos offered a definition of noise from the world of acoustical science. "Noise," he said, "has more frequencies than musical sound and the frequencies are not related." The way in which certain "unrelated"—that is, dissimilar, uneven—clusters of frequencies strike the ear can have dire real-world consequences.

※

Every structure, organic and nonorganic, has a special frequency at which it naturally vibrates when energized into motion. We might think of the situation this way: on some level, everything likes to be still—to be silent—as much as possible. But failing that perfect state of rest, there are specific speeds at which every structure is predestined to vibrate. An ashtray, a car steering wheel, a violin string, and the vocal folds of a child—each has its own fundamental frequency.

What makes for the fundamental frequency of a given object? That object's mass and tension. In other words, the core physical truth of every structure determines the way it dances and shimmies off sound waves into the universe. An object's fundamental frequency is a kind of naked snapshot of identity. By definition, this snapshot also reveals the other structures that the object is most likely to mutually resonate with.

Our auditory systems seem to pursue fundamental frequency as an object's calling card. Manufacturers of mini-speakers with limited bass range know that by multiplying frequencies in the upper harmonic pattern it's possible to make people feel they are also hearing the low, fundamental harmonics with which the upper range is typically associated. But the bass boost is all in the mind. Similarly, when we're playing a five-foot grand piano, the lowest key, vibrating at 27.5 times a second, is barely audible. What we hear when that bottom A is played is, in fact, the upper harmonics overlaying it. And yet, Gaydos says, what we're always straining for, even if only subconsciously, is the fundamental frequency. "We're always searching for the floor of things," he said.

Perhaps, then, we listen for the fundamental frequencies to try and perceive the bodily truth of what's radiating a particular sound. Only the fundamental frequency, the telltale pulse of mass and tension beneath all the noise, can signal to us how we ought to orient our own body in relation to the sound maker.

So what happens in the physics of unwanted sound? I talked

with Andy Niemiec, the director of the Neuroscience Program at
Kenyon College, about the effects of violating intervals between
frequencies like the octave that strike our ears so benevolently.
Niemiec is studying the ways that certain changes in harmonic
structure trigger aggression. In particular, he's looking at the ways
that the harmonic relations in infant cries put them at risk for
physical abuse. "There's the base frequency of the sound,"
Niemiec explained, "the fundamental, and then harmonic over-
tones, multiples of that fundamental. Any complex real-world
sound has this structure. Tap a metal plate," he said to me, "and
you're stressing that plate. That action is going to change the
plate's harmonics in ways we may have evolved to find irritating.
There's a lot of stuff out there that could be taken to argue that
certain changes in harmonic levels relative to each other cause
some sort of physiological change in us."

Gaydos agrees. "Remember, the Earth spins at a particular
frequency, even though we don't hear that frequency as sound,"
he told me. "There are correlations between the earthly vibrations
that we have adapted to as part of our evolutionary process." As he
spoke, Gaydos began manipulating sound waves on Pro Tools,
the software program that is now used to edit most film scores
and other music, creating different, color-coded harmonic con-
figurations and dissonances in celadon, pink, scarlet, and black
patterns evoking the image of our planet as a great vibrational
quilting bee.

※

Recently a few researchers at medical schools in the United
Kingdom began looking at what happens in the brain when we

listen to unpleasant sounds, like chalk on blackboards. Different bands of acoustical energy imprint themselves on different parts of the auditory cortex. By analyzing where the brain maps sounds that the study participants said they disliked, the researchers hoped to identify the spectrum of auditory representations that rub us the wrong way.

The study, which was published in the *Journal of the Acoustical Society of America* in December 2008, measured the effects of seventy-five different sounds, rating them from most to least unpleasant. The two top offenders were sounds that fortunately are rarely heard outside of certain last-ditch drinking establishments: "scraping a sharp knife along the surface of a ridged metal bottle" and "scraping a fork along glass." But female screams and baby cries also ranked alarmingly near the top of the list. (Baby laughter was rated as the least unpleasant sound, followed by "water flow," "small waterfall," "bubbling water," and "running water.") The researchers found that energy in the frequency range of two to five kilohertz will almost invariably be perceived as obnoxious—roughly the same range that Niemiec singled out in his work on aggressive responses to infant cries.

The U.K. researchers suggest that the explanation for our response may have to do with points of sensitivity in our auditory system. We might hear certain sounds as unpleasant because "they contain strong concentrations of energy in a range . . . to which the auditory system is maximally sensitive." In other words, the sounds that drive us crazy may be ones that we hear as loud at almost any level. Our auditory cortex seems set up to favor sounds consistent with the pursuit of silence.

The pitch of an infant's cry may have been biologically

selected because it's so hard to ignore. We may just be faced with two diametrically opposed interests on the part of the screamer and the screamed at. The helpless baby has to hit the most vulnerable point in our auditory cortex to make sure we take away the pain; the screamed-at party, on the other hand, has to smother the noise since it puts them at risk of being localized, then lunged upon by a savage beast or by someone like Jason Everman. Loud sounds—especially in certain frequencies—mean something bad is coming at us or placing us at risk. They have to be silenced as quickly as possible.

Except, that is, when aggression is the aim of the noise.

Once again, as Niemiec reminded me, it's not the frequency per se that's at issue. Aggression arises in response to certain changes in harmonics. A sense that some fundamental frequency is being stressed the wrong way elicits rage. And this returns us to the "228 vibrations" of Hitler's voice. Niemiec pointed out that to the extent Dr. Steer was correct in his measurements, it might mean Hitler sounded like Mickey Mouse. (Not usually a bloodlust-inducing frequency, though parents exposed to repeated viewings of Disney DVDs might think so.) Or, Niemiec added, it might sound like a woman's scream. But then I read another account of Hitler's voice that suggested the secret of his vocal powers might lie squarely in the domain of Niemiec's harmonic studies. This description reported how "at all of his public meetings Hitler begins in a rasping tone; decidedly he is off key. Then he modulates his voice and it becomes a pleasant baritone." Later on, the higher pitch returns. Then the lower. And so on. Perhaps, then, the power to incite aggression in his audiences arose not from the 228 vibrations on their own but from the repeated shift in harmonics, where Hitler stressed his "pleasant baritone" up to the level of a female scream. Leni Riefenstahl, Hitler's filmmaker, wrote in her memoir that the instant she first heard Hitler's voice she had an "almost apocalyptic vision." All at once, she recounted, the surface of the earth spread out before her "like a hemisphere that suddenly splits apart in the middle, spewing out an enormous jet of water, so powerful that it touched the sky and shook the earth. I felt paralyzed." Perhaps Hitler's voice really did create a kind of noise that suggested disruption in the cosmos.

Among the most intriguing explorations of the cosmic roots of noise is a study done in 2005 by Mark Whittle, an astronomy professor at the University of Virginia. Whittle undertook to analyze the sound of the big bang itself. His analysis revealed that the sound would not, in fact, have been an explosion at all.

Creation itself, it seems, was completely silent. Because the initial expansion consisted of a perfectly balanced, radial release of energy with, in Whittle's words, "no part catching up with any other part—there were no compression waves, no sound, just quiet brilliant live expansion." However, variations in density in the pre-creation universe had carved what Whittle describes as gravitational valleys and hills. As the gases of the big bang fell into these "cavities" and ricocheted around, sound waves were created. With the passage of time, more gas fell into deeper caves, making for more long, deep sound waves. Over the first tens of thousands of years, as gravity released the longer pressure waves into the spectrum, the pitch dropped. Gravity, in Whittle's universe, plays the part of a pianist at the keyboard of the primordial landscape. He characterizes the overall noise of the big bang as "a moment of silence, followed by a rapidly de-scending scream which builds to a deep roar and ends in a deaf-ening hiss."

Perhaps our revulsion for certain harmonic changes has its origin in the birth pangs of the universe.

※

There are two main ways that sound can have a negative impact upon us. One relates to specific associations we bring to a noise. The second, which is only just beginning to be explored, has to do with the inherent acoustical properties of certain sounds. In many but not all cases, the two species of disagreeable sound overlap. But whether the issue with a particular sound is associa-tive or intrinsic to the noise, or both, the problem is that—at least if it's loud enough—time does not diminish its sting. A thundering growl is as much a signal to us that we better hide as it was to our ancestors. Lidia Glodzik-Sobanska of the New York University Center for Brain Health told me that the problem with alarming sounds is that while we are quite good at psycho-logically adjusting, if we hear them often enough, our physiolo-gies *never* habituate. No matter how thoroughly our conscious minds might know that a loud siren rushing by is not coming for us, our blood pressure still spikes, our pupils still dilate, and our hair cells still flatten and twist.

There are two phenomena that trigger a baby's startle reflex: a sense of falling and a loud noise. In both cases, a baby responds by arching its back, flailing out with arms and legs, and grabbing out with its thumb and first finger. In other words, noise, exactly like being dropped, makes a baby feel it has lost its anchor in space and is plunging down. No wonder the word "noise" derives from *nausea*—specifically seasickness and the sense of dizzy disorientation it implies.

※

There is plenty of evidence for the negative consequences of noise. But the more I understood about these, the more I wondered why we would make so much of it intentionally. To get a handle on this conundrum, I went to visit a few contemporary environments in which people were relentlessly jacking up the volume.

CHAPTER FOUR

Retail: The Soundtrack

Dateline August 11, 2008, Barton Creek Square

From the dark opening in a black wall stamped with gray shutters came a pounding bass throb. I thought of the words of Michael Morrison, a professor of marketing I'd recently spoken with. "It's so difficult getting a 'wow' from customers entering a retail space today," Morrison had lamented. "The challenge of producing the 'wow factor' is placing a whole new amazing focus on the acoustical element in store design!" I stepped closer to the entrance and felt the waves of noise taking control of my body; it was as though a muscular DJ had just slammed down inside my chest and grabbed hold of my entire cardiovascular system.

"Wow," I said out loud.

"Right?" Leanne Flask, a blond sound designer with many clients at the Barton Creek Square mall in Austin, Texas, nodded. "Let's go." She waved me forward. We passed a pair of pubescent girls twitching in place in the spotlit darkness, and entered the sonic abyss of Abercrombie & Fitch.

⌗

Their flagship store is planted on Fifth Avenue a few blocks from my office, and from time to time in the months prior to my visit to Texas, I would wander by the entrance and take in the *thump, thump, thump* that emanates all day long from inside. The store often has a velvet rope set up outside, guarded by towering, chiseled men who eye the line of shoppers with cool menace. Many days the line wraps all the way around Fifty-sixth Street, filled with tourists from all over the world, mostly young but sometimes old, patiently awaiting their turn to get inside and buy some mass-produced clothes. Okay, I get it: it's hot, it's exciting, it's sexy. But I didn't *really* grasp why so many people of all different backgrounds would be drawn to shop in an environment where the sound was kept at a truly punishing level. I couldn't fathom why it was that, as Professor Morrison gushed, "People *love* that space everywhere they go!"

⌗

Shopping and noise have been associated since the first shill hawked his wares. In ancient bazaars (and a number of modern-day souks) salesmen shouted out the nature, quality, and prices of their goods; the loudest voice promising the best bargains often drew the biggest crowd. It's basic, big-lung competition. But except for a few connoisseurs of street noises (such as Irving Howe, who wrote approvingly in *World of Our Fathers* of markets where you could "relax in the noise of familiars"), the loudness of the scene was not itself a draw. Newspapers describing the peddler trade in early-twentieth-century New York almost invariably

attach the adjective "noisy" to this form of commercial activity—
in close conjunction with "aromatic," "unsightly," and "dirty."
When Mrs. Isaac Rice, who founded America's first society to
fight noise pollution, took a trip down to the Lower East Side in
1908 to hear the "unnecessary rackets in that section," she pronounced it the "saddest place" she had ever visited. To end the
"noises made by the hucksters" she proposed that residents of
the tenement houses "display different colored cards to indicate
the peddlers they wanted to buy from. A red card could attract the
vegetable vendor, a yellow card, the fruit man, and other colors
other tradesmen." Through this means she hoped to minimize
noise in neighborhoods where people were already condemned
to insufficient sleep "owing to their long toil." A few decades
later, most people applauded Fiorello La Guardia's campaign to
eliminate pushcarts—in part because it meant confining the
noise of commerce to the new indoor markets the mayor had
built. And when a *New York Times* article in January 1940 reported on the belated closing of the East Side pushcart market, it
noted that "only a few sentimental New Yorkers" regretted the
fact that Orchard Street, Hester Street, and Rivington Street
would no longer "resound to the raucous cries" of "bull-voiced
peddlers." Still, the clamor of the pushcarts was not the thunder
of Abercrombie & Fitch. I decided to contact A&F to ask them
about their sound strategy.

Unfortunately, my questions made "corporate" fall suddenly
as silent as Trappist monks after compline. But eventually I discovered DMX, the sound-design company responsible for implementing A&F's auditory will. Leanne Flask, an executive with
DMX, invited me to Austin, where the company is headquartered,

to discuss the thinking behind Abercrombie & Fitch's acoustics, and to give me a tour of the mall.

Flask is a stylish blonde with a big, apprehensive smile. The day I met her, her right arm was encased in a lavender-colored cast, the result of a volleyball disaster. As we drove to Barton Creek Square, Flask told me that DMX had started out in the mid-1970s marketing an uninterrupted music service that was beamed into stores by satellite. Music design for retail was then in its infancy: most providers, Flask explained, took the approach that just throwing on a CD did the trick. "You would have a store selling teen ballet slippers playing classic rock." There was a complete disconnect between product aura and store sound.

Today, the DMX Web site describes the company as "an international leader in multi-sensory branding" that enables clients to express their brand's "unique personality and create an unmistakable identity." These days, Flask explained, acoustical branding is much more than a matter of loading up an iPod for a client. "We hand-design how every single sound flows from song to song seven days a week, twenty-four hours a day." DMX provides clients with "mood, energy, texture." In her experience it was incredibly difficult for people to grasp that these elements had no connection to the most popular artist or the most popular song. What was it about then? I asked. "It's all about connection." She swung into a parking place in the mostly deserted mall lot and dug in her cowhide-pattern purse for a pair of sunglasses. "I've lived my whole life in music. I love what I do." She looked up at me. "This power to heal and connect and bring people together who otherwise wouldn't be . . . That's amazing."

ACOUSTICAL RAPTURE

As Flask and I began to loop the store, she hollered the odd factoid above the din. Pointing to a set of cellblock-like dressing rooms, she explained that though it sounded here as though the music had been cranked louder, it was just due to the fact that the dressing rooms lacked the stacks of clothing that provided a measure of sound absorption. I stopped to write a note, whereupon a young girl twitched up out of nowhere to ask if she could help us, then jiggled swiftly away when we shook our heads. Flask aimed a finger after her. "She thinks we're managers reviewing the store and she's freaking out. If you ever want to torment the people working in an Abercrombie & Fitch store, just come in with a little notebook writing things down." We started moving again. Flask yelled a few more insights in my direction. I gestured helplessly toward my ears; her remarks had been entirely drowned out. She started to shout louder, then gave up.

At last we staggered back out of the gates of the store to a position far enough away that we could hear each other without screaming. She glanced back at the storefront. A sympathetic human weariness passed across her features. "Everything's very dark inside. So they use the music to make it lighter." I nodded encouragingly and she gathered steam. "So all the music—everything's like very, very uplift-y. It's like—I'm going to start my day in a club!" She adopted the expression of someone being ecstatically strangled. "That's a branding tactic."

When DMX got the Abercrombie & Fitch contract, corporate management told her that the store "needs to feel like a place where everyone's having fun *all the time*. A happy place with a positive, happy feeling. Like a party. So for us, we have to be careful. Because there's a feeling they want you to express and it's not what they've done with the visual design. I have to look at what they already have and figure out how I can make it feel like an upbeat, uplift-y, happy, positive place when everything's really *dark*. So I'm going to have to go to extremes of happy and energetic." She looked back once more at the vibrating blackness.

While Abercrombie & Fitch technically targets fifteen- to twenty-eight-year-olds, Flask believes it's really going after the college freshman and those who idealize the freshman lifestyle. "It's the mentality of first time away from home," she said. "It's like, '*Woohoo!* I'm going out at night and I'm not going home afterward!' "

I inquired to what degree sheer loudness was part of the equation she had to work with. She cast me a look like I was making fun of her. "We have to be *very* aware of exactly how every sound will be heard at the levels they're going to be played at," she said. "So if a song is going to start splattering at a certain level, we can't use it." She went into a lengthy technical digression about how they gauged the risk of splatter in different acoustical conditions.

"But how is all this about creating a connection?" I asked, gesturing toward the booming storefront. Flask paused. "This isn't about using music to create a connection," she conceded. "It's about using music to create an event."

All of this seems designed to push a simple, primeval trigger: Abercrombie & Fitch uses loud music and spotlit darkness to induce a state of celebratory arousal. Indeed, if you walk around your local branch of Abercrombie & Fitch, you may feel that there would be something downright frigid in considering your purchase too closely. Far better to release your inner "Oh my God I'm away from my home!"

※

This is not, of course, a use of noise that Abercrombie & Fitch invented. Despite what Flask said, this too can be understood as a means of creating connection, only it's less between people than between the individual and a state of group ecstasy.

※

Iegor Reznikoff is a specialist in ancient music at the University of Paris who has a fondness for medieval chanting and spelunking. In 1983, he went on a visit to Le Portel, a Paleolithic cave in France. When he walked into Le Portel, he began humming to himself, as he generally does when he goes into a new room, to "feel its sounds." Reznikoff was intrigued to discover that when the walls were adorned with painted animals, his humming became louder and more intense. Working with Michel Dauvois, a colleague, Reznikoff went on to demonstrate that ancient paintings on cave walls around the French Pyrenees are positioned in synchrony with points of heightened acoustical resonance. In the course of subsequent explorations across France, Reznikoff found that there was almost no resonant point in caves once inhabited by Paleolithic peoples that did not contain at least some painted markings—and, conversely, that the positioning of some of the markings could only be understood in relationship to sound. Moving through the caves in total darkness while using his voice as the only sound source, Reznikoff would come to "a particularly resonant place," turn on the light, and invariably find a sign, "even in a place unsuited for painting."

Reznikoff believes that this intersection of painting with acoustically hyperresponsive stone walls reveals how the shaman heightened the emotional power of ritual through amplification and echoes. (The resonance at these sites is, indeed, powerful enough that when he himself made sounds in the caves Reznikoff felt his whole body vibrating in tandem with the gallery.) Sound effects enhanced a sense of communion with both the space and the images painted there. Such synchrony would also have boosted the shaman's effort to identify with specific animals. By making a sound near a picture of an animal, Reznikoff discovered he was able to make it seem that the animal itself was calling out.

Reverberation, echoes, amplification, and resonance were all part of the prehistoric wise man's bag of tricks for inducing a state of high emotion and minimal reason. This, it seemed to me, was getting closer to the territory of the mall.

NOISE AND THE PERENNIAL HUMAN ENERGY CRISIS

Flask and I wandered on through Barton Creek Square and stepped into The Limited, a loud, throbby, high-contrast space, which to me sounded like Abercrombie & Fitch on a light Zoloft regimen. I asked Flask to analyze the store's acoustical message.

She lowered her eyes a moment, and nodded to the beat. "The Limited girl is a little older. She works all day, but then she goes out, without having the time to drive home and change her clothes. She's probably just out of college, just entering the work-force. This works."

After Flask conjured up the busy, vibrant life of the Limited girl for me (I sort of did and did not want to meet her), I wondered aloud whether the noise strategy of the mall today did not, after all, just come down to sex. Was what we were hearing simply a matter of different stores taking on the acoustic personae of giant bullfrogs in a fecund swamp at springtime? A kind of precopulatory croak-off between—

"There's a lot of sex," Flask broke in. But it was also, she added, a matter of energy dynamics. "All of the energy of the loudness makes you feel very energetic." She raised her voice several notches. " 'George, did you see this shirt! Did you see this?!' It raises the ambient energy in the store. It feels like excitement, and starts a whole reaction of people. There's a circuit of energy! The music is fast and loud so you move through the store more quickly without using as much energy."

Indeed, one of the only repeatedly validated effects of music on shoppers relates to tempo. A faster beat makes shoppers move more quickly, while a more leisurely tempo slows physical movement through a store. The principle is derived from the effects of military music on the speed of marching soldiers. Not only does the process of falling into step with a drumbeat make the pace of the marcher subject to manipulation and lead to general arousal; recent research has demonstrated that when people are moving in synchrony to a beat, their behavior is more compliant to the collective will.

Things were beginning to fall into place. Loud, strong, fast beats pump energy—and social conformity—into any number of environments.

One of the earliest newspaper mentions of Muzak is found

in a *New York Times* article from January 1939 entitled "Pier Equipped for Music Night and Day to Make Longshoremen Work Happily." The Isbrandtsen-Moller Company, an operator of cargo liners, decided that its workers on Pier 30 in Brooklyn would perform better "under the influence of sweet music." Muzak, which began in 1934 with a technological innovation that enabled phonographs to be played over electric power lines, quickly morphed into an audio-entertainment service for hotels and restaurants. The possibility of streaming music into workplaces opened new horizons for company marketers. An executive with Muzak applauded the policy decision by Isbrandtsen-Moller, declaring that "a heavy bag of coffee would assume a new aura of romance in an atmosphere charged with ebullient melodies urging the workers on." Muzak's program department determined the precise content of the "musical reproducing system" that broadcast dinner-and-dance music to the stevedores, loaders, and other members of the pier office force. It knew "the psychological time for 'lift' music and other categories fit for a worker's wandering emotions."

Shortly after the practice was adopted, however, and despite reports by the vice president of Muzak and Mr. Isbrandtsen that all the longshoremen were euphoric, local union leaders decided that the real purpose of the program was to speed up the pace of workers. The union called a strike that killed the music in double-time.

A couple of years later, however, during World War II, the notion of "riveting to rhythm" gained traction across the nation. Westinghouse discovered the acoustical secret to raising energy levels at work by accident, when the manager of the company's

Newark plant began playing records to test radio receivers. After the project was completed and the receivers were turned off on the plant floor, workers began complaining that they felt more fatigued than when listening to "I Do, Do You?" and "Let's Get Away from It All," and asked that the practice be reinstated. In response to lingering criticism by labor advocates, business leaders insisted that instead of "spurring a tired horse," they were helping to end boredom. Music, they contended, was a healthy distraction, particularly popular tunes that hit a metronome count between sixty-five and ninety beats per minute. By 1941, William Green, the president of the American Federation of Labor, could say, "Music is the friend of labor—it lightens the task by refreshing the nerves and spirits of the workers."

EAT THE BEAT

Zagat, the restaurant-review company, reports that noise is consistently customers' number-two complaint nationwide, ahead of high prices and second only to poor service. In 2008, more than a third of New York City patrons cited noise as their foremost complaint, up from 2002, the first year for which data is available, when only 21 percent ranked noise at the top of their list of dining grievances. Ten years ago, the *San Francisco Chronicle* was the first newspaper to incorporate a noise-rating system into its restaurant reviews: one bell indicates a sound level of less than sixty-five decibels, and the scale ascends through another three bells to the category of "bomb," representing eighty-plus decibels of din. Michael Bauer, the *Chronicle's* senior food and wine writer, says that he may now have to institute a "double bomb" rating, and reports a sharp decline in the number of San Francisco restaurants rating less than four bells, equivalent to loud factory noise.

※

The first rigorous study of the effects of fast music on the pace of dining was conducted in the mid-1980s. Customers exposed to slow music spent significantly longer at table: an average of 56 minutes as opposed to 45 minutes. Another study, performed around the same time at Fairfield University, demonstrated that people increased the speed of their chewing by almost a third when listening to faster, louder music, accelerating from 3.83 bites a minute to 4.4 bites a minute. Stoked with data of this nature, chain restaurants, such as Dick Clark's American Bandstand Grill, developed computerized sound systems that were preset to raise the tempo and volume of music at hours of the day when corporate wanted to turn tables. "A lot of the managers try to turn music down because they think it's too loud for people eating," said Don Blanton, who developed the system for the grill. "So we've put in an automated system."

※

Loudness has been linked to a more profitable rate of food consumption more by intuitive association than because of hard evidence. (Indeed, one study indicated a decline in the amount of money spent at the tables that turned too quickly.) But when it comes to consumption of alcohol, the data confirms expectations. A study completed in the summer of 2008 in France by researchers at the Université de Bretagne-Sud found that when music was played at 72 decibels, men consumed an average of 2.6 drinks at a rate of one drink per 14.51 minutes. When the sound level was cranked up to 88 decibels, the numbers spiked to an average of 3.4 drinks consumed every 11.47 minutes. Reasons for this acceleration may include an increase in ambient energy, the difficulty of talking—which makes it easier to just signal the bartender for a refill than to engage in conversation—and perhaps actual changes in brain chemistry.

It has already been proven that acoustic stimulation heightens the effect of MDMA, better known as Ecstasy, to a degree that influences the drug's toxicity. Since most people are taking Ecstasy in environments where sound levels are rapturously elevated, this is a worrisome finding. Though the mechanism is not fully understood, a recent study by Italian medical researchers demonstrated that even low doses, which did not in themselves affect electrocortical parameters, when administered in conjunction with sound equivalent to a typical discotheque, spiked electrical activity in the brain sufficiently to produce what might be called a sizzle-and-fry effect. Furthermore, when animals in the experiment were drugged in silent environments, their brains reverted to normal levels of electrocortical activity within twenty-four hours. When loud sound was added to the mix it took a full five days for their heads to straighten out.

But there's a larger point here: noise heightens other forms of stimulation, especially other forms of overstimulation. There's also evidence that loud acoustics make us crave more overstimulation. A group of men presented with an array of foods balanced across a salty-sweet spectrum reported pleasure from the high-sugar flavors at far greater rates when listening to loud music than when dining to a background of soft music. In other studies, researchers have shown that when people eat potato chips while wearing headphones that amplify the overall noise level of their crunching, they rate the chips as crispier, fresher—more desirable—than their counterparts chewing without an electronic sound boost.

✠

So retailers turn up the volume to get people moving through the store and build in-store excitement. Restaurateurs crank up the sound to turn tables and build (literal) restaurant buzz. There was one other environment that came to mind when I thought of places that had been much quieter in the not-so-distant past— sports arenas. The modern-day gladiator is dependent on acoustical steroids.

NOISEBALL

In October 2008, Louisiana State University's Tiger Stadium (nicknamed "Deaf Valley") was touted in the *Athens Banner-Herald* as "one of the loudest places in the nation." University of Georgia coach Mark Richt called the stadium "a place you can't hear yourself think. A place that I can truthfully say is the loudest place I've ever been." Meanwhile, *Sports Illustrated* put Arrowhead Stadium in Kansas City at the head of its list as "Toughest Place to Play" for an opposing team—because of how loud the Chiefs fans get. Rod Smith of the Denver Broncos remarked that the first time he played at Arrowhead "it scared the hell out of me—and that was just the national anthem . . . I thought they were going to attack us. I thought 70,000 people were about to come out of the stands and get us." Crowd noise at Autzen Stadium in Eugene has reached 127.2 decibels, which would make the fans' experience resemble that of roaring in concert with a Boeing 747.

Qwest Field in Seattle, built in 2002, claims the title of loudest roofed stadium in the NFL. Paul Allen, owner of the Seattle Seahawks, instructed the architects to design the stadium to reflect a maximum of crowd noise back onto the field. He also installed a special seating zone with metal bleachers for the most raucous fans called the Hawk's Nest, which would enable the stamping of feet to reverberate as violently as possible. When the Giants played at Qwest Field in 2005, they were called for eleven false-start penalties—attributed to crowd noise that made it impossible for them to communicate.

It's small wonder that supporters of different teams are constantly accusing opposing home teams of electronically boosting the sound of their fans. Mike Sellers of the Washington Redskins recently said of Qwest Field, "That place had to be miked up, because the last time we played there, it was ridiculous. We couldn't hear ourselves talk. For a stadium that small, it can't be that loud." Fred Micera, the Qwest Field audio engineer, pronounced Sellers's charge an insult to the Seahawks fans, saying they had no need of artificial enhancement. (It can be done, though: a few years ago the New Jersey Nets were found to have been amplifying the sound of a crowd by broadcasting the prerecorded noise from another game.)

Outside of electronic escalation, there are structural tricks for maximizing the levels of ambient noise. Open-air stadium architects will sometimes add extra balconies and increase balcony overhang to heighten the reflection of sound into the stands and onto the field. Different materials can be used in construction to maximize reverberation. And yet, as Jack Wrightson, president of WJHW, an acoustical-design firm responsible for many of the best-known stadiums in the United States, told me, "The building doesn't make the crowd. You can enhance, but you can't turn a bad crowd into a good one with just building materials." The classic example, Wrightson said, is Denver's Mile High Stadium where, in 2000, Bronco fans entered the *Guinness World Records* for the loudest single crowd roar ever recorded. At one point the NFL began penalizing home teams when the noise went above a certain decibel level that was deemed an interference with quarterbacks barking commands to their lineup. (Wrightson pointed out that the NFL crowd-noise regulations are almost entirely ignored. "Nothing a crowd likes more than getting a penalty called on itself," he said.) But there was nothing special about the Mile High Stadium from an architectural point of view, Wrightson went on. "It's all about the crowd."

Yet the crowd is not just tens of thousands of spectators howling, clapping, stamping, and pounding. It's also every electronic and nonelectronic device that adds to the noise they can make with their own lungs. Some stadiums give out noisemakers like cowbells, maracas, and clackers. Barkers sell whistles, megaphones, handheld sirens, air horns, stadium horns, sports horns, and "super loud air blaster necklaces." And then of course there are the endless official stadium noise amplifiers generated by PA announcements, PA music, PA advertising, PA fireworks, PA applause, and general PA crowd incitement.

As for the athletes whom all this noise bombardment is intended to energize—they are playing in conditions that exceed by hundreds of percentage points what the Occupational Safety and Health Administration states is safe for the roughly three-hour duration of a game. Not only do extended balconies and enclosures beam whatever sound the crowd can make directly onto the fields, the roar is, as former Colts defensive tackle Larry Tripplett put it not long ago, "right in your ear. With the helmet that sound gets in there and rattles around." To prepare for these conditions, NFL and college players now regularly practice with rock music played at earsplitting levels as well as with noise machines parked along the sidelines that mimic the noise of a coliseum full of bloodthirsty spectators. While these machines are designed to help teams adjust to the distractions of fan noise, they are also used at the players' request, according to New York Giants coach Tom Coughlin, because players believe the noise helps them keep their energy level high. Between the noise of the games and the artificially generated noise of the practice field, many of today's professional athletes will suffer premature hearing loss.

CHAPTER FIVE

Sounds Like Noise

A German friend who lives part of each year in the United States told me recently that when he was first getting acclimated to the States, noise was one of his biggest problems. Not the noise in the streets, the stores, or the restaurants, but the actual word "noise." He could not get used to the way that people would use the word "noise" to signify a loud, offensive sound (as in, "I can't stand the noise here!") and also to refer simply to the sound something made (as in, "Don't you love the noise of that fountain?"). People might have thought him hard of hearing when he kept asking, "Do you think we're hearing a noise?" German, with its *geräusch* (sound) and *lärm* (nasty noise), preserves a clear distinction between creating a sound and emitting an unpleasant one.

The word "noise," as we know by now, derives from the Latin root *nausea*. How did that notion transfer to sound as such? The neutral usage crops up in late Middle English in England—around 1400. It would seem plausible that the switch occurred in the acoustical equivalent of a population explosion: too many disparate sounds heard together make for an experience of noise.

But that's not the whole story. What about noise-canceling headphones? These work by analyzing the waveform of background noise then generating an equivalent counter sound wave. Active noise control actually involves making *more* sound so that we hear less noise. And even without technology we all know that sometimes it's much harder to hear a person we're speaking with when there's one person with a *penetrating voice* standing next to us than when there's a whole group of people chattering in our vicinity.

"We're pattern recognizers," Wade Bray, an acoustical engineer with Head Acoustics, remarked to me. "When you're driving a car and there's a low-level rattle somewhere, even if the engine is making a loud, steady roar, the rattle is going to be the thing that bothers you. If you wanted to mask that sound, you'd be doing something so that the peaks weren't as high or as low. Total pattern always trumps objective level of sound. That's where human impressions and the loudness meter disagree." As an example, Bray asked me to imagine a quiet neighborhood in which two or three cars go by every ten minutes compared with a busy neighborhood where twenty cars might pass in the same time period. "There's going to be less peak value and less modulation in the quiet neighborhood." For that reason the two cars are often going to be more disturbing than twenty.

This is not, of course, a phenomenon unique to the human brain. There's an ancient evolutionary basis for the preference. We can see it in action today in the red-eyed tree frog, a creature that uses acoustical pattern recognition to perform the extraordinary feat of fast-forwarding its own birth to escape death. The normal hatching period for these frogs lasts four to seven days. A group of biologists and engineers affiliated with Boston University has spent the last several years in Panama studying how it happens that when the eggs sense that they're about to be attacked by a predator, embryos can expel themselves from their jelly capsules ahead of time and start doing their best to survive as preemie tadpoles. The answer, they've discovered, lies in their ability to recognize patterns in vibration or sound. Snakes are the biggest threat to the eggs, and when a snake strikes at the clutch, its rippling vibrations start the embryos firing out into the water. That may not be surprising, but the biologists discovered that raindrops and wind produce vibrations on exactly the same frequency spectra as the snakes. So how can the eggs tell the difference? As it turns out, the vibrations made by the snake produce a regular on-off pattern as the reptile reaches for an individual egg, withdraws to munch its frog caviar, then reaches in again. The gap between the vibrations makes for a pattern that tips the eggs off: hit the ejector button and get the hell out. The random pattern of raindrops and wind is a sign to eggs that they can mature at their leisure. (Maybe there's a clue in this phenomenon as to why we're often soothed by sounds of falling water.)

J. Gregory McDaniel, the Boston University mechanical engineer who explained all this to me, is a big man with a rock-cracking laugh and a jaw off Mt. Rushmore. He is now using the pattern-recognizing tree-frog eggs as a model to create "biologically inspired" sensors for the U.S. Army. Soldiers will scatter them like tiddlywinks every meter or so across areas in Iraq and Afghanistan where they want to be able to monitor the history of patterned vibrations, like mine burying, before they drive through. "The army told me the sensors had to cost less than a dollar a piece!" McDaniel repeated more than once before giving his cliff-breaking laugh. "Now we're starting to make them so you can put 'em in water to detect patterned vibrations there. Just like the eggs!" Vibration-monitoring devices based on frog embryos may soon be saving troops and ships around the world.

Just as we're instinctually predisposed to be disturbed by sounds that stick out from the ambient flow, when we hear lots of different sounds simultaneously, the result can be not just less jarring but actually more calming—closer kin to the family of silence—than even low-level sounds we hear separately. Hence the sleep-inducing patterns produced by white-noise machines that bring together all audible frequencies at once. Or the musical productions produced twenty-four hours a day by the infrastructure of our great cities.

❈

At a meeting of the American Association for the Advancement of Science in 1931, Dr. William Braid White, director of research and acoustics for the American Steel and Wire Company, created a nationwide stir when he proposed that the roar of cities actually had a musical undertone. Dr. White encouraged every member of his audience to go to the twentieth story of a New York skyscraper, open a window, and lean out. "Let him then listen carefully to the noises that float up to him from the street below," Dr. White instructed. "After a while he will notice that the crashes, bangs, and clatters that, upon the street level, come as a succession of shattering blows upon his ears, now begin to blend into a single continuous roar." Having reached this point of higher acoustical consciousness, the fellow hanging out of the window was commanded to concentrate still further until he made out "a low bass hum below the main roar." This, Dr. White argued, was the "ground tone" of New York, based on innumerable small elements, which, while individually disagreeable, together made for a genuinely musical tone. (New York's, he said, was pitched between A and B flat in the low bass.)

Every city in the world, Dr. White claimed, has its own special ground tone. Chicago, for example, though filled with people who are just as noisy as New Yorkers, seemed to Dr. White "more lighthearted." Though the Loop was "crowded to suffocation," the lake acted as a damper—all the more necessary because the streetcars were noisier and the sound of the elevated "far more pervasive." All in all, Dr. White was inclined to place Chicago's ground tone at E flat. London, on the other hand, had "a heavy hum" close to the lowest C, because it was a city of "low buildings, wood paving blocks, moist atmosphere"—and a "law-abiding population" not prone "to displays of excessive excitement."

Dr. White confessed that his discovery might not carry overwhelming scientific relevance, but he contended that if we listen for the particular character of music made by our respective blendered city noises, we might achieve insights into both the innate psychologies and environmental influences acting upon residents. There were also, he implied, benefits for the listener: all you need is a little distance in order to begin receiving something of the concertgoer's pleasure from an experience of sound that might otherwise strike the ears simply as noxious clamor.

I thought about frog eggs, snakes, Dr. White's experiment, and about sound and offensive sound. When does a multiplicity of noises add up to a musical undertone as opposed to a galling cacophony? If a mall roof was stripped off, and Dr. White was elevated to a point high above it, how would he characterize the nature of the place from its sound?

But the phenomenon in question goes far beyond the mall. The sound designer DMX lists restaurants, hotels, entertainment complexes, health and fitness centers, and a handful of prestigious universities among its clients. Supermarkets, hospitals, building lobbies, parking garages, public restrooms, and most airports today have sound streamed through their waiting areas and corridors. Even the depths of our swimming pools are now sometimes amplified with music, as I discovered when a conference on noise took me to Foxwoods Casino. It's very, very loud everywhere you turn at Foxwoods, and the blanket of green trees beyond the casino confines are off-limits to guests. The only "escape" permitted is gambling. I consoled myself that once I dove beneath the water of the pool I would steal a break for as long as I could hold my breath. To my shock, when I dipped beneath the water I found that speakers were playing there as well. Muzak, at the height of its popularity, used music primarily as a backdrop to visual displays. Today, so-called foreground music, which is played at higher volumes and features original artists with vocals, bass, and percussions intact, is the soundtrack of choice.

The new noise is all about trying to demodulate and defy any larger pattern of environmental sound. Usually this translates into being loud, but not always. Designers are now dedicating themselves to provoking moods and emotional connection from sounds of every dimension made by individual products themselves. Sonic branding is fast becoming a major business. More and more product noises are now manipulated to punch up the consumer's desire to purchase. The purr or roar of an automobile engine. The sound of a golf ball. The click of a camera. The crunching of foods. The sound of the lipstick-container top popping off and the lipstick sliding up. Already these sounds are being analyzed and enhanced. Everything we buy is going to join the acoustical menagerie endlessly bleating out its sonic identity to every passerby.

Going back to Dr. White, I would propose a definition of noise as sound that you can't get distance on—sound that gets inside your head and won't go away. Hypersonic sound, a relatively new technology that dispenses with the loudspeaker altogether by shooting a super-focused ray of sound directly at its target, is only an extreme version of what most of the new noise is trying to do. When the acoustical laser beam of hypersonic sound hits the ears, it feels as though a projected voice is speaking inside the "listener's" skull. I got beamed by one playing party dance music in the Massachusetts Institute of Technology Media Lab. As the person holding the flat-black tablet-style speaker pans the beam across you, you hear the sound pass from ear to ear *through your head*. Big wow factor. There are numerous online diaries and pleas from people who may or may not be paranoid schizophrenics discussing hypersonic sound as one more proof of a conspiracy involving a huge time and energy commitment by extremely scary forces to take over their brains and drive them to suicide.

For all of us, the effect of sound we can't get away from can be literally dizzying. When it is loud enough it can disturb the vestibular system in the inner ear on which our sense of equilibrium depends. Even when not actually inducing vertigo, there's a loss of psychological balance that comes from being taken over by a sound; our aural back and forth with the world is gone and we are shaken into the larger vibrations.

※

One afternoon at rush hour I went to Grand Central Station. I stood in the middle of the terminal, beneath the great vaulted ceiling with its twinkling stars, listening.

At midnight on January 2, 1950, a series of extraordinary, spontaneous protests brought to an end a 13-week program in which canned music, along with 240 commercials per 17-hour period, were broadcast through 82 loudspeakers positioned throughout the terminal. The program had been a profitable public-private partnership: the New York Central Railroad was making $1,800 a week (almost $15,000 in today's terms) from leasing the soundscape of Grand Central Station to Muzak and the advertisers who worked with it. But the commuters rose up, insisting on their inalienable right not to be exploited as "captive audiences," demanding their "right not to listen." They made dire prophecies that if this practice were tolerated, the trains themselves would be next. They enlisted psychiatrists to argue that the constant sound was deleterious to the nervous system, and advertisers who testified that the initiative would besmirch the integrity of the business of advertising. They refused to be silenced and began preparing legal briefs.

And suddenly, amazingly, the railroad backed down and abandoned the program. "We just threw in the towel," one unnamed railroad spokesperson declared. The manager of the terminal concluded his announcement of the termination of the public-address system broadcast by thanking "all our passengers for giving us the benefit of their sincere opinions on the subject, pro and con, for it is only after a thorough airing of the issues that such matters can be decided."

⚒

I stood a few moments, letting the great reverberating waves of sound wash over me. I heard the rolling wheels of suitcases; the unfolding crinkles of maps; the scuffs and squeaks of shoes on the big, polished light tiles; the chink of an umbrella onto the stone; a broken sentence, "Anyway—*here you are*"; an impossibly low, faint bellowing of some train announcement. Above all, I heard the different frequencies of thousands of melding voices floating up to the great blue-green barrel vault dancing with golden stars and the silent bestiary of the zodiac, swelling and ebbing in one great sublime roar. I stood there and shut my eyes. As I listened, I knew I could only have been in this one place in all the world.

⚒

After my visit to Grand Central, I knew we couldn't blame all noise today on evil anonymous retailers, restaurateurs, and the corporations who supply them. How did we ever get to the point of giving the acoustical shock troops such a wide field of opportunity? What is the nature of our complicity? As the commuters in Grand Central once demonstrated, *life doesn't have to sound this way.*

To get a better handle on why we let things come to such a pass, I still had to travel to the extremes of loud; to people who choose not just to pound with sound but to pulverize—to turn themselves and others inside out with noise. For if I now understood some of the motivations for amping up the volume, I had yet to grasp the rationale behind the pursuit of noise for noise's sake. I suspected that this principle underlay a great deal of the day-to-day sound of today. Noise has become our way of "just saying no" to many, many things. I wanted to zero in on the cultural and technological developments that have driven us to make sonic punishment a badge of freedom.

First, however, I needed a break. I felt as though I'd been on an exhausting tour to some not very nice places. Come to think of it, I had. Now, like any other weary traveler, I wanted to put down my guidebook and take off my shoes. I needed refreshment: an out-of-the-way café shaded with umbrellas, serving lemon ices; an inviting spring shadowed by a willow tree; a hidden garden graced with old gray statues and lichen-ambered stone benches. I craved a little quiet time.

CHAPTER SIX

Silent Interlude

Having neither time nor money for a holiday flight, I decided to go on a tour of oases of silence near my midtown office. As a matter of principle, pursuing silence should be pleasurable, like hunting for prize wild mushrooms or bathing in mild seas, not painful, like striving to flatten one's stomach or to maintain a stern budget.

Wherever you live there are ways of finding silence—it's just that these ways are often not as pleasant as they should be. Silence is still around, but often it's been marginalized to the point where it conveys the prospect of eternal silence a little too vividly. Abandoned, broken-glass-strewn lots behind barbed wire, vacant buildings, and mortuaries might be quiet, but at what cost?

That said, the basic strategy for locating the remaining sites of silence in your hometown is to envision it as the Costa del Sol. The beach is out of the question. All the places people are naturally drawn to for work, recreation, and shopping are going to be impossibly loud. But a short distance inland cuts the crowds down to a dribble of locals and suddenly one finds oneself in an authentically foreign place. So ask yourself: What is the interior of the place I live? Where do surf and sand stop? What's the road no one bothers to drive? The bench where no one sits?

In many cities, the land underneath the yawning arches where old bridges sink their foundations is a place of refuge, as are the tops of undistinguished skyscrapers. In smaller towns, historical societies and libraries with inadequate Internet connections are almost invariably deserted. Museums of unfashionable subjects are a good bet anywhere (you can almost always hear a pin drop in collections attached to schools of medicine). Cemeteries on weekdays, wherever you live, are an obvious but reliable refuge. Just remember to keep asking, Where's the culture pulling everyone? Now turn around and walk the other way. Keep walking.

Manhattan might not seem like the most promising foraging ground for a couple of hours of silence, but I'm in an especially fortunate area for hunters of that aural truffle. My own circuit is small and more effortless than it might be in many ostensibly quieter communities.

POCKET PARKS

Within a ten-minute walk of where I work there are two marvelous and one better-than-nothing example of the pocket park. Pocket parks—also known as miniparks and vest-pocket parks—are small patches of landscaped nature generally built on vacant building lots or scraps of urban land that fall between the cracks of real estate interests.

I began my morning's pursuit of moderate silence at Paley Park on East Fifty-third Street, just across Fifth Avenue from the Museum of Modern Art. Opened in the spring of 1967, it is one of the oldest pocket parks in the United States. It is named for William Paley, the former chairman of CBS, who financed and oversaw the park's design on the site of the old Stork Club. When he announced his plans to create the park, Paley described it as a "resting place" and a "new experiment for the enjoyment of the out-of-doors in the heart of the city." It proved an enormous hit from the moment it opened, and has remained popular ever since. The *New York Times* called it "a corner of quiet delights amid city's bustle." Early visitors waxed enthusiastic about the relief it provided from the din of the streets, and the "acoustic perfume" of the park's waterfall.

To enter Paley Park, you ascend a few steps from Fifty-third Street into a narrow gap between tall buildings, flanked by ivy-covered walls. (The park's landscape designer, Robert Zion, described them as "vertical lawns.") Almost instantly, the waterfall at the far end of the park—twenty feet high and running with some 1,800 gallons of water per minute—entirely drowns out the street noise. The morning I visited, the park's tall, scraggly honey locusts were still bare, but the gray pots scattered around the park were bright with clumps of yellow tulips. From the entrance, the rectangular sheet of brown stone at the far end of the park over which the white water flows resembles a movie screen, but as you come closer you realize that the backdrop is in fact composed of countless small brown-and-gray irregular stones that sometimes slow and highlight the pattern of falling water. It's beautiful. Like the other two pocket parks in my neighborhood, there's no real quiet. Water masks the grinding city sounds. It works: the effect on the spirit is one of silence.

Jacob Riis is credited with having invented the idea of the pocket park in 1897, when he was secretary of New York City's Committee on Small Parks. The committee issued a statement declaring that "any unused corner, triangle or vacant lot kept off the market by litigation or otherwise may serve this purpose well." New York abounded with possibilities at the turn of the century, but Riis's idea went largely unrealized. The real surge in implementing the concept occurred in postwar Europe, London and Amsterdam in particular, where the staggering numbers of bombed-out building sites provided the opportunity to create an array of small parks at less cost than reconstruction. Pocket parks thus came into their own in literal gaps in the fabric of the city. In New York, their proliferation began in the late 1960s during the Lindsay administration, under the stewardship of the commissioner of parks Thomas Hoving. Noting the profusion of small parcels of empty land in the city—Bedford-Stuyvesant alone had 378 vacant lots along with another 346 abandoned buildings—Hoving saw that even a modest allotment of parks money, less than 10 percent of the annual budget, would be enough to acquire and develop 200 pocket parks across the city.

Hoving recognized how great a difference these small oases could make in the lives of the communities where they were situated. They offered the city not only "lungs" and a respite from noise but opportunities for collective action on the part of the surrounding communities that Hoving enlisted to reclaim the land. Hoving saw that the communal act of making these spaces of quiet itself promoted harmony.

Greenacre Park, where I walked next, on Fifty-first Street between Second and Third Avenues, is larger and to my mind still more exquisite than Paley. At the far end of the park from its Fifty-first Street entrance, an even higher waterfall tumbles down over great uneven blocks of rough-hewn brown granite. The steps leading down to each of the park's three levels are themselves edged by a stream of water running over irregular stones. The lovely, pale branches of a Japanese magnolia tree scribble at the western border of the waterfall, and this afternoon a large ornamental pear tree up above was gorgeously festooned with white blossoms. Miraculous.

I sat down on a white metal chair on the lowest level of the park, nearest the waterfall. Having individual chairs, as opposed to benches, was part of what made the pocket parks novel—and successful. Several studies undertaken a few years after the opening of Paley Park to look at the use of public plazas and other open areas in the city found that their effectiveness was directly tied to their "sit-ability"—defined both by availability of seating and the ability to shift the position of one's seat at will. Our sense of the quiet of a place depends on being able to comfortably pause within it wherever the mood takes us.

The white magnolia petals before me were open, long and gently droopy, like starfish cut from slightly damp summer chemises. The last time I'd really looked at a tree was a month earlier when I'd visited my brother in California and he'd taken me on a hike up in the Angeles Mountains. I'd noticed then how, at steep points in a narrow trail when our feet dislodged a tiny parade of gravel, the trunks and roots of the forest seemed to close directly over the sound.

There's an old notion that trees quiet the noise of our self-obsessing and help us engage with the world beyond. John Evelyn, the seventeenth-century English gardener and diarist, was involved with a long campaign to defend England's forests from the ax. In one of his impassioned appeals, he invoked the unpleasantness of walking along the "expos'd" roads of France. Without the shade and delimiting presence of trees, he declared, travelers "are but ill *Conversations* to themselves, and others."

The longer I sat in Greenacre Park, the more thoughts of other hours I'd spent in nature enveloped me. The act of remembering can itself create a greater silence, wrapping the present in layers of the past that sound doesn't penetrate.

At last I rose and walked on to 1221 Avenue of the Americas, a pocket park that allows you to walk through a plastic tube that takes you "under the waterfall." It's a bit too gimmicky, but it's still a welcome respite from the street.

PICTURES OF PAINTINGS

I was very close to the Museum of Modern Art, but it was a Friday and I knew the museum would be a madhouse, so instead I found a random stoop nearby, plopped down, and drew out the postcards I'd brought with me on my walk: small, pocket park–style reproductions of works by Giotto, Vermeer, Chardin, and Hopper. I stared very hard at the images. After a time, the stillness of a certain work of art will communicate itself, apart from specifics of the artist's vision. The bustling din on the street around me began to subside. I'm a skittish meditator, but there are numerous ways to achieve the silent states of mind that stereotypically come through closed eyes and open palms. We all can find something that stills our mind when we concentrate upon it.

The French Enlightenment philosopher Denis Diderot once made a peculiar but fascinating observation about what happens to us when we stare at a painting. He said that the beholder of a work of art is like a Deaf man watching mutes sign on a subject known to him. The metaphor suggests that staring at a painting places us in a communicative silence. (Not every work of art has this provocative effect. Diderot was also one of the first thinkers to focus on the problem of visual noise. He described the paintings of François Boucher, master of louche frivolity, as creating "an unbearable racket for the eye." They are, Diderot said, "the deadliest enemy of silence.")

Certain paintings and sculptures can trick time. And if we lose ourselves gazing on a work of art, we may find a glimmer of the experience Keats had before the Grecian urn: "Thou, silent form! dost tease us out of thought / As doth eternity."

THE ENDANGERED SILENCE OF PAINTING

We all like to learn more about what we're looking at, but when is the last time you found yourself able to stand for any length of time before a great painting without either your own handset or the insect murmurings of another visitor's electronic guide? You may learn a great deal, but you won't come to know "the foster child of Silence and Slow time," as Keats put it.

There's a still more frightening cognitive question that's being raised by some researchers in the new field of neuroaesthetics. We know that the architecture of our brain circuitry dramatically shifts with repeated experience. Two primary modes of visual processing are the so-called "vision-for-action channel" that takes place in the dorsal processing stream, and the "vision-for-perception channel" that transpires in the ventral processing stream. Computer and video games, along with other televisual formats, trigger the former almost exclusively. Crudely put, this means that what is seen sparks an instinctual reaction (a physical motion on the joystick, for example), rather than mental reflection. Overstimulation of the dorsal processing stream means that eventually vision demands a moving target in order to focus. Basically, as one recent study suggests, if a child accumulates untold numbers of "pictorial micro-interactions with moving images," he or she may lose the neurological ability to explore a static painting. Without repeated exposures to unmoving, quiet works of art, the inner silence that can be transferred by that stillness is lost on the individual. The unheard music simply goes unheard.

PLACES OF WORSHIP

When I finally rose from my stoop and stowed my pictures back in my pocket, I went to church. There are many complaints that believers and nonbelievers alike might level against God in the big Western city today, but one thing you have to concede is that He is supreme at keeping the places where He is worshipped silent. The vast majority of churches in a city like

New York are usually empty. The withdrawal of faith from the contemporary urban house of worship has left some awfully big dark holes filled with quite glorious, ecumenical silence.

I decided to visit St. Bartholomew's on Park Avenue at Fifty-first Street—a beautiful, cavernous chamber with long panes of stained glass above the altar. It was entirely quiet except for a very faint sound of an organ. It was almost completely dark, with not another soul in all the pews. I then walked north a few blocks and went into St. Thomas on Fifth Avenue. Magnificent. There was the famed eighty-foot-high ornamental screen behind the altar with all its spotlit carved apostles—everything was quiet, with not more than five or six other people in a space that can hold hundreds. I sat in one of the pews thanking God, or God's absence, for the quality of silence that remains behind. Silence in a deserted temple is to God as the imprint left by sleep in some soft bed is to the departed dreamer.

⚜

When I left St. Thomas, my time was up. I had to get back to work, but I'd gotten at least an injection of minimal silence. I felt both calmer and less enervated. I could now face my journey into the heart of loudness.

CHAPTER SEVEN

Soundkill

One hundred and thirty miles from Cape Canaveral, just off Martin Luther King Boulevard, near the border between Seffner and Mango, in a stretch of central Florida blistered with low-end strip malls and stamped with a waffle-iron grid of asphalt, stands Explosive Sound and Video, the principality of Tommy, the King of Bass. The Sunday before Memorial Day, Tommy, who owns the loudest music-playing, driving vehicle in the world, was hosting a double competition in his parking lot: a dB Drag Race and a Bass Race. Tommy hosts only one or two events a year, and the combination of this rarity with the fact that it had been some time since he'd broken a windshield had sparked a healthy turnout. "He's going to let it bust today," a member of the online forum FloridaSPL (for "sound pressure level"), "the LOUD-EST Website in the South," told me, nodding confidently at the 150-plus people clustered around different vehicles scattered across the lot, three or four of which were emitting an interplanetary vibrational hum. "The crowd's decent, the time's right, he can control it—I mean, why wouldn't he break his windshield today?"

I nodded knowingly. "He's gotta bust it." I raised the beer I'd grabbed from Big Red's cooler after watching MP3 Pimp demo his special something on a long-haired lady. "He's gonna massacre that windshield."

As I threaded the labyrinth of energy-radiating boom cars in front of Tommy's—swampy heat and bass merging into a brain-swamping blast—my thoughts turned to their loud-lovin' ancestors: the Italian futurists.

❅

"As we listened to the old canal muttering its feeble prayers and the creaking bones of sickly palaces above their damp green beards, under the windows we suddenly heard the famished roar of automobiles. 'Let's go!' I said. 'Friends, away! Let's go!'" So wrote F. T. Marinetti, poet and revolutionary, in his 1909 manifesto announcing the founding of the new artistic movement he dubbed futurism. The futurists were dedicated to annihilating all cultural monuments to the past—indeed to eliminating the past itself—in the name of speed, machines, and noise. Luigi Russolo, one of Marinetti's comrades-in-loud, wrote his own manifesto a few years later called "The Art of Noises." Russolo declared that noise was born in the nineteenth century with the invention of the machine. "Today, noise is triumphant and reigns supreme over the sensibility of men," he joyfully boasted.

Plenty of people before the futurists made noise on purpose, but no one had ever constructed such elaborate and provocative philosophical arguments on its behalf. The futurists proclaimed noise to be the soundtrack of liberation. We've been dubbing that soundtrack over our lives with revolutionary impunity ever since.

The flip side of the futurists' lust for noise was their loathing of silence. Ancient life was nothing *but* silence, Russolo complained. And the whole of nature was no better. He bemoaned the fact that apart from "exceptional movements across the earth's surface, such as hurricanes, storms, avalanches, and waterfalls, nature is silent." Marinetti lumped silence in with what he called the moribund "idealization of exhaustion and rest"— the "rancid romanticism"—that provoked his movement's first public action on a serene Sunday afternoon in July 1910.

Marinetti and a contingent of his *rat-tat-tat* pack climbed to the top of the clock tower in Venice's Piazza San Marco. It was no accident that they'd chosen to launch their movement in one of the world's most famously quiet cities. Leaning over the tower's balcony, Marinetti's disciples proceeded to dump 800,000 pamphlets titled "Against Past-loving Venice" down onto the heads of the bewildered public below, while he howled through a megaphone: "Enough! Stop whispering obscene invitations to every mortal passerby, O Venice, old procuress!" The content of the leaflets went further, calling upon Venetians to transform their city into a commercial and military metropolis: "Burn the gondolas, those swings for fools, and erect up to the sky the rigid geometry of the large metallic bridges and manufactories with waving hairs of smoke." One has to admit, it's got panache.

Of course the futurists didn't appear out of nowhere. Voices celebrating the noise that man makes in the act of "denaturing" the Earth have existed since the beginning of civilization. The words of William Faux, an English farmer who traveled through the American west in 1819 to weigh the advantages of resettling there, are typical. Referring to the effect of forest fires lit by the "White Hunters" to help them shoot animals, Faux wrote, "The everlasting sound of falling trees . . . night and day, produces a sound loud and jarring as the discharge of ordnance, and is a relief to the dreary silence of these wilds, only broken by the axe, the gun, or the howlings of wild beasts." Manmade noise often signals the defeat of nature. What the futurists did was to link this idea with a deeper philosophical mistrust of silence.

Twenty years before the first futurist manifesto, Friedrich Nietzsche wrote in *Twilight of the Idols* that he meant to "*sound out idols*" with the "hammer" of his philosophical interrogation. Nietzsche's idols consisted of all those comforting, hypocritical fantasies by which we delude ourselves about the character of the world and mute the healthy energies of the human spirit. Nietzsche expected to be answered by "that famous hollow sound which speaks of inflated bowels—what a delight for one who has ears behind his ears . . . in presence of whom precisely that which would like to stay silent *has to become audible*."

Nietzsche's commitment to broadcasting "that which would like to stay silent" echoes in all those latter-day liberation movements dedicated to "making a noise" about unjust power relationships and giving voice to those who've been gagged. Part of why we fell in love with being loud is because quiet is associated with "being silenced" and with being given "the silent treatment."

This is, of course, a formula for explosion. At the start of the First World War, the futurists were on the vanguard agitating for Italian intervention. In his most regrettable formulation, Marinetti declared war to be the "world's only hygiene" and wrote a letter describing his own battlefield experience with unpunctuated ecstasy. "Cannons gutting space with a chord *ZANG-TUMB-TUUMB* mutiny of 500 echoes smashing scattering it to infinity . . . Violence ferocity regularity this deep bass scanning the strange shrill frantic crowds of the battle Fury breathless ears eyes nostrils open! load! fire! what a joy to hear to smell completely *taratatata* of the machine guns screaming a breathless under the stings slaps *traak-traak whips pic-pac-pum-tumb* weirdness . . ."

Marinetti's rhapsody to war sounds like the birth of gangster rap.

꘎

Of all the sounds that the futurists fired praise upon, the noise of an accelerating car took first prize. Marinetti's original manifesto records the hour of the movement's awakening: "We went up to three snorting beasts (cars), to lay amorous hands on their torrid breasts." The futurists' launch happened to coincide with the moment when the Italian automobile industry under the leadership of Fiat achieved a level of glamour and commercial importance that made it a European industrial force. While the futurists were rising to prominence, Rome was becoming, in the estimation of some, the noisiest city on Earth—because of its car traffic. Marinetti idolized the car as nothing less than the metallic angel of the future's annunciation: "A racing car whose hood is adorned with great pipes, like serpents of explosive breath—a roaring car that seems to ride on grapeshot is more beautiful than the Victory of Samothrace."

Speed. Noise . . . Noise. Speed. There's an intrinsic relationship between the two that the futurists reveled in. After all, it's when an object vibrates quickly enough that motion becomes sound. A fast-moving life is a noisy life. A powerful machine is supposed to be loud. The ur-connection between acceleration and amplification idles under the hood of the boom-car phenomenon.

Long before there were boom cars, there were drag races. In 1989 Eddie Lopez, a chunky twenty-one-year-old trash collector from Long Beach, became perhaps the first boom-car driver ever to make a direct link between the energy released in racing and that discharged in "booming." Justifying the $1,200 in noise fines he'd had to fork over to the police, on top of the $5,000 he'd sunk into his vehicle's audio equipment, Lopez asked a *Los Angeles Times* reporter, "When hot-rodding was in, why did you want to speed?"

Hot-rodding is not dead, but there are incalculably more roads today on which it's possible to boom than to race. And when people's physical horizons feel constricted, there's a tendency to want to expand acoustically. Early in the twentieth century, Theodor Lessing, a European writer and philosopher who became a major activist on behalf of silence, had already noted this phenomenon. "A coachman who cracks the whip, a maid who shakes out the bedding, a drummer who beats the drum, detect in their noises a personally enjoyable activity and a magnification of their own sphere of power." Ecce the boom-car driver.

⌗

Though the boom box had historical precedents dating back to the 1920s, the loud portable radio—noise in motion—first hit the scene in a big way in the late 1970s and early 1980s. It was

then that hip-hop and the boom box exploded together. Immortal-
ized in the hands of Radio Raheem in Spike Lee's *Do the
Right Thing* (the noise of Raheem's boom box playing Public
Enemy's "Fight the Power" inside Sal's Pizzeria triggers the racial
confrontation at the film's climax), the boom box became a
weapon of resistance against the system. It serves as a textbook
illustration for how self-expression, when it happens in the form
of noise, translates into self-assertion—which in turn threatens
property boundaries. The bigger your sound, the more territory
you dominate.

Boom cars first began to receive media attention in the late
1980s, when the phenomenon had already been gaining popularity for several years. Contests with names like "Sound Quake"
and "Thunder on Wheels," sponsored by car-audio manufacturers looking to promote their "Ground-pounder" products, helped
galvanize the fever, and open the wallets, of fledgling boomers
like Eddie Lopez. Though it originated in Southern California, it
quickly moved east—and almost immediately became subject to
hefty fines in multiple states. From the start, boom cars drove
people crazy.

But people driving boom cars may have been reacting to a
frustration of their own. It was also in the 1980s, according to
the Texas Center for Policy Studies and Environmental Defense,
that America's urban traffic came definitively to exceed roadway
capacity. In the years roughly corresponding to the rise of the
boom car, from the early 1980s to 2003, driving delays in twenty-
six major American cities surged by an astounding 655 percent. I
read that number and can't help thinking of Theodor Lessing's
idea that when people feel caged up, they get loud. Boom-car

fever corresponds with the period in which traffic around the country began grinding to a halt.

That doesn't change the sense of being under siege experienced by people at home when the boom cars quake by.

For several months, I'd been reading posts on the Listserv of Noise Free America, an antinoise-pollution organization, where boom cars are considered absolute evil. Every few days, Noise Free sends out an e-mail blast linking to a story involving the arrest of someone for assaulting a person who has complained about the noise of his car; or an article about an attack on a police officer who stopped a vehicle for loud music; or the announcement of a new link between boom cars and drug dealers; or details on the discovery of guns inside a boom car. In the accompanying comment threads, boom-car owners are invariably referred to as THUGs or Boom THUGs—and the posts often drip with a bile typified by one that went up the week before I traveled to Tampa. "These criminals are the sort of human garbage that are the life's blood of the boom-car pestilence," it read. "Unfortunately, it's not legal to shoot them all and feed their rotting corpses to wolves. The wolves could use the food, and we could use the peace and quiet." Okay . . . Unquestionably, the assault by four individuals on one woman is abhorrent. But were the "human garbage" who perpetrated the crime really the "life's blood of the boom-car pestilence"? I didn't like the noise of boom cars in my own neighborhood the least little bit. I hate the way my windows rattle when they thump by. By now I'd read droves of articles that led me to empathize with the far more severe suffering that boom-car noise sometimes inflicted on others.

But still I couldn't help being disturbed by the off-the-road rage I encountered in the echo chamber of the Listserv.

❀

By contrast, the forums of the boom-car enthusiasts were relatively quiet. Indignation was certainly expressed on FloridaSPL about antinoise legislative efforts, but their biggest complaint was the way all boom-car owners were lumped together. There were even occasional surprising metaphysical disquisitions on the site, such as a posting under the "Rants" category by CalusaCustomConcepts titled "Who Cares About Words?" which began, "Do words have any meaning? Are the words we use important? What are words anyway? Aren't words the translation of the concepts we imagine? If words are concepts translated into sounds with assigned meanings, then words are expressed ideas."

How could I not be intrigued? I made contact with Casey Sullivan, the site manager of FloridaSPL, in an effort to hear their side of the story. Sullivan presented the Memorial Day event at Explosive Sound and Audio as an ideal fact-finding opportunity. He also arranged for me to get "drive arounds" with several forum members on the night before the contest so that I could experience the boom cars in their natural cruising habitat.

And so it happened that at nine on a Saturday night late in the spring I found myself standing in a parking lot outside Tampa staring through chain-link fencing at a patch of tall reeds that waved back and forth like a metronome, listening to the drone of I-75, waiting for a call from MP3 Pimp. The call came, and I bolted for my vehicle, heading to a Shell station across the road from a Hooters restaurant, in search of a tangerine-colored vehicle with a fractured windshield.

BOOM-ERANG

When I reached the station and spotted the one orange car, I thought there'd been some mistake. The vehicle was hardly bigger than a Matchbox car. This could not be the machine of a Boom THUG. The hose was stuck in the tank and there was no one behind the wheel. I got out of my car and walked closer. The windshield was, indeed, finely cracked in many places, creating an effect, in the overhead fluorescence, of delicate ice-crystal calligraphy. A moment later, a large man in long shorts pushed out of the station store, sucking meditatively on a tall soft drink.

Robin Butler, aka MP3 Pimp, is an ample man in his mid-twenties, with honey skin, light eyes, and a softly curling beard. He looks like a biblical patriarch, only gentler and more self-conscious. We shook hands, and he invited me into the car. The second I yanked open the door on the passenger side (it was broken) and swung in, I realized I was entering a whole new realm. This was not a car interior in any sense I'd ever experienced. Everything had been stripped of its original elements and reconstituted Frankenstein-style—swollen with foam, fiberglass, black speakers, and a profusion of colorful wires. The entire rear half of the car was obscured by immense black audio equipment; the dashboard seemed to consist only of dark metal cavities, coils, and protrusions with a little digital box at the epicenter, like the control panel of a retro-sci-fi vessel. MP3 Pimp turned on the engine. I reached across for my seat belt.

"No belts," MP3 Pimp commented. I glanced down at the torn sockets by my hips, and we pulled out onto the highway.

As we drove, MP3 Pimp occasionally reached up two fingers to push back the duct tape propping different sections of the windshield to prevent them from falling across our laps. I asked him what had triggered his involvement with car audio.

"Just hearing people with bass driving around—just ever since I can remember hearing it, I remember responding to that sound. And I've had something since I was seventeen. Nine years. But as for something as ridiculous as this . . . maybe two years."

And was it really true that his windshield had cracked because of sound?

"Yup," he nodded. "Fourth windshield this year. See these dents in the metal?" He pointed up at the ceiling. "Also audio-related."

And what is the police response? I inquired.

He shrugged. "They don't really bother you too much, as long as you're respectful. If you drive by a cop with your music on and you turn it down when you see him, he knows it's you, but you're being respectful. They might pull you over to check your registration, make sure everything's in order, but as long as you're being respectful, it's okay." He told me that the people who participated in the shows were rarely the ones creating a public nuisance.

"So the ones creating the problem are a minority?" I ventured.

"Well—actually," MP3 Pimp hesitated. "No. The people who go to shows—most of us are respectable. They call it 'bumping responsibly' . . . But you get the kids: they have a loud system in their cars, and they want everybody to know, so they play it loud all the time. Unfortunately, they're in the majority because a lot of people who have car stereos don't come to shows. They don't even know the shows exist. Some people do it for fun. Some people just like it loud, like me. And some people do it to impress other people, like girls or whatever. Some people abuse everything."

And would the strict new antinoise ordinances that had just been introduced in nearby Sarasota affect the attitude of police toward boom cars around Tampa?

"You know, it changes everything once you have the law looking at you." He glanced over at me. "Especially when you're breaking the law."

I nodded thoughtfully. He glanced at me again. "Anytime you want me to turn it on, let me know."

"Crank it up," I said. After all, the sound itself was why I was here.

MP3 Pimp bent forward and began pushing buttons in the lunar panel. Numbers and words lit up and disappeared.

❖

For the first few seconds of music, I felt very pleased with myself. It was loud, but I could take it, and I enjoyed the rap bass line. I got it. It was fun. MP3 Pimp was still fiddling with buttons. And then, suddenly, the entire system turned on. I felt as if I had been launched in thunder and fire from an ejector seat—only the seat hadn't ejected and I remained inside the thunder and fire. I felt my organs collapsing. I didn't hear sound. I just experienced my bones and heart bursting apart through my skin. My hands slammed to the sides of my head and I bent forward, vaguely aware of MP3 Pimp's finger pulsing a button by my temple; the sound declined.

"I don't want to cause you pain," he said.

"Thank you," I managed.

Recalling the sober audiologist who had recently told me that a single exposure to 140 decibels can cause permanent hearing loss, I straightened back into my seat. "How loud was that?" I finally asked.

"Oh it gets a lot louder than that," MP3 Pimp chuckled.

"How loud?"

"I don't know exactly. The loudest I ever heard it is 158.6, and that's on average, over 50 seconds. What you heard right then is 141, 142. It's definitely loud. But it gets louder."

Some perspective on those numbers: a pneumatic riveter at a distance of four feet produces 125 decibels. The decibel system is logarithmic, with every increase of 10 decibels signifying a ten-fold increase in sound. If you are 3 feet away from a rifle when it fires, the sound you hear is approximately 140 decibels. If you are 75 feet away from a jet at takeoff, you are exposed to 150 decibels. Standing 30 feet from a jet at takeoff you hear 160 decibels. The explosion of Krakatoa from 100 miles up in the air or a jet engine heard from one foot away is 180 decibels.

"What do you think of the groups that say all boom cars are evil?" I blurted out.

"I've never looked at one of the forums before, to be honest. I've read some e-mails that I guess a guy from one of them was sending out, and it's kind of funny because they have no idea what they're attacking," he said. "They don't even know who they're trying to be at war with." I asked him what he meant. "Just because somebody has a gun—like a hunter, say—doesn't mean they're going to shoot at people. And just because I have a stereo in my car doesn't mean I'm going to drive by your house every night and bother you. It's like saying that all people who listen to rap are thugs. But I look on it as a sport. Not an athletic sport obviously, but it's a hobby that became a sport. It keeps me entertained and busy when I'm not working or with my family."

We waited for another FloridaSPL forum member to join us in a truck stop while the single headlight of a police helicopter beamed down over us, the chopping of its blades drowning out the highway. "They're looking for somebody," MP3 Pimp said. "They're looking for *somebody*." He sighed. "While we're waiting I can show you the car."

He pointed at the inside of the door. "Took the stock panels and turned them into something they're not. Took fiberglass and molded it. Cut out the rear deck with an angle grinder. We use like spray foam everywhere, and whatnot. You want to seal off everything as much as you can to keep all the pressure up front. And then . . ." We walked around back and he opened the trunk. Five car batteries festooned with red-and-blue wires were wedged into the space.

"Wow."

"There's another one under the hood and one in the corner by the passenger seat, so seven batteries total. They weigh about forty pounds apiece. It actually weighs down the car a lot. Causes everything over here to drop about four inches. We also paint all the windows black; keep the light that's inside in; keep the light that's outside out. That way nobody can see in."

⌘

Big Red emerged from the seat of a giant, elevated red truck that looked like every boy's fantasy. He was a colossal wallop of a man with a small head, buzzed hair, a mustache, little indentations in his face that looked as though they might, like the dimples in MP3 Pimp's roof, have been "audio-related," and a giant black T-shirt airbrushed with a skull. From the other side of the cab hopped a petite woman with plush red hair and a soft, lilting Southern accent ("Big Red's Lady," MP3 Pimp joked, as he somewhat sheepishly explained that they all went by nicknames).

Big Red immediately broke into an anecdote in a surprising, twittery voice. "She watched me put that duct tape on the windshield," he laughed.

"Inside?" MP3 Pimp asked.

"No, not inside. She don't like it loud inside. It gives her headaches."

"I stay away from it when it gets loud-loud," Big Red's Lady said. "I get migraines. I like to still be able to hear and enjoy myself for the rest of the day."

We moved into Macaroni Grill. Cheesy string music fluttered around us.

Big Red made a general announcement as we sat down. "Science has proven 100 percent of all divorces can be blamed on marriage." MP3 Pimp asked him whether he and Big Red's Lady were married.

"Noohoho," said Big Red.

"He's been married twice," said Big Red's Lady. "I've been married once, and not to each other. And you've seen the baby that's with us sometimes—that's his second marriage. He has a seventeen-year-old by his first marriage. I have a twenty-four-year-old, a twenty-year-old, and a seventeen-year-old."

"You've got five kids, three failed marriages, and a relationship," MP3 Pimp noted, in an astonishing split-second calculation. "That's a beautiful thing."

"And an ex-husband who likes guys," Big Red's Lady added. The table went quiet. "Yeah . . . Don't go there."

"No," Big Red said quickly. "If you're going to go there, you have to go all the way. An ex-husband who lives with his male roommate that has another boyfriend. We stop by from time to time." Big Red chuckled.

"We do." Big Red's Lady nodded. "We actually take advantage of the male roommate, because he's great with computers."

MP3 Pimp caught the others up on our conversation so far that evening. "I've been explaining to George how not everyone who's into car audio is a douche bag."

Big Red launched in. "I mean as far as proposing a law—I'm all for it. Putting a fine in place for people who drive through a residential neighborhood at three o'clock in the morning banging their stereo. They deserve to get a ticket or double the fine of the ticket. But to take somebody's car because you can hear it from twenty-five foot away at three o'clock on a Sunday afternoon when you're getting off the interstate, that's a little steep."

For a brief time, Sarasota had become the most costly city in the country in which to violate a municipal noise ordinance. On a first offense, if a vehicle was audible to a police officer from twenty-five feet, the car would be impounded and the violator hit with a $74 fine, in addition to a $125 towing fee. On a second offense, the fine jumped to $250 on top of impound fees. By the third offense it was $500, and the car was impounded for ten days.

"What really gets me is it's a misdemeanor," Big Red continued. "Nonmoving violation misdemeanor. So if you're going to impound a vehicle for a misdemeanor, why not impound for failing to give right of way to an emergency vehicle? Or for talking on a cell phone while driving down the highway? Those can kill people. The stereo blast is not killing somebody. I understand it can be annoying. But, I mean, I'm forty-three years old, I own my own business. Do I like to get out there on the highway and turn it up every now and then? Yeah, I do. Do people around me get perturbed by it sometimes? They probably do. But you know what? If somebody walked up to me and said, 'Can you turn that down?' or 'I really don't like that selection or choice of music can you change it?,' I have no problem doing that." (The question of how exactly anyone could walk up to Big Red and do anything other than get pancaked as he roared down the highway was not directly addressed.)

"I've been doing this for twenty-five, twenty-six years," Big Red went on. "I was living in Maryland and I drove by the local radio shop one Saturday and they had some demo vehicles out there. And I just thought, as loud as they were, how pretty the installation looked, and I've been hooked ever since. I've had seven cars since then and every vehicle I've had has something in it." He pointed at his girlfriend. "The Chevy she drives every day, you wouldn't know it had anything in it. It's all hidden. Then you turn it on—it's got something in it."

"Oh yeah," Big Red's Lady said.

"But like I said, we are people in our mid-forties. We have people we compete with who are in their mid-fifties that do this."

"Oh, there's a huge range of people," Big Red's Lady nodded. "There are eighteen-year-olds to Papa's—what's Papa? Fifty-four, fifty-five? And we've seen people in their sixties."

"All different kinds of backgrounds. We've got retired naval officers are in the sport."

"There's Lawyer Boy," Big Red's Lady added.

"We've got lawyers involved in the sport. I'm a roofing business involved in the sport. We've got county employees—the civil service involved in the sport. We've got the guy who works at Publix in a nine-to-five job saving his money."

"We're not getting the kind of good exposure we need to reverse these laws," MP3 Pimp said.

Big Red's Lady nodded. "Because the exposure the people do see is to do with the drug dealers. They don't see that it's John and his wife out on a Saturday afternoon with the windows rolled down and their stereo turned up, and they just happened to drive by a cop."

Big Red flicked himself forward. "Or Drop Bottom who works sixty hours a week so he can keep his vehicle up and keep it running."

Whatever else, I was loving the *Midsummer Night's Dream* quality of the nicknames. I asked the table at large how early most participants got into the sport—silently wondering, as I did so, when the term "sport" had become applicable to men seated behind the wheel of a stationary vehicle adjusting the dial on a car stereo.

"They're usually kids that are right out of high school," Big Red's Lady began. "But no—actually—there's Mighty Tyke. He's four."

"That's right." Big Red nodded. "We have a guy over in Iraq serving his country right now who's a part of our Team dB Unit, and his son is four or five years old. He has a Power Wheels vehicle that's got a bass system." Big Red chuckled. "Mighty Tyke's Power Wheel's gone 136—which is louder than what you can hear from twenty-five feet away."

"136 with a box and a battery," Big Red's Lady nodded. "It's what—a Grave Digger?"

"Yeah—a Grave Digger Power Wheels with a box and a battery. They literally put Mighty Tyke's Power Wheels on a mike to see how loud it was."

The conversation about Mighty Tyke hitting 136 decibels in his Grave Digger made for a natural segue to the larger subject of the rising volume of car audio. Big Red explained that when he got truly involved in the sport a few years back, if you were breaking 130 "you were the man," whereas, the previous night, someone on the forum had put up a video of a guy who hit 181.6.

"Everything keeps getting louder," Big Red cheerfully marveled. I mumbled something incoherent about the wonder of ever-improving technological capabilities. But all three of my tablemates pointed out that there were specific reasons why the technology of car audio had spiked of late. The most important factor, they averred, was the Internet. Because of the way that parts and know-how ricochet back and forth between members of forums like FloridaSPL, the speed of technological evolution has dramatically accelerated.

Big Red was not the only enthusiast to remind me repeatedly that the extreme environment of car-audio competition has pushed the horizons of possibility for everyone. Car audio has driven the audio industry as a whole, and car audio geared for stereo competition drives the evolution of car audio.

SOUND OFF!

Explosive Sound and Video sits next to a hair salon, an ice-cream shop, and Tire Kingdom in a parking lot that was already grinding with heat by the time I arrived at ten thirty on Sunday morning. A pair of blue tents had been set up to shade an assortment of high-caliber sound-measuring equipment and laptops. Over the course of the next couple of hours, the participants' vehicles rumbled into the lot along with spectators who clustered around the champion cars waiting for audio to be demoed and gazing hopefully at the dark-tinted windows to try and glimpse the special "something" each had hidden inside. The men, clutching giant plastic cups or dark bottles, seemed to fall generally into the category of short on neck and bald (save for a sneeze of facial hair) or stringy and towheaded. There were plenty of women as well, but with one or two exceptions, they were all girl-friends, wives, or the catchall "lady of." Everywhere there were tattoos and T-shirts emblazoned with multiple skull or single crucifix motifs.

By noon, a critical mass of competition vehicles had arrived in the plaza. I wandered around and found MP3 Pimp about to perform what is known as "hair trick." Hair trick involves finding a long-haired woman who will lean her head into the window of a car demoing its audio. A young woman with very lengthy red hair was just bending over the passenger side of MP3 Pimp's vehicle as I approached. He turned on the audio and her orange hair began flying up in the air, like a free-floating wildfire.

"I love it," she squealed when he turned the car off. "That's the best feeling in the world!"

"Why?" I asked.

" 'Cause your whole head tingles and all your hair's moving and you can see it all moving!"

"And you can finally justify having so much hair," a spectator observed.

"I can finally justify having so much hair!" she concurred.

⚒

The dB Drag Race qualifications were at last getting under way. For the onlookers, this process consisted primarily of watching a huge bald man with a shredded auburn goatee, in a tank top that read GORILLA HEAVYWEIGHT, lumber over to cars and stick a sound meter on a hose through the windows of dozens of them one by one, as if he were hooking them up to an IV in preparation for a transfusion. Once Gorilla Heavyweight had positioned the tube, the window rolled back up from the inside, and at the conclusion of a countdown from the judge, who held his fingers above the decibel-monitoring laptop, the audio behind the dark glass switched on to strike a tone barely audible from outside the car.

After watching this for a time (qualifications were to continue for the next four and a half hours), I glimpsed the man I suddenly knew to be Tommy, the King of Bass, McKinnie. He had just emerged from the garage of Explosive Sound and Video and was walking to a low, gleaming black-and-silver truck sitting under its own special canopy, with the words HO PROBLEMS stamped across the front windshield and KING OF BASS on both sides.

Even watching Tommy, the King of Bass, move from a distance, one knew oneself to be in the presence of a master of something. A handsome, mildly pumped-up man in his thirties, wearing a black Explosive Sound and Video T-shirt and a matching black baseball cap with the brim reversed, he had that hunter's poise, that charged balance—of complete alertness and utter relaxation—the self-assured élan of a successful professional athlete who knows his body will perform exactly as it has to when it has to. Only in this case that body is prosthetic, the chassis of a low-slung 1995 Isuzu packed with enough audio equipment to kill by sound alone.

McKinnie has been competing for ten years and purports to be undefeated in all car-audio competitions. He has taken his truck everywhere across the United States and prevailed at the world finals four years in a row, from 2005 to 2008. In 2007, for the first time, the finals were hosted over the Internet, with three locations in the United States (Florida, Indiana, and California) going "face-to-face" live online with France, Greece, and, perplexingly, Norway, to see who had the Earth's loudest vehicle. Answer: Tommy, the King of Bass. A lot of times, McKinnie told me, "they call the King of Bass 'the Case' because I have twenty-four of everything. Twenty-four midis. Twenty-four tweeters.

Twenty-four woofers, and twenty-four amplifiers." His truck is known as the Loch Ness Monster, "because you always hear stories about it, but you never see it." Nine-tenths of the year, the Loch Ness Monster remains deep within Tommy, the King of Bass's, garage. He never drives it or brings it out, unless it's going up on his trailer to a show. When I looked inside, it was like looking into Ali Baba's cave—a black vortex gleaming with countless silver cones, odd lustrous disks, gorgon's hair of wires, and plates of dark metal.

The truck can hit in the 160s constantly for a minute straight. But there is no judging category that technically goes that high, so he runs in the 150 to 159 class, "What we call 'Balls to the Wall,' " McKinnie said with a nod. "You know, 'Run what you brung and I hope you brung enough.' " A pretty woman in a bright-white T-shirt and mirrored sunglasses who looked like a somewhat less pampered version of Scarlett Johansson, and who proved to be McKinnie's girlfriend, appeared with a high black velvet crown studded with a rainbow of rhinestones. She handed it to McKinnie, who placed it casually on the hood of the truck.

"I'd say my entry into the sport began when I was in junior high before I got my first car," McKinnie remarked. "Guys that considered they were loud in the neighborhood—or considered they were loud in the streets—every time they would drive by, I would run to the door and my parents would think I was crazy. I said, 'One day that's going to be me, riding around shaking everybody's houses and restaurants.' I just always wanted a loud stereo." He added that once he had his first car with his first audio system, he drove it loud enough that he was barred from

every restaurant in town on account of shattering their glass—
Burger King, McDonald's, Taco Bell. Even the car wash ("which
I'd never actually used, because my truck was always too low")
banned him because he drove by one time and broke its window
with the power of his sound.

ॐ

McKinnie's story reinforced what I'd heard from MP3 Pimp and
Big Red the night before, and what I would hear from a dozen
competitors—longtime and first-time alike—over the course of
that afternoon. Everyone had craved a loud stereo more than
anything in the world basically ever since they could remember
wanting anything. Some of them had purchased their first car
stereos before they could drive, let alone own a car. The crowd
was not especially THUGish. It was, on many levels, diverse—
amazingly so, racially—peppered with both more and less aggressive sorts, mostly in their twenties and thirties (with a handful of
exceptions either side of the age divide) and making more or less
money (though less was certainly the rule).

As Tommy turned away to defend the Loch Ness Monster
from a mob of admirers, Casey Sullivan, the administrator of
FloridaSPL, a genial, gangly guy who looks all of sixteen, and his
partner Buzz Thompson, who resembles a somewhat shorter, no
less voluble, but considerably more coherent version of the
Dennis Hopper photographer character in *Apocalypse Now*, introduced themselves, and told me their version of the history that
Big Red and MP3 Pimp had begun feeding me the night before.

They explained that car-audio competitions began in the
early 1980s with extemporized "boom-offs," along with more eso-

teric contests such as "car-alarm meets"—in which challengers matched up to determine who had the biggest, loudest alarm gadgetry in their vehicles.

Over the next decade, two things happened. First, a new generation of speaker and amplifier technology powerful enough to survive multiple high-volume sessions—and loud enough to excite audiences in ways that sound quality alone never quite mustered—began to appear on the scene. Often the men behind the new subwoofers were home-garage tinkerers who never wrote down their secrets and who made their mark by, as Thompson put it, "getting dirty, spending money, and taking time." Eventually, if they were lucky, they got recruited by major manufacturers, who helped make a handful of American companies the elite standard of the car-audio scene. Second, sometime in the 1990s, a new strain of powerful subwoofers from China began thumping into the markets. Because they were so strong—and so cheap relative to high-quality equipment—competitions began to torque in the direction of loudness alone. Availability and affordability of extreme subwoofer technology set the stage for the arrival of dB Drag Races.

One day in 1994, Tim Maynor, with Jonathan Demuth in tow, showed up at a bass competition. At that time sport participants were required to compete playing a song the match sponsors had chosen for them, which happened that afternoon to be the first song on the *Flashdance* soundtrack. Maynor and Demuth had analyzed the first track of *Flashdance* pulse by pulse to find the frequency at which it peaked and where the peak occurred. By abandoning all pretense of playing a recognizable snippet of the song, and instead hitting a button at the exact second when the music was loudest and playing only that one tone, they immediately gained three decibels of sound. The crowd, which Demuth told me numbered in the thousands, went wild.

Their discovery opened the floodgates. Everyone started converting their cars into "one-note wonders," or "burp vehicles." Soon thereafter, McKinnie related, "dB Drag Racing got out of hand. Everyone lost the highs, lost the pretty stuff, the pretty-looking stuff, and it was all about how loud can you make your car be."

The dB Drag Race cars can't even play music. If they do, they will break their speakers. (Sometimes destruction is the goal. The world finals occasionally include a Death Match class, in which competitors run head-to-head for five minutes. The last car standing wins, and both cars get buried in smoke from frying audio entrails.) Indeed, the vehicles themselves, let alone the audio systems, cannot withstand the pressure exerted by the burp button. It's not coincidental that Maynor and Demuth were also the first team to replace their vehicle's factory-installed windshield with a steel plate.

And yet, Demuth told me, in putting too much "scientific-ness into it," they took out the fun—and began losing sponsors as well. That's when the organizations approached McKinnie and told him they'd come up with a new format—the Bass Race—and wanted him to compete. There was to be no more "burping." Contestants had to play music for thirty seconds and remain within a certain decibel range the whole time.

For all its musical appeal, the Bass Race is not appreciably quieter than SPL. Last year McKinnie broke thirty windshields. (He told me, regretfully, that in Florida insurance would only cover three a year.) In fact, while current peaks of the Bass Race may be closer to 161 than the 181-plus top scores of dB Drag, the bodily experience of Bass Racing for everyone involved may actually be louder. This is because, in the modified cars of the dB Drag Race, materials like three- to six-inch windshields and special reflection panels guide the energy wave to the exact spot on the dashboard where the judge's microphone is grounded. Recent changes in regulations have begun to factor in the catastrophic consequences of car-audio showdowns for the hearing of participants. The dB Drag Race competitors in the classes of 140 decibels and above are required to operate their cars from outside, remotely. "Adequate hearing protection" is required if you remain inside at lower decibel levels. Similar rules have come into play for the Bass Races. But I didn't see any Bass Racers standing outside their cars the day I was at Explosive Sound and Video—and they were hitting some seriously high numbers. The windows and doors were left open. The protection-free crowd got to "feel the vibe," to merge with the full blast of music.

⌖

A little while after we had spoken, Tommy, the King of Bass, at last demoed the Loch Ness Monster, playing his signature song, Phil Collins's "In the Air Tonight." I was standing about twenty-five feet away at the time. In the first few seconds, I had the uncanny experience of knowing that I was listening to music but being unable to hear the sound *as* music, to experience it as anything other than pure vibration. This is like hearing music if you're deaf, I thought to myself. My pants legs and shirt suddenly felt loose and began fluttering wildly free of my body—somehow as though the agitation was coming from inside me. I had a cell phone in one front pocket of my jeans and my recorder in the other, and they both began massaging my thighs like mini-vibrators. It was extraordinary: not exactly exhilarating but electrifying. I saw the opaque panes of glass in the hair salon—covered with decals reading PERMS, TANNING, COLORING—begin flapping like black sheets. Someone pointed up at the floodlights on poles probably twenty feet overhead—the bulbs appeared to be unscrewing from their sockets. It was like standing on the lip of the apocalypse.

After the demonstration, Buzz Thompson told me with a chuckle that employees from the drive-through McDonald's more than fifty yards away were storming into the parking lot to complain that they couldn't take any orders from customers because of the sound of Tommy's truck. I asked him whether the natural development of the technology combined with the power of the Internet to accelerate that development meant that the decibel levels competitors hit would just keep getting higher.

Thompson reminded me that there is a problem with the dream of perpetual progress in the sport, since it is approaching a realm where the physics of sound begins to create threshold limitations. Already, he said, when you're in one of these cars and they're doing 163 or above, there is so much pressure inside the cars that the air molecules cease to behave like air. The air becomes so thick that you feel as if you are moving underwater. Come to think of it, much of the music I'd heard sounded as though the speakers were submerged. Essentially, Thompson said, at 163 and higher the air has ceased to be air. Competitors today were already hitting in the low 180s. But once you hit around 194 decibels, sound ceases to be sound. Basically sound crunches the air and then releases it as it travels. At approximately 194 decibels, the pressure is twice the pressure of the atmosphere. That means there are no more air molecules to disperse. There is no more back-and-forth cycle. There is no more sound. There is only a forward-driving force of further compression. If SPL or Bass Race competitors one day hit 194 decibels, they will succeed in creating a shock wave. This is the realm of sonic booms and earthquakes.

⁂

Even after all of the explanations I'd heard of why people were drawn to the sport of loudness for loudness's sake, I was still missing something. I got that there were more rules and regulations to car-audio competition than I would ever have dreamed possible, and that competition—however arcane the terms—was driving the amplification. But I pressed Thompson to give me his take on what lay at the core of the obsession.

"It's just so sensual!" he moaned. "It's sound! It's feeling! It's the attention you get! There's so much to what you're doing when you add a subwoofer to your car! And once you do it, you always have a taste for it. You find someone with louder, and you say, 'Wow that louder is better than my louder.' Every single guy out here wants to be louder. Nobody out here says, 'Wow, that's loud enough.' "

That made sense. Yet of course this sensuality, the sensuality of "hair trick" or "balls to the wall," was not, to put it mildly, everyone's sensuality. And, to an extent, Thompson's analysis

amounted to saying, "These people are just born this way." True
enough, but I craved an answer with more reverb. I was standing
next to Thompson sucking on the beer I'd been offered by Big
Red's Lady, pondering what, if anything, it would mean when scientists identified the genetic marker for "noise fetish," when
Thompson, who'd been waxing on about the feeling of 150 decibels inside an automobile, abruptly cried, "The entire state of
Florida is designed to be driven around in! You can't walk anywhere! You need a car to conduct your life down here. Every
sixteen-year-old in Florida looks forward to getting a car! The car
is your *life*."

And suddenly the click came. What was that sixteen-year-
old listening to before he got into his first boom car? When his
headphones were off and his ears were naked to the stagnant air,
I mean.

Let's leave the boom-car drivers demoing that special something in the egg-frying parking lot. We need to find somewhere
quiet where we can think about this a little harder. Thompson's
last throwaway lines point deep into the sound of our age—all the
way to the realm of acoustical weapons. And even to the blessed
white inner sanctum of the iPod. Another way to think about the
noise we make today is as an effort to immunize ourselves against
the noise pain we're all suffering from anyway. Another way to
view our new noisiness is as a diverse global initiative in soundproofing.

CHAPTER EIGHT

Freeway to Noise

A recent European Environment Agency report estimates that within the European Union alone, traffic noise regularly exposes upward of 67 million people to decibel levels exceeding safety recommendations in terms of both hearing and cardiovascular health. (The United States has been slower to track this problem.) Traffic is the most pervasive noise on the face of the planet. While we might have mentally habituated to its depredation, as we now know, we will never physiologically acclimate to it—and our behavior, unconsciously or no, reflects that bodily failure to adjust.

When I thought about my time in Florida, I thought about traffic and noise. Whether in my hotel off the roaring ribbons of I-75, or on any one of my innumerable, interminable driving expeditions (since it was impossible to go anywhere without driving), what I heard was traffic. Oh, and any interior I entered was either playing loud music or blasting me with televised information. No wonder people who live in this kind of sonic environment want to boom through it! At least then the noise you're subject to—that low-frequency, vertebrae-vibrating bass earthquake punched up on your special something—buries the sound of your surroundings.

Indeed, much of the "unnecessary" noise people make is responding to existing sonic pain. We instinctually try to turn the tables on the sound that's playing havoc with our equilibrium. A neat example of this can be found in the history of the Mosquito™.

A few years ago, a diabolical English inventor by the name of Howard Stapleton developed a product called Mosquito Teen Deterrent to disperse young people engaged in antisocial behavior. The device emits a sound near the upper end of the human hearing range—around 18,000 cycles—that almost everyone over the age of twenty has lost the ability to perceive. The Mosquito's promotional literature describes the product as "the solution to the eternal problem of unwanted gatherings of youths and teenagers in shopping malls, around shops and anywhere else they are causing problems." Thousands of Mosquitoes have been ordered and installed in Europe and North America. Demand seems to be on the uptick—along with outrage among various civil-liberty groups that have tried to legislate against the device for infringing on the rights of the teens, not to mention small children who are unwittingly blasted with sonic repellant. While the selectivity of the pain dealt out by the signal may be a factor of the pitch, the pain itself reflects the fact that the sound is being played at levels hitting ninety decibels—louder than standing next to an idling bulldozer. Stapleton says it's not loud enough to cause hearing loss, likening it rather to "a demented alarm clock." But here's the thing: almost immediately after the Mosquito began to catch on, the high-frequency tone was co-opted by U.K. adolescents to create Teen Buzz, a cell-phone ringtone that would go unheard by teachers and anyone else old enough to object. The sonic weapon became one more acoustical device youth could turn back on those trying to silence them.

If you're used to thinking of punishing sound as a good thing, it's natural that you start thinking about how to share the pain. When I spoke with my boom-car aficionados, one name kept cropping up as a kind of idol of the car-audio competition world: Tom Danley. He was described, with a kind of awed chortle, as the individual who took subwoofer fever to its extreme. Danley was the inventor of the Matterhorn: the largest subwoofer in the world. "You've gotta hear about the Matterhorn!" Buzz Thompson told me.

Danley's company, Danley Sound Labs, which is based in Georgia, features on its Web site a biblical "verse of the day." When I first looked at the site the scripture reading was from the second book of Samuel: "How great you are, Sovereign LORD! There is no one like you, and there is no God but you, as we have heard with our own ears." Danley traces his own fascination with low-frequency sound to the time when he was nine years old and his grandfather let him go into the pipe loft in a church. "I didn't know whether to run or stay—but I stayed!" he recounted. And he began building his own speakers shortly thereafter.

His colleague, Michael Heddon, told me that Danley had been considered "the Guy" for subwoofers since the glory days of the mid-1980s to the 1990s. "Journey, U2, Bon Jovi—all those guys used Tom's subs," Heddon said. "The Michael Jackson

Thriller tour had all Tom's subwoofers doing the heavy lifting." Cirque du Soleil uses his products in several venues in Las Vegas. IMAX is a customer. Danley has built loudspeakers for the home theaters of Bill Gates and George Lucas, and for many houses of worship.

It is not surprising, then, that when the military wanted a new weapon comprised of a massive subwoofer, Danley was their man. Hearing about this from Heddon, I tried to remember the food chain: Car-audio competition inspired the development of more powerful audio for everyone. More powerful audio inspires more powerful audio-based music. Ultimately we realize that what we've made to punish ourselves is virtually a weapon. Take this one notch further and it can be an *actual* weapon.

The Matterhorn boasts forty subwoofers powered by forty thousand-watt amplifiers. By deploying this speaker, the military would be able to create a sound wave to conceal the noise of a stealth aircraft launch. Another use, Heddon told me, would be to back the Matterhorn up to the entrance of a cave. "I'll assure you that no one is staying in that cave, because they can't." The monstrous energy of the weapon's sound would remain almost completely intact as it thundered forward great distances. "The Bible says all creation sings, but all creation *vibrates*," Heddon noted. "This kind of sound—let's say 150 decibels at 10 or 15 hertz at the mouth of the cave—that messes your eustachian tube up. You can get vertigo—all kinds of weird stuff."

Indeed, as Hillel Pratt, a professor of neurobiology at the Technion, the Israel Institute of Technology, has reported, the simulation of the vestibular organ by frequencies below audibility induces a discrepancy between the visual system and the

processing systems for everything from temperature and body position to the sense of touch and the activity of the heart. The
soundtrack and the images of our film of the world are knocked
violently out of sync. Once more, we're back in futurist country.
The vestibular organ, assaulted by powerful low-frequency noise,
signals an experience of intense acceleration—of speed. The individual subjected to the Matterhorn becomes overwhelmed
with motion sickness even when standing dead still.

"There's really nothing like it in nature," Heddon said. "There's
just nothing that emits massive amounts of continuous, low-
frequency energy. When you get into big amplitude, low frequency
and continuous, then you start to get into stuff that's scary. If I
hit you with a blast, I can stop you because your heart is knocked
out of rhythm. Let's say you hit a cave with the Matterhorn—you
could create a cave-in."

Abruptly, Heddon stopped. He'd begun by saying most of the
data on the Matterhorn was classified; now he suddenly seemed
to hear himself, and with no transition, switched course. "We're
just helping people have a good time with IMAX," he said.
"They're blown away by what we do. We're fortunate. We're just
blessed."

❊

I hung up the phone feeling pretty vertiginous myself. As I was
listening to Heddon, I'd recalled a report I had read on the use of
amplified noise at Guantánamo Bay. The report contained some
interesting details about dissonant harmonic changes along the
lines of Andy Niemiec's work (in this case, dubbing Meow Mix
commercial soundtracks over the sound of crying babies). One

line stood out. When James Hetfield, co-founder of Metallica, heard that U.S. interrogators were using Metallica's "Enter Sandman" as an instrument of torture on prisoners at Guantánamo Bay, he laughed. "We've been punishing our parents, our wives, our loved ones with this music forever. Why should the Iraqis be any different?"

PODOPHILIA

When I think of the iPod, I think of Audiac.

In 1960, Dr. Wallace Gardner, a dentist in Cambridge, Massachusetts, collaborated with one of his patients, an acoustical expert named Licklider, to develop a new technology for pain management. Audio analgesia, patented under the trademark name of Audiac, purported to transform dental treatment into relaxation by way of loud sound. To be given Audiac, dental patients donned a pair of giant, heavily padded headphones like the ones worn by navy pilots. Then they would lie back on the chair and choose from one of eight musical selections ("Bali Hai" was a favorite) that had been mixed into a tape of "masking sound" similar to a waterfall. Whenever the dentist approached a sensitive spot, the patient twisted the knob to increase the volume of sound. The worse the pain, the louder the noise. According to Gardner's research, 90 percent of patients said that Audiac reduced the pain of filling a cavity to the level of a mosquito bite. A couple of thousand were in use in dental offices across the country less than a year after Gardner got his patent. Soon Audiac was being brought to hospitals for use in childbirth and minor operations.

Audiac was actually invented to deaden the pain of noise itself. Because of a punctured eardrum, Dr. Gardner was tortured by the sound of his own dental drill. Licklider developed a way of diminishing the suffering by creating a louder, masking noise; the pair realized that the "controlled sound" of Audiac would "overlay the pain message to the brain" no matter what the source.

It's not quite clear what scuppered the bright future of Audiac. The American Dental Society of Anesthesiology mounted a hostile campaign against the product—whether out of genuine concern about the side effects of the device (not just potential hearing damage but reports of patients entering into a hypnotic state) or from a desire to save their own investment in drug-based anesthesiology, it's difficult to say. Obviously, the pain relief of Audiac came at a cost. But at least one contemporary firm, Sound Pain Relief, is now trying to resuscitate audio analgesia, invoking more fashionable explanations for its effects, like cross-sensory masking.

⚏

Reading back through newspaper reports of public response to the release of the Sony Walkman in 1979, the precursor of the iPod, it's striking how often devotees of the device praise the Walkman as soundproofing against painful noise and the afflictions of modern life in general. This feature got as much attention as did its ability to supply music "wherever you want," which Sony had focused on. Users claimed the Walkmen made commuting tolerable and provided relief from "the awful sounds of the city." Anthony Payne, a New York TV producer interviewed by *Time* magazine in 1981, declared, "There are buses, airplanes, sirens . . . You have to replace them with something louder, by force-feeding your own sounds into your ears." A Manhattan computer executive called the Walkman "a great way of snubbing the world."

We also come once more upon the connection between noise and speed. The Walkman's very name contains the notion of motion. But the association went beyond walking to encompass any movement that enhanced the sense of personal freedom. Howard Bogaz, a carpenter *Time* interviewed while he was roller-skating in Venice Beach, summed up the appeal: "I take it when I ski or on long drives. I'm into my music! The sun is out, the wind is blowing, and you're on your wheels!" When Sony initially released the Walkman in Tokyo, the launch centered on demonstrations of people listening while roller-skating, riding bicycles, and jogging. One of the popular television commercials for the product presented the Walkman as an instrument to make your body "fleet." A woman in a leotard is shown engaging in graceful, dancer-like stretches in a light, airy room; after a few seconds, a male voice announces, "Now you can lose inches off your waistline effortlessly"—the woman pauses to switch the cassette player at her waist for a smaller model—"thanks to the new Super Walkman from Sony; the world's smallest cassette player." She resumes her motions.

Sony's Walkman was sold as the ultimate portable music device, but it also used sound to transform the experience of mobility.

The iPod upped the phenomenal success of the Walkman to the point where people speak of an iGeneration. The iPod appeared in 2001. As of the fall of 2009, Apple announced that 220 million had been sold worldwide. By way of comparison, sixteen years after its release, Sony had produced a total of 150 million Walkmans. Part of the explanation for the iPod's extraordinary success may lie in the way that it amplifies the idea of personal sound as a surrogate for motion. With its enormous capacity for storage, the iPod is no longer about taking music anywhere you want; it's about letting the music take you anywhere that processed sound goes.

In the same years that the iPod was taking off, and one began seeing cords dangling from more and more ears like bits of cranial wiring come unstuck, my own walking habits changed. My office is only five blocks from Central Park. When I first began working in midtown, at the end of the 1990s, I could get to the park in six or seven minutes. Today, at lunch hour or the end of the day when gridlock is at its height, it can take me fifteen minutes to walk the distance. The park is no longer an easy, quick break from the urban grid. It's a thirty-minute back-and-forth commitment, and I walk there far less now than I used to.

It's difficult to get statistics on the increasing congestion of pedestrian movement in major cities, but indubitably walking in any of the world's major cities has become a more choked-up affair. New York City population growth began declining in the 1960s, with the largest drop, a whopping 10.4 percent, between 1970 and 1980. Then, between 1990 and 2000, the city grew an astonishing 9.4 percent—a figure you have to go back before the Second World War to approach. Though the numbers aren't quite as high, the population of inner London falls and returns to growth in close parallel with New York's trajectory. Tokyo, which also saw a steep decline in population for several decades, has seen growth every year since 1997.

Perhaps the iPod took off when people's actual freedom of movement became compromised to a degree never before experienced in history. We might go one step further and speculate about a larger overload, a mounting congestion of stimuli that drives us to try to recapture the lost sense of untethered acceleration through sound.

Even if we hesitate to tabulate precise correlations, I think it's fair to assume that part of the iPod's appeal is that it allows people to interpolate inside their headphones a sense of speed and motion that's clogged up one way or another in the outside world.

❊

Those who love the iPod are keen to sing the praises of the device. And what they have to say about their passion is remarkably consistent.

When self-professed "heavy users" are questioned about what makes the device so addictive, they often mention access to endless great tunes, but very quickly the argument shifts. For many people, it seems that iPods are less about the individual pieces of music they allow one to hear than about the overall sound they weave—the acoustical superhighway they open. People talk about how the iPod provides continuity through sound, stitching together experience through music. Over and over, people describe the iPod as providing a soundtrack for their lives. "It makes everything harmonic," said one fifteen-year-old. "Every-thing that was confusing it makes smooth and flow together. It gives the perfect soundtrack for your life. It makes everything become clear." Stitching together fragmented experience and feelings, the iPod injects a new sense of flow into everything we do. It drives *us*. The iPod covers over the gaps, the silent holes in our day-to-day being, as nothing before in history. The iPod gives the user 24/7 access to audio analgesia.

In my own conversations and in interviews I've read in which people talk about why they love their iPods, one no longer hears, as one did with the Walkman, about the need to block out awful city sounds. Instead, what comes up again and again is the ability of the iPod to "filter out distractions," including people talking on cell phones, playing digital games, and playing music too loudly on their own sound devices—as well as the magnetic pull of In-ternet noise on users themselves. The iPod is touted not for its ability to mask over old infrastructure sound but for the way it blocks out the discretionary din that got plastered on top of that layer and defines the new noisiness of the digital age. Based on how people speak about their iPods, it would seem that today the nexus of pain is not so much any single loud noise as it is our diffraction between multiple stimuli engaged in a continual "boom-off." Rather than ranting about the "alienation of the iGeneration," we have to ask ourselves what we did to make our larger soundscape so disposable that it became the sonic equiva-lent of fast food.

And still, as with the Audiac that tried to end dental pain by increasing noise, the cure in the end may be worse than the disease.

POD-COSTS

If you poke around the Internet, you'll find numerous stories about people on foot or riding bicycles being hit by cars, purportedly because they were wearing iPods and couldn't hear the approaching machine. Swinton Insurance, a large U.K. firm, recently declared that one in ten minor traffic accidents are now attributable to "Podestrians," pedestrians listening to personal sound devices. Most of the time, the Podestrians aren't hurt themselves, according to Swinton, but cause rear-end collisions when one car slams on the brakes to avoid hitting the walker wearing headphones.

We haven't quite evolved beyond the need to take the acoustical measure of our environment. When Dirksen Bauman, a professor of Deaf cultural studies at Gallaudet University, began telling me about a group of people who'd abruptly lost their hearing, I assumed he was going to describe the psychological experience of being suddenly cast into silence. In fact, each person in this group, recounting their initial shock at having gone deaf, commented that they did not think to themselves, "Oh how terrible—I can't hear anything." Rather, what they experienced was a deep sense of "*Where am I?*" "Their whole sense of place, the cues they use, the foundation of how they situated themselves in the world around them, were gone, without them even having realized until then what that foundation had been based on," Bauman said.

Our ears may have been more sharply attuned to this problem when sound devices first became popular. Shortly after the Walkman's release, the dangers of blocking out the soundscape occasioned a number of legislative initiatives to restrict their indiscriminate use. Within two years of the Walkman's appearance, nine states banned the use of headphones while driving. Woodbridge, New Jersey, went further, passing a law forbidding pedestrians from listening to headphones when they stepped onto the street: $50 or fifteen days in jail was the penalty for violating this law. A member of the New York City Council tried to have a similar bill passed there. But what seemed a growing movement soon trailed off. Enforcement was too difficult. The allure of noise in motion was too great. Some people would say we all became more nimble at gauging where we are in space without hearing the world around us. I suspect we just got habituated to being more clumsy and collision-prone.

⌖

But what about the more obvious problem of losing the ability to hear at all? There have now been multiple studies indicating that the use of personal sound devices at sufficient volume poses the risk of hearing loss. What has been far trickier to ascertain is the number of people who regularly listen to their MP3 players at levels that threaten hearing. By and large, what studies have reported is that there are young people who regularly listen to their iPods too loudly; but the numbers, while significant, are not alarming. That, of course, depends on your definition of alarming. The most authoritative recent study, a joint undertaking by the University of Colorado at Boulder and Children's Hospital Boston, places the percentage of teens who listen to iPods at dangerous levels somewhere between 7 and 24 percent of the population.

More interesting than the parade of statistics on high-volume iPod use are the findings about how young people react to learning about these hazards. The UC Boulder/Children's Hospital Boston study found that teens who are told most forcefully by their peers and others about the dangers of loud iPod use respond by . . . turning up their iPods. The more these teens were made aware of the damage they were doing to themselves, the more damage they did.

It's a poignant finding. The teens' response points toward the built-in limits of antinoise activism. At a certain point, whether out of evolutionary aggression or our general cultural predilection for challenging whatever threatens our right to make some noise, we react to being told to turn down the volume by doing precisely the opposite.

What, then, should we do? Educate people less about the dangers of noise so that they won't feel that their right to be loud is being threatened and will keep noise levels lower of their own volition? Perhaps when it comes to certain teenagers, yes. This would be a version of the legalize-drugs argument. But the noise problem may be even more complicated than the drug problem—on many levels.

For one thing, we don't really have a handle yet on the ways the new noisiness is damaging our hearing. For another, the whole debate about safe levels of sound may be basically moot. According to Jim Hudspeth of Rockefeller University, who studies the biophysical and molecular bases of hearing, even lower sound levels that are tolerable for a short period can be damaging over the long run. "Living in New York City, we're very aware of noise all around us that's not immediately painful, but the question is whether spending hours and hours with that exposure causes permanent damage," Hudspeth said. "Remember when the Walkman came along and it was a big deal? Now we have the iPod, and it's ubiquitous. With the iPod, people have something stuffed in their ears all day long—at work, while commuting, even while exercising and having meals, they have those wires stuck in their ears. Well, even if their level of sound exposure is moderate, it's not clear that sufficient duration of exposure won't cause real damage."

Once again, the issue may be less about literal loudness than about constant inundation. It might prove to be that surprisingly few hours a day at a surprisingly unpunishing sound level is enough over time to dramatically degrade our hearing. If you thought it was hard telling your teenager to turn down the music on their personal sound device, try telling them to turn it off altogether. "Turn off your iPod at least eight hours a day or ten years from now you will not have any high-frequency hearing!" I can just see the volume dial spinning smoothly round and round to drown out the sound of *that* warning.

CHAPTER NINE

Home Front

At this point I thought that I understood a little better why our world sounds the way it does. For a combination of evolutionary, commercial, infrastructural, and sociocultural reasons, there's more continual, inescapable noise than ever before. And the new noisiness that's tipped us over the edge into the land of loud may be the hardest to mitigate of all. Why? Because we ourselves crave that noise to keep us feeling energized, youthful, focused, free, fast—and protected from all the other noise we can't control. But that doesn't make the need for silence any less profound. How can we opt out of the world of noise? What can we do in practical terms to soundproof our lives other than by just making more masking noise?

In a summer of a thousand bass-heavy thunderstorms, I traveled to Dearborn, Michigan, to attend Noise-Con 2008. The conference billed itself as an event "facilitating interaction among a wide spectrum of noise control professionals." I listened to lengthy papers on subjects it had never occurred to me anyone had ever given the slightest thought to, such as "The Effects of Wear Estimates and Prediction Practices on the Production of Planetary Gear Whine" and "The Influence of Body Cavity Acoustic Modes on Booming Noise During Acceleration." Some of the essays sounded as if they could have been lifted from a poem by John Ashbery, such as one from NASA entitled "Vibration Response Models of a Stiffened Aluminum Plate Excited by a Shaker." Others smacked oddly of lines cribbed from a 1950s etiquette book: "Ceiling Performance Is Best When No Touching Is Allowed." Then there were the more cocktail-party-minded presentations, like one on mitigating noise from a private racetrack. (Its author told me he had recently done a study for a major theme-park operator on roller-coaster noise in response to complaints from surrounding communities. The main thing this study discovered was that by far the most annoying noise at the theme park came not from roller coasters but from musical concerts.) The event also boasted many, many papers on airplane, airport, vehicle, and road noise, along with a special session by a somewhat mysterious body known as the Noise Control Foundation. I learned a great deal. What I was most interested in, however, was not the papers but the vendors.

The conference brought together just about every major player in the soundproofing industry. I wanted to learn what was happening at the cutting edge of the business and came armed with a simple question: What could we do—more precisely, what could *I* do—to shut out the world and create a reasonable approximation of complete quiet?

Scores of vendors packed the mega-ballroom exposition hall at the Hyatt Regency Dearborn. Many of them were sloshing back drinks and seemed to be enjoying the kinds of uproarious conversations that would have been equally appropriate at Noise-Pro 2008. There were snake-oil-style soundproofers in loud suits manning booths arrayed with tiles and slabs of peculiar layered materials, canisters of sprays and foams, odd metal bits, rubber mats, door panels, as well as over-magnified, bleached-out photos on poster board of function venues, housing developments, cement blocks, trees, and pretty, pigtailed girls with their fingers to their lips above the word "QUIET." Men and women who looked as though their products had been concocted for late-night-TV sales spots jostled up next to earnest northern Europeans dressed like influential architects and standing before black boxes projecting gray needles, faceless heads wearing headphones, and laptops in suitcases with screens displaying sharp, dancing green lines and complex spectral grids. Though there were exceptions, by and large Americans seemed to be making the stuff that actually got glued to, hammered on, or squirted into walls, floors, and cracks to cut sound down, while the Europeans were the sound-measurement jocks—devising ultrasensitive decibel counters, vibration analyzers, and software systems to figure out exactly what kind of noise problem you were dealing with.

I paused a second before a neat display of rough, pasty tiles at the booth of the International Cellulose Corporation. A bald, tan guy bent forward to read my name tag.

"How are you doing, George?" he asked.

"I'm doing well," I said. "How are you?"

"I'm fine," he said. "If I was any better, there'd be two of me. And you don't want that. Even I can only stand one of me."

"So, listen," I said. "I've got noise problems all over my home. What can you do for me?"

"George," he said regretfully, "we only sell through licensed applicators, architects, and acoustical engineers. But . . . are you familiar with our new SonaKrete?" I shook my head. "It's our new premium acoustical finisher and probably the product we're most excited about right now. Unbelievably effective. George, they're using this everywhere. Courtrooms. Restaurants. They're putting it in the Freedom Tower. It occupies the niche between textured sprays and European-type plaster finishes that might sell for $35 a foot. Whereas this is $8 to $12 a foot." And what exactly was SonaKrete? I asked. It was, he replied, an extremely smooth, "architecturally acceptable," acoustical treatment that was "getting famous for doing custom, integral colors that soak right into the material." It looked good to me, and I could just hear the commercial: "SonaKrete: The Krete That Made the Freedom Tower Fall Silent."

I moved on to the Material Sciences Corporation. The written material I read on this company explained that "Whether it's cars, dishwashers or computers, we live in a world where quiet equals quality in the minds of consumers." Was that really true? There are stories about how, when quieter vacuum cleaners were introduced into the market, customers wouldn't buy them because the sound suggested feeble suctioning power. "Put simply," the promotional literature concluded, "at MSC we manufacture quiet." While I tried to figure out how I felt about the idea of manufactured quiet, the booth team approached saying that they wanted to talk about Quiet Steel™ roofing. Quiet Steel has been a successful product for years now in the realm of automobile manufacture, where it's described as one of the company's "family" of NVH damping products. (NVH: noise, vibration, and harshness—I love the idea of getting rid of harshness along with noise and vibration. The reverse would be a QSC product. Something offering quiet, stillness, *and* compassion.) MSC's booth displayed little steel plates hanging on chains from stick-and-post arrangements in the manner of Chinese gongs. The salesman explained that it was "basically laminated steel, two layers, with polymer in between." It can be used, he said, "wherever there's radiated noise. Automobiles. Washing machines. Driers. Vacuum cleaners. Now roofs as well!"

He gave me a little wooden hammer and invited me to strike an untreated steel plate, and then give a whack to Quiet Steel. I did. The first plate, of regular steel, made a nice, reverberating cymbal sound. Quiet Steel made just a little, discreet, dent-thud. I half expected the Quiet Steel plate to say "Excuse me" after its polite little sound emission. The vendor excitedly told me that he had a washing machine treated with Quiet Steel and had recently left coins in the pockets of his pants. "My wife could barely even hear them clattering around inside the machine!" he marveled.

The danger, of course, with such effective noise, vibration, and harshness damping is that you might not hear sounds signaling that you're in the process of demolishing your product. At another point in the conference I heard about what happened when John Deere proudly introduced soundproof cabs into its

agricultural machinery to combat the very real problem of farmers suffering noise-induced hearing loss. The machines were a
hit—until farmers realized that they could drive across an entire
field in their air-conditioned, stereo-equipped cabs dumping
engine parts without realizing anything was wrong until they'd
totaled the machine. That put a damper on silence as a selling
point for heavy farm equipment.

At the 3M booth, a big guy with a flat face and a loud bang of
a voice told me that the hottest new thing in soundproofing was
microperforated film. It's a new film that has holes in it that you
can "tune" for absorption, I was told, and should be commercially
available for large-volume usage ("like carpeting all the systems
under an automobile hood") in the next couple of years. When I
asked where microperforated film could go, I was told, "Where
can't it go might be a better question. It absorbs all sounds anywhere you put it. And you can print on it." What exactly does it
do? I asked.

He told me that while most sound absorbers today are fiber
based—using materials like fiberglass, polymeric foams, and
materials based on polyurethanes and acoustic tiles—there are
"environmental implications" for many of these substances,
since they release particulate matter into the air. Microperforated
film, on the other hand, is a thin flexible sheet that can be
stretched over anything with no loss of particulate matter. The
sound hits these micro holes (you can control the cavity depth,
which influences the sound-absorption spectrum) and the un-
desired frequencies get sponged up while other frequencies
vibrate in a "free span" portion of the cavity.

Microperforated film might have been, as the 3M man told

me, "as hot as nanofibers were a few years ago," but there was one word I heard whispered over and over in the Hyatt ballroom. Actually, two words: "Green Glue." With all the high-tech products being flogged at Noise-Con, nothing was as omnipresent as this "viscoelastic material" (a gunky green plastic ooze that's a dead ringer for the substance in the Dr. Seuss masterpiece *Bartholomew and the Oobleck*). It comes in tubes and buckets and can be squeezed in between just about any two surfaces to make a sound-killing oobleck sandwich. The noise waves pass through the first material, hit the layer of oobleck, and, as the company's diagrams reveal, turn into a series of hapless red lines squiggling any which way they can in order to flee the oobleck. As Green Glue puts it: "the vibration energy" is "dissipated and gone." Green Glue is probably the top-selling soundproofing product in the world today and was acquired last year by the massive French multinational construction materials firm Saint-Gobain. As Green Glue reveals, soundproofing doesn't have to be all that state of the art in order to be pretty impressively effective.

Indeed, until very recently the art of soundproofing, even at its most sophisticated, boiled down to a handful of principles: blocking sound through mass or distance; reducing or damping sound by absorbing the waves in some kind of material, like heavy curtains; and decoupling the sound source so that it can't transmit sound waves. Soundproofers may quibble, but basically from an end user's point of view you're either trying to knock out the noise or to suck it up. Dan Gaydos's description of sound as a "brute force" might have been lifted from the annals of soundproofing; many of the basic tactics have the ring of military phraseology. Soundproofers speak of "isolating the noise," "flanking noise paths," and "neutralizing or deadening sound vibrations" before they ever manage to invade your home. In broad outline, at least, these principles have also been known for a very long time.

PULL OUT YOUR PLUGS

We began soundproofing by blocking the entry of sound into our own heads. Probably the earliest literary reference to sound-proofing occurs at the moment when Odysseus ordered his sailors to plug their ears with beeswax as their vessel approached the Sirens. True to the snake-biting-its-own-tail relationship be-tween desirable and undesirable sound, this first-ever mass soundproofing event was not dedicated to protecting the sailors against obnoxious noise but to safeguarding them from a sound so enticing that it might tempt them to their deaths. Odysseus himself exchanged silence for stillness—getting roped to the mast but keeping his ears free to enjoy this once-in-a-lifetime serenade.

The Greeks became adept at all manner of acoustical tech-niques in the process of navigating sound problems in their theaters. We still don't fully understand how the interplay be-tween sound and silence worked in these structures. Exploring the astonishing acoustics at the giant theater of Epidaurus, which enabled some 15,000 spectators to make out actors' lines without a single subwoofer, researchers recently found that the stone seats actually serve in part as sound *blockers*. By tracking the way in which voices carry from the stage up through tier after tier of limestone seats, scientists found that natural corrugations

in the rock filter out lower frequency sound (such as the distracting noises of an audience stirring) while bouncing the higher
frequencies, within which most human speech transpires, all the
way to the back of the space. In its early iterations, soundproofing was less about creating quiet than about ensuring that the
noise we wanted to hear wouldn't get lost in the crowd.

There were, of course, many improvements in soundproofing
methodology over the next hundreds of years, but the ability to
mute a room really took hold in the muffled interiors of the nineteenth century. By the early 1800s, the soundproofing profession
had grown enough to have its own jargon. It was then that the
definition of "deafening" came also to mean rendering a floor or
partition impenetrable to sound by way of "pugging" (packing
empty space with materials ranging from earth and sawdust to
hair and cockleshells). There were still kinks to be worked out in
soundproofing technique, to be sure. The writer Thomas Carlyle
discovered these, to his hair-tearing regret, when he tried to build
a quiet study in his home.

Carlyle was a vociferous Victorian pursuer of silence. He
often dissolves into raptures on the subject, as he did to one cor-
respondent in 1840, writing "SILENCE, SILENCE: in a thousand senses I proclaim the indispensable worth of Silence, our
only safe dwelling-place often . . . This shallow generation knows
nothing of Silence: that is even the *disease* of it; will be the death
of it, if not cured. 'Self-renunciation' too, that is *Silence* in one of
its senses." He is less uplifting on the subject of noise. In the midst
of a rant against a "vile yellow Italian" organ-grinder who plied his
street and ruined his summer, Carlyle wrote, "The question
arises, whether to go out and, if not assassinate him, call the po-

lice upon him, or to take myself away to the bath-tub and the other side of the house."

Carlyle was not alone in his struggle for quiet. Rather, he was part of a surge of intellectual professionals in Victorian London who were making their homes their principal place of employment—and requiring a new standard of silence outside the walls in consequence. Street musicians were often their biggest complaint. Some did, indeed, station themselves before the homes of people they knew hated their sound, demanding money in order to leave. But many of them were also indigent immigrants desperate to make a little loose change. This was not the production of noise for noise's sake. And the foreign-born status of many of these musicians triggered ugly racial profiling. The *City Press* described street musicians howling "like apes and baboons escaped from the Zoological Gardens, and looking much like these creatures too." The mathematician and inventor Charles Babbage became so fixated on shutting down street music—he called it an "instrument of torture"—that he provoked an uprising. His neighbors grew so weary of his loud pursuit of silence that they broke his windows, shadowed him in a screaming mob, dropped dead cats across his doorstep, and threatened his life.

Considering the fate of Babbage, Carlyle might have been merely being prudent when he damped down his public activism against noise and focused on pursuing silence in his own home. In danger, he claimed, of being driven mad by itinerant musicians (along with the songs of a neighbor's "Demon Fowls"— Cochin China roosters), he decided to soundproof his study on the top floor of his home. At first, he was all excitement, writing a friend, "We are again *building* in Cheyne Row: a perfectly soundproof apartment this time; deaf utterly, did you even fire cannon beside it, and perfect in ventilation; such is the program— calculated to be the envy of surrounding 'enraged musicians,' and an invaluable conquest to me henceforth, if it prosper!"

"If it prosper," indeed. Quickly, the noise of the soundproof operation itself became a wretched commotion: "Irish laborers fetching and carrying, tearing and rending, our house once more a mere dust-cloud and chaos come again." Carlyle fled the operation—and the house—leaving both to the directorship of his wife, who was relieved to be free of her husband's oppressive noise consciousness. "Now that I feel the noise and dirt and disorder with my own senses, and not through his as well, it is amazing how little I care about it," she wrote.

Before the dust had even settled, it became clear that, despite the use of sound-mitigation strategies that would be perfectly respectable today (such as double walls and a specially designed slate roof with sound-deadening air chambers beneath), the project was a fiasco. Carlyle characterized the efforts as "totally futile." Ultimately, he declared the room to be by far the noisiest place in the entire house. Even its vaunted perfect ventilation was a bust. Shortly after its completion, Carlyle climbed to the study and shut himself up inside to smoke a pipe in mournful contemplation of his ruined dreams. Fortunately, his absence was noticed before much time had passed. A housemaid found Carlyle splayed unconscious on his study floor, overcome by smoke fumes.

Worst of all, the whole experience had darkened his view of human nature. His fantasy of a soundproof room, Carlyle now realized, "was a flattering delusion of an ingenious needy builder."

In combination with shoddy building and crippling expenses, the moral depravity evidenced in the work of his soundproofers made the room "a kind of infernal 'miracle'" to him, his "first view of the Satan's invisible world that prevails in that department as in others." It was a fate fit for a Greek myth. Carlyle's dream of a soundless room left him with both the noisiest room in his domain and an embittering recognition that corruption thrives even at the heart of man's noblest calling: the pursuit of silence.

※

And still, despite Carlyle's failure, the rise of so-called brainwork went hand in hand with the refinement of soundproofing technology. Even earplugs got better. The old problems of irritation from beeswax and the skanky decomposition of sheep tallow were overcome by composite plugs mixed with cotton wool. Franz Kafka grew reliant on a new line of such plugs to muffle daytime noises and had them specially sent from Berlin—though he lamented to his fiancée that they were still rather messy and wished that the tiny steel "sleeping balls" a Strindberg hero slipped into his ears could be found outside the author's imagination. By the early twentieth century, Carlyle's fantasy of a room that would be impervious to sound even if a cannon were fired beside it was closer to becoming a reality.

Floyd Watson, author of a pioneering 1922 work on soundproofing techniques, reported that during the First World War a room was built to insulate the sounds of machine guns being tested. It was a room inside a room, actually: four inches of ground cork lined its wooden walls; a double layer of flax boards padded the ceiling. Bullets were shot into a big heap of absorptive sand.

The insulation worked well enough that neighbors across the street had no idea what was happening inside the building until one of the gunners forgot to shut the double-pane windows after opening them to fan out the billowing clouds of powder smoke.

Exciting developments in soundproofing were happening around the world. Scientists in Utrecht, Holland, claimed to have built a room so free of noise that a person could hear his own heartbeat. When Shepherd Ivory Franz of the George Washington University Government Hospital for the Insane went to check it out (psychological investigations were to take place there, among other experiments), he was elated. Diagrams of the room Franz published in the journal *Science* depict what appears to be a box made of multiple frames resting on a fat plank. Lines radiate out from a list of materials in the middle of the box indicating the wall-within-a-wall layers of soundproofing each frame represents: korkstein, wood, lead, trichpiése (some kind of woven horsehair), porous stone, and air space. That's not even to start on the sheet-lead-and-carpet buried floor. Franz confirmed that while it was true you might also be able to hear your own heartbeat in certain rooms that were *not* noiseless, this would only occur after "very violent exercise," while in the Utrecht chamber all it took were "a few swings of the leg or arm" to make "heart sounds quite distinct." So quiet was the room, he reported, that "one hears a subjective buzzing similar to but of less intensity than the buzzing produced by large doses of quinine." (That buzzing was probably the same tinnitus-type noise that John Cage mistook for the sound of his nervous system more than forty years later when he made his famous visit to Harvard's anechoic chamber, a special soundproof room designed to suppress all reverberation. "There is always something to see, something to hear," Cage wrote after this experience.) The lesson of the Utrecht room seemed straightforward: given sufficient layering and distance, you can kill any sound. But the pursuit of silence through soundproofing wasn't only about piling one deadening material on top of another. There was also the quest for the one all-purpose, ideal soundproofing technique: the elixir of noise-lessness.

At the close of the nineteenth century, Samuel Cabot, a Boston manufacturer, had discovered the power of cured eelgrass packed between thick paper sheets to stop sound by creating a "thick, elastic cushion of dead-air spaces." Using the trademark name Cabot's Quilt, he was soon boasting of the substance as the Green Glue of its day. "Every Hotel, Flat, Lodge, Hospital, School, Auditorium or similar building should be sound-proofed," proclaimed one advertisement Cabot placed in a 1918 issue of the journal *Western Architect & Engineer*. "If it isn't sound-proof it's a failure. Cabot's Quilt has made more buildings really sound-proof than all other deadening materials combined." In 1929 British engineers rediscovered Cabot's product as their own invention. (The history of soundproofing is littered with instances of convenient forgetting.) A captain affiliated with the sound locators of the London Territorial Air Defence Brigades got credit in the *London Times* for realizing the soundproofing potential of this fireproof, nonverminous seaweed. Imported to Great Britain from Nova Scotia in the form of mats that were attached to ceilings and walls, it became the definitive sound absorbent for the quintessential silent institution: the English bank.

At a London trade show in 1930, Trystan Edwards, a town

planner and architectural critic, exhibited a model for an entirely "silent house." The house boasted a miracle door that could "even be slammed silently." (Begging the question of the dangerous rage that might be provoked absent the satisfaction of that argument-closing clap.) Sir Banister Fletcher, president of the Royal Institute of British Architects, lauded the idea and called for architects to consider it as they built near the loud, crowded thoroughfares of London.

On both sides of the Atlantic, anxiety about metropolitan population explosions helped drive the soundproofing renaissance. Even the stolid United States Bureau of Standards, concerned by studies that forecast a spike in the density of urban dwellings, jumped on the bandwagon of experimenters trying to devise a truly silent apartment. The bureau's exhaustive tests of acoustic properties of different building materials led to the official proclamation that air space between the two halves of a compound partition was the most effective sound snuffer in the world.

Along with private homes and financial institutions, courtrooms, hospitals, and prisons were early beneficiaries of the advances in soundproofing. In the latter, soundproofing was brought in as a humane gesture to protect quieter inmates from noisier ones, as well as to cultivate religion. Not religion through silence, however. A new chapel at Sing Sing featured a breakthrough rolling soundproof partition that enabled it to simultaneously host two religious services, one Catholic and one Presbyterian.

From the turn of the century on up to the Second World War, optimism about the capacity of soundproofing technology to meet the challenges of the new, machine-driven din abounded. In a spring fever, the *New York Times* tied the prospect of new soundproof spaces to amatory bliss: "We don't need any more faculties for divorce. What we do need are a few old abandoned telephone booths large enough to accommodate two, fitted up with a rustic seat and sound-proof, where the city lover can sit undisturbed and repeat the old, old story that no age has been able to supplant." More sober authorities, such as R. V. Parsons, an acoustical engineer with the New York City Noise Abatement Commission, which was established by the city health commissioner in 1929 and was the first such body in the nation, announced that "Preventing noise at its source and insulating against it are both possible now—not in some Utopian future."

A few unfortunate members of the commission were tasked with measuring the efficacy of a soundproof room that had been developed in collaboration with Bell Laboratories against a biblical checklist of urban noise plagues. All day long, day after day, the experts huddled in this special chamber, blasted by one noise type after the next, gauging how well the room performed. Most wracking of all was a sound replicating the roar of heavy traffic "punctuated by the penetrating discord of sirens and automobile horns." After health commissioner Shirley Wynne visited the room—bluntly labeled a "torture chamber" by one of those present—he left visibly shaken, deeming himself "a martyr to the cause of humanity" for having agreed to participate in the research.

Health benefits of soundproof buildings were being studied around the world just as the construction of such buildings was becoming logistically feasible. Sometimes the results of this research were surprising. The most curious finding emerged from a test begun in 1930 by scientists from the Tokyo Hygienic Laboratory. Doctors Fujimaki and Arimoto compared the physical condition of numerous sets of white rats, half of which were raised in rooms protected from loud noises and half of which were raised in a noisy environment. In their first experiment, involving two groups of 20 rats, they discovered that rats raised under an elevated railroad over which 1,283 trains passed each day were more nervous, grew less, had higher infant mortality rates, lower fertility, and ate more frequently than their noise-proofed cousins. However, there's a twist: nasty and brutish the lives of the noise-battered rats certainly were—but they were not especially short. At least not by white rat standards. In fact, the rats raised beneath the elevated lived a full 53 days *longer* in aggregate than those shielded from sound. Given that you're talking a three- to four-year life cycle on average, an extra 53 days is nothing to wrinkle your whiskers at.

Fujimaki and Arimoto were startled and redid their experiment with other sets of rats, subjecting the noise-nurtured packs to other types of clamor. They raised one group of twenty white rats in the pressroom of the *Nichi Nichi*, a Tokyo daily, while housing the other set in a soundproof room. Another time, the noise rats went into a room where a bell buzzed continuously. On each occasion, the results were the same: the rats raised in noise were nervous wrecks with all sorts of collateral health problems—but they also lived considerably longer than their quiet-cradled kin.

What does this mean? Might it really be the case, as some present-day healers claim, that sound waves contain juvenating vibrational powers? God knows, but it raises the old question: At what price longevity? An extra 53 days or 1,283 trains per day overhead for your whole life? I'd opt for early checkout. Still, the

Tokyo experiment presented the researchers with a quandary.
Perhaps there could be such a thing as too much soundproofing.

※

This question has become more salient in recent years. While
the vast majority of what I saw at Noise-Con 2008 amounted to
riffs on materials and tactics developed early in the twentieth
century, there are new products—better mousetraps—all the
time.

Even Carlyle's loathed Cochin China fowls might have lost
their alarming power today, as I learned reading Super Soundproofing Community Forum, one of several blogs sponsored by
soundproofing companies. When I read the query of a forum
member who lived in a well soundproofed apartment, but fretted
about the sound made by a noisy cockatiel that he himself had
bought and didn't want to cover with a sound-deadening blanket,
I thought to myself surely this individual is doomed. But no. A
fellow forum member informed this person about a birdcage company that made an entirely enclosed, transparent, sound-trapping
cage. Turns out that there are dozens of almost completely soundproof acrylic models on the market, and they're hypoallergenic
to boot.

Noisy neighbors remain more of a problem. Often one or the
other of you has to basically agree to go into a cage. But here as
well there are surprising new possibilities. Super Soundproofing
Community Forum lists suggestions for soundproofing a backyard by constructing high, specially treated walls around the
space, and for quieting a barking dog by playing "laughing dog
tapes" at it—sounds that supposedly are the canine equivalent of

laughter and have been shown to soothe dogs. The saddest posting I read came from someone asking whether anyone knew of a
soundproof mask or helmet that he could buy. But even this desperate individual was helpfully informed by a moderator: "You
can make your own out of Super Soundproofing Mat—closed
cell vinyl nitrile acoustic foam. It's kind of like making a 'Policy
Hat'—encloses the entire head and has only a mouth and eye
holes." A site administrator added in a separate posting that
Super Soundproofing technology was "secretly working on such
headwear," and that if the original poster was serious they'd like
him to come in to test "some of our creations."

※

Beyond product proliferation, a few new technologies are
changing the parameters of what's possible in soundproofing.
Noise-cancellation technology is the most commercially relevant
of these at present. And researchers have been working to extend
its application beyond headphones to devices like the already
patented Silence Machine, which is designed to be fired at any
troublesome noise source, such as construction sites and night-
clubs. By generating a counter sound wave exactly out of phase
with the incoming noise, it creates a "personal sound shadow" for
the user. At the far edge of the technological pursuit of silence,
scientists are even working on an "acoustic cloak" using something
called sonic crystals (artificial composites of "meta-materials")
that would operate like dense clusters of very tiny cylinders to
deflect all sound from around an object in the same way, scientists say, that "water flows around a rock in a river."

But even if the acoustic cloak should one day prove possible, would we *really* want to snuggle into this garment? When I think of the cloak of silence, I can't help thinking of the Cone of Silence from the 1960s television series *Get Smart*. Whenever agent Maxwell Smart has a piece of top-secret information to impart to his superior, Chief, Smart insists that they enter the Cone of Silence. But the technology is faulty. The only effect of the Cone of Silence is to make Smart and the Chief completely inaudible to each other, while everyone outside the cone can hear their every word with crystalline clarity.

If we have learned one thing about the pursuit of total soundproofing it is that whatever degree of blessed silence we achieve, we will not be satisfied.

This reminds me of a story I heard not long ago.

THE QUIETEST HOUSE IN THE WORLD

One afternoon, I was standing in the park at the end of my street with Andy Pollack, an architect, watching our children hurl themselves with great crows of delight into a heap of dirt. Pollack is a big, friendly guy with a wide smile who looks as though he's just slightly outgrown his body. In an effort to distract ourselves from the likely ingredients of the particulate matter that our boys were dive-bombing face-first, he began telling me about his experience of the soundproofing business from an architect's perspective. One of his war stories concerned a client with unlimited funds who was building, in Pollack's words, "a very, very, very large house" (14,000 square feet) on a high vantage point in prime Long Island.

It was to be, he went on, not only large but also "an exceed-

ingly well built house, and my client was a stickler for quiet. He
said to me, 'I want you to hire whatever consultants necessary,
buy whatever materials you need, do whatever you have to do,
so I can have *the most* quiet house.' " Pollack embraced the
challenge. "We took it upon ourselves—the contractor and myself—to make the quietest house in the world."

They hired a top consultant who could give them specifica-
tions beyond what they already knew. It's difficult to decide
where to begin describing the steps taken to silence that house.
Soundproofing extras on top of the rigorous noise-abatement
measures Pollack's firm incorporates into all its work ultimately
ran in excess of $100,000. To keep sound from transmitting be-
tween walls, Pollack and his team built in such a way that no
stud had a wall on both sides of it. Every other stud attaches to
the wall opposite, so that each wall is isolated. That's not unheard of, but on top of this they stapled a rubber sound blanket
to each stud to further dampen sound waves. They insulated
every cement board that went onto the studs with a special min-
eral fiber. In the basement, where the client wanted a media
room, they built a room within a room completely separate from
the structure that held the house up. Not only did this room not
touch the ceiling, it didn't touch the *floor* because its underside
sat on little rubber isolating feet. "You can sit in there and watch
Star Wars with THX sound and no one in the kitchen above
would even know," Pollack said.

Another thing that's always a problem in this kind of house is
that ducts will transmit sound. So in addition to having special
dampers put on each duct, they built in such a way that no room
in the gigantic compound was connected to another by ductwork.

They added special "door details" to keep sound from leaking under the sill. All the windows were, he said, "double insulated, *very* custom windows, very, very well made—completely sound-proof." He did all this and much more and when it was through, "the house could not have been quieter," Pollack said. "The house almost feels like it's pulling the sound out of your ears."

The great day came when the client was to walk through the front door of his completed, absolutely soundproof home for the first time. As it happened, the front door opened onto a kind of enclosed porch. The client walked through this door and—froze. "Andy, I hear a hum," he said. "I hear a hum! I thought I said no noise." Pollack pointed out that it was a very faint hum and that you left it behind the moment you entered the house proper. The client held his ground. "It's the front door, and I hear a sound."

Deep underneath this house is a mechanical room. The house has a geothermal heating system. All the air-conditioning for 14,000 square feet comes from cold water that gets pumped out of the ground, heated, then put back into the ground. This translates into thousands of gallons of water going from the ground up and back. That's a lot of infrastructure, and, by using extras like a sound-isolated Sheetrock ceiling for the room, Pollack had managed to reduce what would otherwise have been a low roar to a barely perceptible hum. But you still needed a motor sucking air from outside so the room could breathe, and when you walked into the front door you could just make out the sound of that motor through a vent. Here was the thing: the house was on a bluff known for its windiness. There were almost constant breezes. Even a light wind, he said, would have been plenty to mask the sound of that hum; but since no sound at all was getting through from the outside, there was no natural, atmospheric cover for even the tiniest sound.

"Now we've got a situation," Pollack went on, "where everything else is so quiet that a pin drop is noise. In the dead silence, you could hear *everything*." A guest came to visit and brought a small baby. The client placed them in the wing of the house at the farthest point from his own bedroom—but because the whole house was so quiet, he could hear the baby crying from thousands of feet away. He called Pollack to complain. Pollack tried to explain that it was audible not only because baby wails were designed to cut through anything but also because there was *nothing else to hear*.

The worst moment came when the client called to say that he heard a hum in his office—designated the inner sanctum of silence. This room was situated far, far away from the mechanical room. Everything possible had been done to ensure that here, at least, in this contained space, no noise from anything else in the house could conceivably leak through.

"Are you sure you hear a hum?" Pollack asked.

"I'm sitting in the office now," the client said, "hearing it."

"Are you sure it couldn't be the fan of your computer?" Pollack asked.

"No," the client said. "Impossible." The computer—no doubt the quietest model on the market to begin with—had been completely isolated. "It's a deliberate hum," the client concluded. "You have to come out here and figure it out."

Weighed down by a sense that he'd been defeated at last, Pollack drove out to Long Island. He got to the house and trudged through room after room into the inner sanctum, and shut the door behind him. He heard the hum. The computer was not in use, and its central processing unit, or cpu, was nowhere visible; it had been, as the client declared, "completely isolated." And yetthe hum sounded like a fan. Distinctly like a fan. Pollack approached the gigantic, thick antique desk in which the cpu had been sequestered. He opened up the desk and there, he recalled, "was this cpu just *wailing*." It had been so thoroughly enclosed within the massive piece of furniture that it couldn't breathe and the fan was running desperately all the time. Moreover, the client was used to working in an office where ordinary background noise would have masked the machine's efforts to self-ventilate. Now, for the first time, he was hearing the sound of a device that he used all day.

⚶

The poor little computer hard drive panting away in the desk of Pollack's client is an allegory for what happens when we try to create complete soundproofing: somebody ends up getting smothered. Their gasps for air will grow louder and louder until we surrender the fantasy of total noise control. Because, in the end, we are born into this world screaming as loud as our tiny lungs can howl, yet simultaneously terrified of loud sounds and demanding silence in order to sleep. Because we are human and hardwired at the deepest strata of our reptilian brain to detect noise, and failing to detect it, miss it, and call whatever we do hear noise nonetheless.

⚶

Indeed, if there's nothing else to hear, at a certain point our own ears will often begin to make sound. When I talked with Jim Hudspeth about the dominant role played by the ears' built-in amplifiers in the hearing process, he remarked that 85 percent of normal ears can produce one or more tones continually in a quiet environment. "Our own ears make noise?" I asked, incredulously. "Yes," he said in his own unflappable tone. "That sound is typically over months, or years. They aren't interrupted and the signals don't change over time."

These so-called "spontaneous auto-acoustic emissions" (perhaps the swankiest of our bodily emissions) are, in fact, currently a major area of study for Hudspeth and others because they shed light on how our ears amplify sound. In a quiet place, the ears of many vertebrae become unstable and start sending off tones. The notion is not, Hudspeth told me, that the tones are useful in and of themselves but that they represent a situation similar to that of a PA system in an auditorium. Ordinarily, the PA system is turned up enough that it will be able to amplify a voice, but not so excessively high that it begins to oscillate. The amplifier of the ear, also, constantly adjusts itself to deal with ambient sound. In a quiet environment it turns itself on. "In a really quiet environment," Hudspeth went on, "the amplifier keeps turning itself up in response to the lack of input until it goes unstable, starts to oscillate, and begins to emit sound." If we were really able to soundproof our lives, we might have to start dealing with regular feedback noise from our own ear amplifiers as these cranked higher and higher to try and make out something to hear.

Granted, in the current aural climate, the prospect of mass outbreaks of spontaneous auto-acoustic emissions is nothing to lose sleep over. For most people, as Hudspeth explained, a far more likely scenario is that "overstimulation from a loud environment will damage the hair cells enough that they can no longer contribute effectively to the active process at all." In layman's terms: we're frying our amps, dude.

BOUTIQUE SILENCE

By the time I'd gotten through speaking with a slew of sound-proofers and exploring dozens of products, I realized that, yes, if you have the money and the time—but mostly the money—you can find a way to soundproof just about anything. Yet I'm uneasy with the notion of quiet as a consumer good. Jeff Szymanski, an acoustical consultant who took part in the Noise Control Foundation panel, described how he'd recently gone to purchase a dishwasher and got caught up comparing the noise output of different machines. In the end, the issue he had with buying a quiet product, he said, was that "the quietest products are also the most expensive. So right now it's seen as a premium, as in—if you're into luxury you can buy noise control." I rankle at the thought of silence as a rich man's reward.

There's a further problem, one that pertains even if state-of-the-art soundproofing were one day to be made as cheap as sub-woofers. I definitely think everyone could use more soundproofing in their lives. But—as I said at the outset of this book—I don't actually want to hear as few sounds as possible. The opposite! I want to hear as *many* sounds as possible. What kind of sound-proofing is going to help me with that?

Once again, the new noisiness is a problem both because of

the silence it destroys and because of all the other, flickering sounds it takes away. The further I went in my research, the more I found myself forced to reckon with how often I liked hearing the noises of people going about their rounds of domestic being in the same way that I liked listening to birds. I like the *tings* of glass and tableware, the pastiche of voices, swinging doors, and lifting blinds. Of not necessarily brilliantly played instruments being practiced. And of impish children streamering gales of silliness over even my most solemn ponderings. That unpredictable panoply of unprocessed sound—when not too loud and when *sometimes* broken up with something like silence—is part of why I continue to live in a city.

Yet if so much of today's noise really is discretionary, what better solution than to distribute automatic quiet kits to everyone, enabling them to manufacture their own discretionary silence? Arm us all with Silence Machines and we can go around zapping every noise we find obnoxious in our vicinity—creating "personal sound shadows" right and left and not having to worry anymore about how much noise our environment may be making. Free choice of whether to zap or zazz for everyone!

You're right, but . . . I have a confession to make. When I really think about it, I don't actually feel much better about a world in which everyone has their own personal Silence Machine, sealing them in private silence cones, than I do about one in which everyone is walking around with their iPods turned up loud. Soundproofing, after a certain point, is just another way of cutting oneself off, and I don't want to feel cut off. More than that, I don't want to feel like I *want* to be cut off. More than that,

I don't want other people to want to be cut off, either. Here we all are, after all.

Soundproofing is terrific like bulletproof flak jackets are terrific. But wouldn't it be better still if we didn't have to worry about getting shot all the time?

If the technology on display in the grand ballroom isn't a magic bullet for the pursuit of silence, what *is* the answer?

⌖

Before I left Dearborn, by chance I experienced an hour of almost total silence. One of the perks of attending Noise-Con was that its organizers had arranged a special tour for us of the Ford Rouge Factory and Application Research Center. We were to be given behind-the-scenes insights into, among other things, the way in which the latest line of Ford S-150 trucks had managed to reduce noise, vibration, *and* harshness so that they ran more smoothly and quietly than ever before.

As matters turned out, the summer of 2008 coincided with the moment when the crisis in the auto industry came home to roost. When my busload of Noise-Con conventioneers got to the plant, we discovered that Ford had suspended production of all 2009 trucks for at least ninety days. The vast, vast factory was dead. Looking over the factory floor from an elevated observation deck that laps the perimeter of the space was like looking into a white metal forest, crisscrossed here and there with orange bars and yellow girders. Hundreds of black hoses hung motionless from the ceiling. The conveyor belts were frozen, conveying nothing: "Little town, thy streets for ever more will silent be."

Massive clean saurian machines loomed soundless and still. Every fifteen minutes or so, a little plant vehicle would emerge from somewhere, swirling off into the depths of the white forest for who knew what purpose. It was an awesome and terrible sight, even if, like myself, you hold no particular affinity for the car industry. No form of soundproofing for the auto industry could ever approach the efficacy of bankruptcy.

I stood there a long time. At last, a heavy, forlorn woman in her fifties—some kind of official Ford tour guide—appeared next to me, sighing, gazing down at the floor. She waved her hand vaguely toward the massive machinery just beneath us. "Here, in the chassis area, with all the parts being brought in—door holders going back and forth, drills and guns—I imagine all the workers would be wearing earplugs," she said. And then as inexplicably as she'd appeared, she slowly drifted away.

I remained for a time, and then slowly orbited that great space. The only sound in the entire factory came from video screens planted at regular intervals. These were playing loop tapes on which faces would suddenly appear announcing, for example, "Welcome to steering-wheel installation! I'm Don." Or: "Hi! I'm Bob. I'm a windshield installer. Welcome to windshield installation." The chipper voices of these spectral workers floated up like soap bubbles in the deserted Rouge Factory, then popped into true silence.

⁂

On the bus back to the Hyatt, I stared out heavily filtered windows at endless, multilane highways—the Great Horizontal

Wall of America—while the air-conditioning roared around me. What's the answer? I asked myself again.

Well, it's obvious, isn't it? If the key isn't to soundproof one's personal life—because one cares about sound in the public sphere—the true road to silence must lie in a change of public policy. We must all go out as good, concerned citizens and support enlightened legislative reform to combat noise. We have to steel ourselves to fight small battles and big wars—taking on individuals, corporations, politicians. We have to drive home the damage noise does to everyone and demand our right to live lives that are noise free just as we have a right to smoke-free environments. We progressives must hold vigils and marches and take back the night from the Loudites! Let's all stand up right now, cup our hands to our mouths, and start making a noise about noise!

I had to stop myself before I got not only carried away but carried off. Spoiling for a brawl, I headed out to see what the hell was going on in terms of noise policy.

CHAPTER TEN

This Is War!

The pursuit of quiet through policy certainly makes for lots of loud headlines. The moment I plunged into the subject, I came across a huge front-page article in the *New York Times* titled "Clamor Against Noise Rises Around the Globe." Noise, the article announced, is now recognized as "the most ubiquitous and most annoying" of all forms of pollution and is "under new attack on many fronts." At stake are "countless billions of dollars and possibly the mental and physical health of millions of people." The article describes a new movement to combat noise pollution involving the United Nations; federal, state, and local governments; science and industry; the legal profession; and private citizens. It cites a study in which rabbits and rats subjected to urban noise for just 10 percent of each day gave birth to defective fetuses at a rate *twenty-five times* greater than that of rats living in quiet. In addition, it reports a huge spike in mental illness around Heathrow Airport. In the United States alone the cost of noise is upward of $4 billion a year "in compensation payments, accidents, inefficiency and absenteeism" due to noise trauma, according to the World Health Organization. On the upside, an environmental conference at the United Nations has identified noise as a vital area for "international study and control." Congress is introducing a host of new federal noise-control measures. The signs of progress come none too soon. Dr. Vern Knudson, an internationally renowned acoustics expert and chancellor emeritus at the University of California, Los Angeles, predicts that if noise levels continue to increase the human race will go the way of the dinosaur.

The only problem is that this article was published on September 3, 1972. Attempts to defeat noise through policy have been breaking on the horizon for more than a century. On October 1, 1935, when Mayor La Guardia officially declared war on noise—particularly that produced by traffic, cabarets, and loudspeakers planted on the sidewalks in front of stores—150 leading city organizations backed the initiative, and within the first four days of the drive the police issued a total of 5,317 warnings. By the end of the month, this figure had ballooned to 20,546, along with 175 summonses. Thousands of letters from citizens poured into La Guardia's office applauding the campaign. New York's Finest went the extra mile to investigate complaints as unusual as one from a woman in the Hotel Pierre who reported that she was going mad because a seal was keeping her awake all night. Instead of giving her the flipper, the police tracked down the offending animal in the Central Park Zoo and arranged for it to be transferred to Brooklyn. The war appeared to be a success. Yet a few years later, with the battle still raging, the press pronounced it a "brave but pathetically ineffective anti-noise campaign."

War on noise was declared repeatedly in London in the 1920s and '30s. Mussolini declared war on noise in Italy in 1933. (He'd been inspired by a cartoon in *Punch* depicting him in imperial toga proclaiming the achievements of his regime above a caption that read: "Make Rome as Quiet as It Is Great.") I learned to my surprise that my great-grandfather James Jackson Putnam, a Boston neurologist and psychologist, had been part of an international congress of some five hundred physicians and lawyers convened in 1912 with the express goal of "abolishing noise" as a "barbarous" threat to civilization. The Germans launched a war on street noises in 1908. A "crusade for quiet" in New York City made headlines around the world in 1906.

The history of antinoise policy often reads like an enthusiastic chronicle of the reinvention of the wheel. Time and again, health experts have run studies revealing new findings about the damage caused by noise to our hearing, cardiovascular, and mental health. As fresh research on these problems is published, courts are persuaded to pass legislation. Police gamely charge out onto the streets to enforce the surprisingly strict new laws. Silence is finally beginning to get its due. And then, one day, someone wakes up and realizes, Hey, everything is louder than it's ever been before.

It's as if the distracting effect of noise renders us incapable of remembering the advances we've already made against noise.

So pervasive is this distraction that at times it even serves the cause of quiet. The most important antinoise regulation in American history, passed by President Nixon in 1972, is a comedy of cascading distractions.

During the late 1960s, state and local governments launched

intensive efforts to control noise emissions from the rail and trucking industries, says Ken Feith, a civil servant who has been working on noise pollution for the Environmental Protection Agency since 1973. Lobbyists went to Capitol Hill to demand protection from the noise laws, making the argument that these were interrupting the free flow of commerce. Congress requested that the EPA investigate the effects of noise on public health and welfare. The study resulted in the Noise Control Act. Russell Train, who served as Nixon's chairman of the Council on Environmental Quality in 1972, told me that he thought the president's chief motivation in enacting a broad platform of environmental measures was to distract public attention from the environmental agenda of his Democratic rivals, and that the only reason noise slipped into this package was because Nixon himself refused to pay attention to details of the legislation.

The Noise Control Act remains on the books to this day— and the EPA is legally obliged to enforce its provisions. (Among other things, it establishes strict noise-emissions standards for transportation vehicles and equipment, machinery, appliances, and other products of commerce, while declaring federal action "essential to deal with major noise sources in commerce control.") But no one seems to remember that the act exists. Ever since the Office of Noise Abatement and Control was stripped of its budget under President Reagan, the progressive act has remained in limbo.

If we look at the history of the fight against other pollutants—smoke, for instance—the trend is generally upward. Ever since the first substantial air-pollution regulation was enacted, just prior to World War I, in response to studies of the long-term consequences of working in mines and factories, the more that scientists have identified health risks, the more these emissions have been regulated. Yet with the exception of the very loudest sound offenders, a chart of the fight against noise would resemble less the progressive ascent to enlightenment than the graph of a wildly swinging stock market.

The easiest assumption would be that noise is simply a less-acute public-health threat than smoke. Relative to global warming, of course that's true. But the overall risk to our health from road traffic noise is 40 percent *higher* than that from air pollutants, according to a 2008 World Health Organization report. Dr. Rokhu Kim, the head of the WHO's noise-related task force, told me that while there's a politically powerful consensus that particulate matter from combustion engines increases cardiovascular mortality, it's still difficult to identify how those particles actually enter the body and jeopardize the heart. At this point, Kim said, "I think it's fair to say that there's a higher biological plausibility for noise as a trigger of heart disease than air pollution."

When it comes to imperiling mental health, noise pollution of course wins hands down. Not only does it jangle nerves, it actually provokes people to murder. In August 2008, for example, a man by the name of Raymundo Serrato was shot to death in Pacoima, near Los Angeles, for playing his car stereo too loudly. A neighbor remarked that Serrato frequently came home in the early-morning hours, booming his stereo. "So I guess he [the shooter], just, probably, had enough," the neighbor said. Noisemakers themselves have a long history of responding to complaints with violence. And even when noise doesn't incite gunshots and knifings, it can trigger ungovernable anger. The U.S. legal system is set up to pit noise haters and noisemakers against each other in an endless series of fight-to-the-bursting-point showdowns.

There are hard-won victories—yet they remain utterly localized triumphs, while noise, by definition, is a boundary buster. And the more rigorous a community antinoise law is, the more vulnerable is the ordinance itself. A perfect example is the legislation passed against boom cars in the city of Sarasota. As of April 2008, if one Sarasota officer could hear your sound system from twenty-five feet away, he could seize your car on a first offense. A year after passage of the new ordinance, I phoned Captain Stitler of the Sarasota Police Department to find out how the legislation was working. He talked to me at length about how strongly the community supported the law, and how effective it had been. I said that was great, and asked him how things were today. There was a pause on the other end of the line. Then Stitler said, "Currently we have been advised by the city attorney's office that we've been challenged constitutionally on the ordinance and at this point we've suspended all enforcement until the litigation is stopped." He is uncertain when, if ever, the law will be reinstated. And even when a community manages to pass antinoise legislation that is both rigorous and durable, local police rarely have the resources to enforce it with any consistency.

The more I thought about the problem, the more it seemed clear that only federal action would be effective. But the government gives noise a level of attention on a par with jaywalking: the EPA's most significant recent action with regard to noise policy has been to conduct a multiyear project aimed at providing better labeling for earplugs, earmuffs, and the like; there is talk of using the Internet to spread awareness.

⌖

It's ironic that the only time when harsh legislation against noise really seems to stick is during *actual* wartime. Beginning one night in 1939, on the basis of a single document stamped by the king, everyone in England was forbidden from "sounding within public hearing any siren, hooter, whistle, rattle, bell, horn, gong or similar instrument" unless advised to do so by authorities as an air-raid warning. In June 1940, the order was extended to include the previously exempt churches, and for the first time in history their bells fell silent. The public understood that quiet was necessary in order for the war workers to rest, and that almost any extra noise might mask a warning signal crucial to the survival of the public or troops.

But surely something other than modern armed conflict could muster popular support for antinoise laws! I craved an upbeat, inspiring story. That's when I recalled the extraordinary figure of Julia Barnett Rice, a society matron in the early twentieth century who managed to quiet New York City by narrowing the definition of noise.

THE QUEEN OF SILENCE

Julia Barnett Rice, dubbed the "Queen of Silence" by the Parisian press, is one of the most remarkable heroines the pursuit of silence has ever produced. She started the Society for the

Suppression of Unnecessary Noise in 1906, the world's first internationally renowned antinoise organization.

A drawing of Rice done around the time she founded the society reveals a woman with a square face, sad dark eyes, low brows, and a heavy crown of black hair. A New Orleans debutante of Dutch-Jewish ancestry, Rice became a musician and a classicist. She also completed an MD at the Women's Medical College of the New York Infirmary. In 1906, she was a forty-six-year-old mother of six living in Villa Julia, an Italianate mansion with soundproofed rooms on Riverside Drive that her husband, Isaac, had named for her and which commanded "the finest view up the Hudson that is obtainable on Manhattan island." Not only was Isaac a trained musician and composer; he made a name for himself in corporate law, earned a fortune as an inventor, and was a chess master who created a dauntingly convoluted opening maneuver dubbed the Rice Gambit. He perfected this move in a noiseless chamber he'd had carved out of solid rock deep underneath the foundations of Villa Julia, reachable only by special elevator. All in all, the Rices are testimony to just how much two people can accomplish who don't have the distracting noise of the Internet to hum along with.

In the summer of 1905, with the windows of Villa Julia flung wide so that the family could enjoy the river breezes, Mrs. Rice noticed a new acoustical blotch on the landscape. Though the tooting of tugboats had always been annoying, they had suddenly become so frequent that she was unable to sleep more than a few hours a night. She didn't know the cause. Inspired by the adage "It is the worst sign of all when men submit to a torture because it is general and not particular," Rice hired a band of students from Columbia Law School to track the din.

The findings of the six students, whom she stationed at different points along the Hudson for a number of nights, were shocking. On a single night in early December, they recorded almost three thousand whistle blasts. At certain moments, her scouts confessed that they had tossed up their pens in defeat because the whistles were coming too frequently to register. Not only did Rice have the students strive to keep a tally of the toots; she had them note what she described as their "endless variety" from "the shrillest shrieks to the deepest of booming sounds," and from split-second blasts to "long, ear-splitting shrieks." In her report, she cited the psychologist James Sully to underscore the injurious effect of this random pattern: "When the sequence is wholly disorderly or arrhythmic, the mind is kept, so to speak, in a state of tip-toe expectation of every succeeding moment," in an "imaginative preoccupation of the attention."

Her final record ran to 33 dense pages covering a range of different weather conditions. Rice was able to show that even on a brilliantly clear Sunday night, the expansive captains had blasted their horns some 1,116 times. She commissioned another team of students to trot up and down the waterways on both sides of Manhattan collecting firsthand statements from policemen, watchmen, and regular citizens about the effects of this noise. To bolster her case, she also talked with some of the more candid captains themselves. Rice found that the vast majority of toots had nothing to do with warnings intended to prevent accidents. Often they were "fraternal"—the sonic equivalent of high-fives between boats. Other times they represented efforts to rouse their besotted crews from the beer-sloshed sawdust of waterside saloons, or to send signals to servant girls cloistered in houses along Riverside Drive. In fact, far from demonstrating a greater emphasis on safe boating, the relentless blasts made it impossible to discern alarms that did matter.

Overwhelming evidence that the tooting was not just obnoxious but superfluous clinched Rice's case. Charging that tugs "murder sleep and therefore menace health," she declared war. From start to finish, it was a stunningly executed campaign.

After the New York City Department of Health absolved itself of responsibility by proclaiming the Hudson a national waterway, she turned to federal bodies charged with docks, ports, and steamboats. When these bureaucracies dawdled, Rice began talking to the police department, heads of medical institutions, and patients inside hospitals on the calamitous health effects of the tooting. In a short period of time, she had amassed statements attesting to the sufferings inflicted by the noise on thirteen thousand poor people. She continued to enlarge her efforts until she was able to bring her case to Washington. Speaking on behalf of all the hospitals in New York City, she was given a hearing at the Department of Commerce and Labor. Congressman William Bennet took up the torch for her. With Bennet's steadfast support, ten months after that initial hearing, she had prevailed. The Board of Steamboat Inspectors in New York, Boston, and Philadelphia announced that all "useless and indiscriminate tooting of sirens and steam whistles" was to halt. When tugs violated the new legislation, they were aggressively fined. When the occasional churlish skipper sought to take his revenge on Rice by sneaking up late at night to points just beneath Villa Julia and blasting off a few toots before swiftly gliding away, Rice hunted the boats down and had their captains hauled into court.

Inundated by letters of support from public officials and private citizens alike, Rice felt empowered to create an organization that would extend the battle to a widening array of targets. Weeks after her victory, she and Isaac hosted a gathering in the soundproof library of Villa Julia at which a roster of city dignitaries applauded the founding of the society. Rice was voted its president in an election at which she cast the only dissenting vote.

She had hit upon a formula for fighting noise that worked. Its essence was encapsulated in her initial statement to the press. "This is not," she declared, "to be an anti-noise society. Much noise is, of course, unavoidable." True to the name of her organization, Rice and her cohorts would tackle only "unnecessary noises."

Her crusade coincided with an intense wave of global interest in maximizing energy efficiency. The same year that Rice founded the society, William James published an essay titled "The Energies of Men," in which he declared that we labor under "an imperfect vitality," failing to properly tap resources of energy that, if we could but access them, would vastly enhance our capacities of work and thought. Noise—the squeaky brake, the grinding gears, the needless whistle blast, friction in all its guises—meant squandered energy.

Rice thus approached the problem as a friend to leaders of the business and industrial communities whom, she averred, were laboring under the illusion that noise was an essential part of progress. Rather than aestheticizing or sanctifying silence, she equated it with the well-oiled, smoothly operating machine. Quiet and profitability rose and fell together.

Moreover, just as the economic sin of smoke made for a visible index of waste, Rice held the evil of noise to be acoustically self-evident. She developed a "graphophone" that reproduced the noises of the city with impressive fidelity. Instead of lengthy explanations as to why certain noises were unnecessary, she simply played them back. This was enough to convince many of their pointlessness.

The next major target of Mrs. Rice's society was the area around hospitals. Armed with letters from physicians and hospital administrators attesting to the retarding, wasteful effects of noise on the healing process, she set about creating the precursors of today's hospital quiet zones. Fifty-nine hospitals representing some eighteen thousand hospital beds joined her directorate. Yet despite manifold abatement measures, Rice discovered that the hospital zones remained noisy. Further investigation revealed that much of the sound came from children who loitered about hospitals to indulge what Rice called "that deplorable craving for excitement" which sought gratification "in the sight of poor, wounded, 'ambulance' cases." She made a minute-by-minute record of the problem. ("3:50 PM—Eight or ten boys hanging about the east gate calling to servants. Pretending to be injured, they walked down into the yard toward the accident entrance. Pounding on fence with baseball bats.")

Rather than having the little ruffians frog-marched down to the police station—Rice pitied their lack of adequate playgrounds—she launched another brilliant PR ploy. In the spring of 1908, Rice formed the Children's Hospital Branch of the Society for the Suppression of Unnecessary Noises. After consulting with physicians, she gave a series of talks to upward of twenty thousand children in which she spoke about the suffering caused to hospital patients by noise. She begged the young people to assist her in alleviating this distress. In exchange for promising not to play within a block of a hospital, nor in front of a residential dwelling in which someone was known to be seriously ill, she offered them official membership in the newly formed auxiliary branch of her society. To help jog the children's memory as to the fact that they were now part of the solution, she issued them all badges and requested that the badges be worn whenever they were playing outside. The badges were stamped with one word in black: HUMANITY.

This campaign proved successful as well, and soon Rice had accumulated a mountain of pledges from the city's children, such as the following heartrending testimonial: "*I promise not* to play near or around any hospital. When I DO pass I will *keep my mouth shut tight*, because there are many invalids there. Nor will I make myself *a perfect* NUISANCE."

❄

The Society for the Suppression of Unnecessary Noises went on to win other signal victories. Rice became an inspirational figure for antinoise movements across Europe, as well as in the United States. Yet for all her acumen, the series of successes doesn't quite tell the whole story. If it did, the society itself would not have fallen silent in the early 1920s. What happened? The gradual withdrawal of Rice's own energies as she grew older certainly took its toll. Yet if the logic of her broader argument against noise was sound, why should her personal leadership have proven indispensable? After much searching I came across one explanation for the society's demise, buried in a 1928 *New McClure's* magazine article announcing that war on noise had been declared yet again: the society's "efforts were baffled," the article's writer declared, "by the introduction of the automobile."

⚒

Julia Rice's own husband, Isaac, was reportedly the first private individual in New York City to own an automobile. He was a trendsetter in the fad that would ultimately unravel most of his wife's efforts to bring quiet to the metropolis. Indeed, Mr. Rice called it a "high-handed outrage" when New York City park commissioner George Clausen revoked his permit to ride it through the serene expanse of Central Park. Rice viewed freedom of choice about his means of conveyance as a basic democratic right. While his wife was chastening tugboat captains around Manhattan's perimeter, Rice was shattering the peace at the island's heart.

Moreover, for all that Isaac and Julia were quiet-loving patrons of art and music, they counted among their children some of the city's loudest, most reckless daredevils. Their daughter Dorothy became the first woman in New York to speed through the city in a motorcycle, and started a craze among the female fast set for racing their snorty machines around town. Another daughter became one of the first female pilots. One madcap flight ended with an eight-hundred-foot plunge into the water off the shores of Babylon, Long Island. With the long fur coat she was wearing over her aviation suit, it was no easy process disentangling her feet from the wreckage, and from her hospital bed she pronounced the whole escapade "very funny."

Were the Rices' autos, motorcycles, and aeroplanes, and the vogues they helped ignite, sources of necessary noise? Surveying the history of the Rice family and noise, I thought of *King Lear*: "Reason not the need."

※

But still, the campaigns mounted by Rice's society were impressively effective for as long as they lasted. Why the initial wave of support for them? Each new offensive was founded in a scrupulous exercise in noise measurement.

Sound measurement also underpinned the next great wave of antinoise initiatives. When cities around the world issued declarations of war against noise in the 1920s, the spurs to battle were often new measurement technologies, such as the Bell Laboratories audiometer, billed as the world's most scientifically accurate sound-measurement device. With one ear naked to the environment and the other fitted to an earpiece connected to the machine, the audiometer's operator turned a dial, thereby amplifying a buzzing sound until that noise was intense enough to mask the noise of the surroundings. The number at that point on the dial became the noise rating for a given location. It thus became possible for the first time to definitively establish the loudest spot in a city. In New York in 1926, this was determined to be the corner of Sixth Avenue and Thirty-fourth Street, where the noise intensity was measured at "fifty-five sensation units above quiet." According to Dr. E. E. Free, a scientist who studied and wrote about noise under the auspices of the journal *Forum*, this degree of intensity meant that to communicate with someone at that corner, "you must shout as loudly as you do to a person who is more than half deaf." One wonders what the audiometer would have revealed four years later when excavation for the Empire State Building began half a block away.

Though this was still not the most objective calculation, it began to change the standards of how the level of sound was quantified. In 1929, when health commissioner Shirley Wynne established the Noise Abatement Commission, engineers traveled the city with what Wynne called "a strangely fitted noise measuring truck, the first roving noise laboratory." The truck covered more than 500 miles and made 7,000 observations at 113 locations around the city, recording everything from "the quiet of remote residential streets to the din of main highways," using the decibel unit. This marked the first broad application of the noise-measurement scale we continue to rely upon. Today, though, what we're using it for is making noise maps.

❈

Noise maps represent the future of the pursuit of silence through policy. Millions of euros and hundreds of thousands of pounds have already been invested in them. But no one seemed able to explain to me what a noise map was. Was it an actual map that showed noise sources or noise levels? When I talked to Jim Weir, a products manager at Brüel & Kjær, a Danish company at the vanguard of acoustical measurement, the closest he came to a definition was to say that it involved "environmental noise monitoring of an entire city." He told me that noise mapping had been around for years at airports. Well, what did the maps set out to accomplish? I asked. "The FAA fines airports for noise," he said.

"So the maps help airports deal with noise pollution?" I ventured.

The maps did help reduce sound, Weir said. Equally important, they reduced complaints. His voice dropped to a conspiratorial register. "I'll tell you what I discovered," he remarked. As far as airport management is concerned, "the pretty charts with color profiles, the ways that noise is presented with pictures and overlays, is *more* important than the microphones." He knew of cases where airport noise had ceased to be a problem the moment the public saw a map of it. "The knowledge of measurement happening can be more important than the measurement," he observed.

I soon saw that I would have to travel to Europe to see for myself what city noise maps looked like.

As Rice herself once wrote: "They order these things better in Europe, where the steam whistle has been largely suppressed. We are indeed a wonderful nation, but have much to learn from the Old World as regards the simple, sane commonplaces of ordinary life, of which protection from unreasonable noise is one of the most obvious."

THE ACTUAL FUTURE

A huge seagull bobbed above me. A handful of cars were nestled in the soft, pale grass. My first glimpse of the low, gray Quonset-hut-type structures that made up Brüel & Kjær's global headquarters on the outskirts of Copenhagen suggested a comfortingly old-fashioned retreat for naturalists. But when I walked into the lobby everything was slick and steely, with multiple silent flat-screen televisions flickering away on every conceivable surface. It was the future, after all.

My chief liaison for the afternoon was Doug Manvell, a young Scotsman with muttonchop sideburns and a mouthful of official title: application specialist and environmental noise management solutions product manager. We had lunch together in the B&K cafeteria with several of Manvell's colleagues and I began grilling them on noise mapping.

Manvell told me that B&K made its money through two channels: legislative and commercial. In 2002, he said, the European Union had passed something called the European Noise Directive. The directive, commonly referred to as the END, put noise on the EU agenda and established a framework for reducing noise across Europe that will continue to be the dominant policy road map for many years to come. The central requirement of the END is that all EU member states create noise maps.

But then what was a noise map? I asked.

Someone at our lunch table said that it involved "predictive modeling of the soundscape." Before I had a chance to ask what this meant, we were deep into the subject of how principles of soundscaping also informed their business's commercial track.

Manvell explained that companies turned to B&K in order to gain a commercial advantage from adjusting the sound of a product. "Typically," he said, "this means a manufacturer looking to do soundscaping within vehicles or other things."

I knew a little bit about the idea of soundscaping motor vehicles. Some years ago, Harley-Davidson was forced to comply with noise regulations outlawing the cycle's earsplitting roar. Yet, as Alex Bozmoski, who headed up Harley's noise and vibration facility at the time, put it, "The experienced Harley community demands a certain distinctive and unmistakable sound." So the company's goal became to make a motorcycle that would still sound like a Harley but be quieter. They damped out whines, knocks, and other undesirable mechanical noises, while adjusting the design to maintain the desired balance of tone, pitch, and beat from the exhaust and engine. At the same time, Bozmoski reported, they maximized "the frequency and amplitude of excitation wherever the rider and machine interface: handlebars, seat and footpegs." Basically, they made the Harley into a giant vibrator. Then they patented the sound. Another case in point involves Jaguar. Some years ago, after surveys revealed that the noise of Jaguar engines was being poorly received by customers, Leyland Motors developed focus groups to study the issue. Although they'd set as their benchmark the sound of a luxury-car rival known for the sophisticated quiet of its engine, they found that Jaguar drivers actually wanted two different acoustical experiences at the same time: one of refinement, the other of power. Jaguar needed to soundscape its engine to create the right balance between the purr and the roar.

Manvell explained that the idea of commercial soundscaping was spreading from cars to building interiors. This could involve something as simple as creating a miniature indoor waterfall in an office reception area to mask unwanted conversation. Or it could mean shaping the sound inside a hospital so that it would be more conducive to healing.

Kevin Bernard Ginn, a colleague of Manvell, explained

that you might walk around a hospital with the Investigator, B&K's new handheld sound meter, recording sound levels and types of noises. (It looks something like a BlackBerry grafted onto a Breathalyzer and runs about 10,000 euros a pop.) Then you could decide which noises and sound levels you liked. "Everything is being made to harmonize more and more," Ginn said.

Manvell added that the same principle might be applied to an entire town square. He asked me to imagine traffic on one side, a park area on another where people relaxed, and a string of restaurants and bars in a third sector where people want to enjoy "the thrill of being in a big city." New measurement technologies would enable someone to go around the square measuring sound in each zone. This data could then be fed to engineers who would look at the discrepancies between the actual sound in a given area and its ideal. Does the park sound relaxing? Do the bars sound thrilling? The engineers could then say, "Okay, maybe now we can adjust this one and this one."

I was beginning to get a sense of what Manvell and Ginn were talking about. In the un-soundscaped, "natural" version of the square he was describing, unless the music of the restaurant and bars was unbelievably loud, the only sound you were going to hear anywhere was traffic. But perhaps this could all be manipulated. Manvell spoke of the entire world of sound, both inside and outside, as something controlled by one gigantic sound-mixing board with someone like him at the dial—constantly adjusting the gain on different features to get the balance just right.

Manvell and Ginn agreed that as recently as five years ago people were claiming that any alternative to physical sound-level reduction was against the ethics of noise control. But positions were softening. As people realized the extreme cost of getting levels down to where experts would deem them completely safe, support was growing for the idea of making the environment at least more appealing.

"The work I've been doing for the past ten years has involved trying to compare a city with a vehicle," Manvell continued. "You have a car—right now, everyone's going for aerodynamics, everyone's going for fuel consumption, everyone's going for color. So *now* we go for soundscaping as another way of positioning ourselves. The city itself, in this sense, is like any other product. Because as a town you're not alone in the world, this leads into marketing questions. The same way some people are dedicated to Ford purchases—they'll never buy anything else—there are people living in Berlin who would never live anywhere else. But there are a vast majority of other people who are not so settled— which leads to cities looking to soundscaping and noise issues not just to protect their citizenry but to attract visitors. In the end, it comes down to that."

As we continued talking, I wondered who would be making the decisions about sonic branding of urban environments in the future.

✠

In truth, the more people I spoke with on the subject, the more I found that the mere sound of the word "soundscaping" generates buzz. Whenever sound professionals start speaking about improving what *anything* sounds like, it has come to mean pretty much whatever the person using the word wants it to mean. Along with the growing commercial interest in soundscaping, there are also idealistic projects unfolding. The best of these often involve collaborations between artists and urban planners who draw on historical soundscaping: the study of types of sounds that characterize an environment over time. With this knowledge in hand, people can work to enhance the audibility of so-called "iconic sounds" of a given neighborhood (old church bells, a town clock, flowing water, or even footsteps). They can support biodiversity so that there will be greater opportunities for hearing the sound of wind in vegetation and birdsong. But the realization of such projects tends to be extremely sparing in the use of technology, and much more concerned with stripping away recent strata of noise than with adding any new sounds into the mix.

Take the work of Max Dixon, an urbanist specializing in soundscapes, who works with the Greater London Authority. Dixon was part of a team that wanted to change the fact that traffic noise drowned out the sound of the fountain at Trafalgar Square. By diverting cars away from just one side of the fountain—the one adjacent to the National Gallery—they not only diminished overall vehicular noise but also allowed sound waves from the fountain a free path to the overhanging portico of the gallery, where they were reflected and amplified for people gathered around the entrance of the museum, exactly the position on the square where one would be most likely to enjoy the liquid concert.

Sometimes soundscaping can also take advantage of cross-sensory perceptions and psychoacoustics to enhance the sense of silence. So, for example, studies have indicated that in areas with sound barriers, there's a ten decibel difference in how annoying noise is depending on the visual attractiveness of the barriers.

An ugly barrier makes for a significantly greater perception of loudness. Other research has indicated that while falling water is often the best way to mask traffic noise, water falling on a metal grating often communicates not a spirit of calm but a reminder of drainage. To convey tranquillity, tests have shown, high-frequency water sounds are best. The most soothing of these are produced by water splashing over small, uneven boulders.

Projects taking advantage of such principles are often simple and worthy of support. But their very subtlety makes them unlikely candidates for the kinds of major metropolitan self-promotions I heard about at B&K. Noting the vulnerability of soundscaping to corporate interests with more tangible profits in mind, Dixon told me that "in the hands of people seeking a cheap 'quick fix' rather than going to the root of the problem, applied electroacoustics could become a nightmare."

The nightmare need not be electroacoustic. Honda recently paid a large sum of money to soundscape a busy road in Lancaster, California. The project—versions of which have already been undertaken in several cities in Asia—involved cutting thousands of tiny grooves into the asphalt so that the road surface would "play" the *William Tell* overture as cars drove across it. (It played best for Honda Civics cruising along at fifty-five.) People living nearby were driven nuts by the endlessly repeated snatch of Rossini and, as the road surface corroded with use, the music became equally degraded.

❊

The reality today is that traffic has washed over the palette of other noises across the world. The exorbitant cost of creating quiet in the world's major cities opens up some awfully big marketing opportunities for the plugged-in vendor with some catchy noise to pedal.

OOMPA LOOMPA-SCAPE

After lunch, I was given a tour of B&K. We milled by endless arrays of microphones of every conceivable dimension, rocket shafts and foamy black eggs able to hear every pin drop; numberless black-and-silver sound-measurement devices that resembled large digital thermometers for taking temperatures of zoo animals; boxes lined with different materials into which objects could be put and shaken to see whether you could still hear them clatter; dummy heads with screws, clamps, and black spikes projecting from them, looking like over-edgy S&M gear, but ostensibly used to test telephone transmission frequencies. There were also many, many laptops showing off the bright color fields of modeling software for indoor acoustics and environmental noise management. These latter represented a core B&K contribution to the noise-mapping initiative.

I walked by an intricate scale model of an airport with a little plane zooming around on a wire, and a helicopter, and multiple tiny pen-cap microphones tracking different airplane noise types and air traffic densities. Most dramatic of all was a life-size car that looked like it had spun into a giant spiderweb—some kind of metal grid laced with dozens of little black bud microphones. This allowed the engineers to hear and predict every vibration in the engine and chassis and then prescribe minute adjustments to create the ideal sonic equilibrium.

Somewhere in the course of my tour, I was handed a glossy

B&K company profile. I flipped back the cover and on the opening page saw a big photograph of a burly man wearing a suede jacket, standing before a blurry barrage of urban neon. He might have been a rough-around-the-edges detective. In fact, he is Svend Gade, of Brüel & Kjær University, a mostly online course platform run by the company. Above his head runs the following quote: "Sound and vibration is all around us. It penetrates every aspect of our everyday world. Our challenge is to keep it from affecting the quality of our life." The point, the brochure explained, is that we are increasingly aware of the myriad effects of sounds and vibrations on our health and happiness; there is no object or environment that couldn't benefit from B&K's techno-silencers.

Even if we are a long way from soundscaping entire cities, B&K presents a vision of how the future war against noise will be waged: with an arsenal of new, officiously harmonizing noises that can be projected over the gap where silence used to be.

THE MAP

A famous story by Jorge Luis Borges describes a land where, Borges writes, "the Art of Cartography attained such perfection that the map of a single Province occupied the entirety of a city, and the map of the Empire, the entirety of a Province." Eventually even these maps failed to satisfy the cartographers, and they created a map that corresponded at every point with the empire itself.

I thought of Borges's story when Doug Manvell finally gave me a crash course in noise mapping. Noise maps, he explained, had actually been around for a long time. In response to an EU directive from the late 1980s, big employers began mapping factory-floor noise to identify zones requiring hearing protection. Then, in the mid-1990s, several German and Dutch cities launched broader noise-mapping projects of their own. In the late 1990s, John Hinton of the Birmingham City Council created a noise map that "was *very* well described—not only in terms of the map itself but in terms of the whole process," Manvell explained. It became the predecessor of the maps eventually mandated by the END.

But what are noise maps? I cried.

To create a noise map, Manvell went on, "you need building heights, then all the road aspects—speed of vehicles, road-surface characteristics, and so on. A whole series of databases." In fact, Manvell observed, while the information is presented in the form of an actual map, the true strategic document is a mass of statistics. The calculations required are so colossal that they were beyond earlier generations of computers. By way of example, he outlined B&K's work noise-mapping Thüringen, Germany. Thüringen, he said, "which is a bit hilly, has 20,000 square kilometers of road-noise networks. We did it on a 50 meter grid with 600,000 individual road objects where the road changes over 5 million topographical data elements. It took 10 hours to do the calculation on 4 PCs, using the fastest software on the market. Buildings were ignored as, if included, their vast numbers and impact on calculation complexity would have exploded the calculation time. That's the danger of pressing the start button. Data costs. A strategic noise map is not an acoustic problem but a data-handling problem. We're making strategic noise maps and they've got nothing to do with maps and nothing to do with noise."

However much this might sound like a Zen paradox, the END requiring member states to produce them—and to meet tight deadlines to avoid massive fines—makes them very real in monetary terms.

After a couple more hours of tutoring, I began to grasp that noise maps basically chart all human movement, transportation infrastructure, major manufacturing, building types, and land contours within a given geographical area. Or at least that's what I thought I understood—until I got more of the story when I talked with Colin Nugent, the EU project manager for noise, who is based in Copenhagen.

⚜

Colin Nugent is a young, handsome man from Belfast with a gentle brogue and an unflappable command of acronyms, an essential skill, given the labyrinth of agencies, committees, steering groups, studies, networks, and centers he must allude to in the course of describing the European pursuit of silence through policy.

In a therapeutically soothing voice, Nugent explained that the first phase of the directive mandated that by June 30, 2007, all member states should have completed noise maps that would chart noise levels during the previous calendar year for all towns and cities with more than 250,000 inhabitants, for all roads on which there were more than 6 million vehicular passages per year, for all rail lines on which there were in excess of 60,000 train "movements" per year, and for all airports with 50,000-plus air traffic movements. "All in all," Nugent observed, "these are quite large sources, but there are a great many of them." In 2012, member states are required to carry out the same procedure for agglomerations of 100,000 and above, doubling the number of cities involved.

But what about actual noise reduction? I asked. Where does that come in?

"Well exactly," Nugent said. "There are also action plans." The END required that no later than July 18, 2008, based on the first noise maps, "competent authorities" would draw up action plans "designed to manage, within their territories, noise issues and effects, including noise reduction if necessary" for all the sources charted in the maps.

In practice, things haven't quite worked out like that. As of spring 2008, eleven member states hadn't reported anything—let alone begun their action plans. Expired and unmet deadlines have continued to pile up ever since. "Plus," Nugent said, "the directive states that if there is a significant change to any trans-port sources—like a major airport that extends a runway for another 1,000 flights or an extension of a major road, that would need to be included in the noise map."

But aren't roads and runways being built all the time? I asked.

They are, Nugent concurred. "So in essence the noise maps we're producing are already out-of-date because the major road network is changing all the time."

I asked whether what had been done so far at least provided the basis for the real business of reducing noise as mandated by the action plans.

"Well, noise reduction is not 'mandated,'" Nugent said. "Member states are required to produce noise maps and action plans, but they're not required to take any actions."

"There are no requirements for any actual actions at *all* to reduce noise?"

None at all, Nugent calmly affirmed. That is left up to individual member states. All that the END requires them to do is to map and produce plans of things one might do to decrease noise based on what those maps show.

I was again experiencing vertigo. If these Borgesian cartographical extravaganzas, which were out-of-date before even being completed, carried no statutory power beyond their own colorful borders, why were they considered so important?

Because, Manvell and Nugent explained, with all their flaws they are yet a powerful tool to persuade politicians to take action. Hence the decision to present all this data as maps to begin with rather than just data streams. Presentation is key, Manvell said. "The visuals are what people want."

Manvell explained how a politician armed with a noise map showing that his district was being exposed to unhealthy decibel levels could go to a national or EU body to argue that the area was entitled to a grant of so many euros for noise reduction. This is why, Nugent explained, his agency worked closely with the World Health Organization. The WHO is revolutionizing our assessments of the disease attributable to noise.

❦

In 2009 the WHO issued a series of reports containing some of the most robust data ever compiled on specific health hazards of noise. These reports are providing the basis for development of a new, stringent set of noise guidelines. They present devastating findings about the impact of traffic noise on the cardiovascular system, in particular. For the first time, such studies have been able to factor for socioeconomic differences that might influence lifestyle health issues. (Previous efforts to gauge the effects of noise pollution have been plagued by the difficulty of filtering out other health risks that are often part of the life package for someone residing near a major roadway or airport.) The studies also pinpoint the effects of noise on different zones within a single house.

It sounds promising. And it would, of course, be foolish to assume that, just because it's never worked in the past, this won't be the time that medical findings about noise translate into a public uprising. Nugent is thoughtful, hardworking, and dedicated. Rokhu Kim and his team are savvy and driven. But there's a long road to travel. To date, as results of noise mapping begin trickling in from Europe and the United Kingdom, it seems clear that the maps are accurate at identifying high-noise-level areas—the kinds of areas that teams of college students like Rice's tootometer scouts might be taught to identify with great accuracy by the naked ear alone. Middle levels are proving more difficult. The identification of low-sound-level zones has barely begun. Mostly, areas are designated quiet by default—points where the maps do not indicate exposure to high or middle levels of sound. Yet many of these areas, Nugent told me, were you to visit them, "would actually seem very noisy indeed." The END introduces the concept of quiet areas in language suggesting that it's been tacked on as an afterthought: states are required only to "aim to preserve" them. In consequence, undeveloped quiet areas can get treated as noise-dumping locations to keep population centers from getting louder. Case in point: a recent plan by British authorities to reroute planes away from the city of Southampton by directing them over the New Forest, a picturesque region where people go for quiet recreation.

One certain result of this report will be funding for new studies, and a rededication to the noise-mapping efforts already under way. This will mean a lot more money spent on noise measurement and modeling for companies like B&K and for the agencies, like Nugent's European Environment Agency, that work with member states to encourage compliance with the END. None of this comes cheaply. The cost of noise mapping Birmingham, England (a city slightly larger than San Jose, California), would run about £100,000 ($165,000). If the contractor is asked to obtain and "clean" much of this data, that figure could easily double.

⌗

In October 1931, Professor Henry J. Spooner, a highly regarded pioneer of the noise abatement movement, gave an address to a society of engineers on the progress of the movement to date. After noting the great success in recent years of devising new instruments to measure sound, Professor Spooner extended a note of caution. "Important as the measurement of noise is for so many purposes, there is a real danger that too much attention may be focused on it, and the suppression of unnecessary, devastating, harmful din neglected," he said. "Happily, Sanitation Inspectors, when they take action against foul-smelling matter or a faulty drain, have not to use a 'yardstick' or the like, to measure it."

※

At the end of our meeting, Nugent and Manvell walked me outside to a pretty plaza near the sea. We began speculating about what had sparked this latest burst of noise-pollution-related activity in which they'd both become professionally involved. Nugent recalled that in the mid-1990s, the WHO had produced another set of noise guidelines that had informed European Commission policy decisions. The driver then, he remarked, was noise complaints. "That was one of the few indicators people had that noise was a problem . . . But if you look at the noise-complaint statistics for the United Kingdom, year on year the biggest single complaint is dogs barking." He chuckled. "That far outweighs everything else. Followed closely by noisy parties, and everything else is *way* below."

"Dogs, neighbors, roads," Manvell quipped.

"Yes, and if you look at roads—road traffic—it's minuscule."

We said goodbye, and I walked away.

It was my last day in Copenhagen, and I needed to clear my head. The ever friendly Danes at my hotel loaned me a bicycle, and I took off. I didn't notice whether the shady neighborhoods I rode through were loud or quiet. I just felt the release of self-propelled speed and wind. I found myself smiling and serene.

After about a half hour, I reached my destination, the Assistens Cemetery in Nørrebro, where the Danish philosopher Søren Kierkegaard is buried. Once inside the gates, I dismounted and walked slowly down the long tree-lined rows of graves, listening to songbirds and looking for his name. It took me quite some time to find, but I didn't mind. It was quiet and the light was beautiful—pattering the leaves and headstones. At last I came upon an old marker with a white crucifix on top and three white stone tablets inscribed with names of many Kierkegaards, Søren among them. I took out my copy of his essay "The Lily in the Field and the Bird of the Air" and read, "How solemn it is out there under God's heaven with the lily and the bird, and why? Ask the poet. He answers: Because there is silence. And his longing goes out to that solemn silence, away from the worldliness in the human world, where there is so much talking, away from all the worldly human life that only in a sad way demonstrates that speech distinguishes human beings above the animals. 'Because,' says the poet, 'if this is the distinguishing characteristic—no, then I much, much prefer the silence out there.' "

CHAPTER ELEVEN

The Dragon Trap

If you look too closely at the complexity of our noise problem, you might be tempted to add your own scream to the mix. Professor Spooner's caution about sound measurement appears in the second report made by the New York City Noise Abatement Commission. The first report, published in 1930, carries a note of plucky optimism. It concludes by declaring that if the citizens of New York want to "do away with unnecessary noise and reduce to a minimum such noises as are necessary" they can do so "if they are willing to take a little trouble." Yet just one year later, after the commission had tried to implement its own recommendations, the mood darkens. The epigram of the 1931 report is a quote from Jeremiah: "Behold the noise of the bruit is come . . . to make the cities of Judah desolate, *and* a den of dragons." Before long the document breaks into a wild-eyed vision in which loud machines, "Frankenstein's monster," are "elected president by a grateful public." Thereafter, "calm gave way to frenzy. Quiet

was lost; the quiet to think and the quiet to feel." Noise itself
"became a minor god."

After my own journey, I could empathize with the commission's despair, yet I found I did not share it. And for a long time, I
was unsure why that was. After all, in some ways the reality of
our soundscape today is *more* apocalyptic than the one the commission envisioned.

One afternoon not long after I returned from Denmark, I had
a chilling conversation with Michael Merzenich, a pioneer in the
study of brain plasticity. Merzenich told me that the entire auditory cortex of many children may now be "rewired for noise" in
ways that have devastating implications for a host of language-
related cognitive functions. And Merzenich was not talking
about basic traffic noise of the sort being studied in Europe. He
talked to me of the white-noise machines given to the parents of
newborns, and a host of random noise generators being switched
on in hospitals and homes following reports that cases of sudden
infant death syndrome decreased when babies were exposed to
overnight noise. He spoke of homes in which televisions are
droning in the background most of the time even when no one is
watching them (reportedly some 75 percent of American house-
holds with young children). He talked of loud fans and air conditioners. And he likened the effects of continual background
noise on children's development of language to what it would
mean for a single parent with a cleft palate to raise a child. In this
scenario, the child's exposure to his or her native language is
muffled. "So what they learn is not English in the sense that you
and I mean by English," Merzenich said, but "noisy English." English in which signal and noise are perpetually mixed together.

On the most basic level, this means that children raised in noisy environments have dramatically slower capacities to process language. But Merzenich raised a more frightening prospect. He told me that he believes this situation, in which increasing numbers of children lack the attentional control necessary to interpret speech at the clip of normal conversation, is one of the main reasons for the increase in incidences of autism. Shortly after our conversation, *New Scientist* reported on a study at the Children's Hospital of Philadelphia that measured the response time of autistic children to a range of sounds and syllables. The study discovered a 20 to 50 percent lag time in the pace of sound processing among autistic children. Since a single syllable in a polysyllabic word might take less than one-quarter of a second to articulate, this delay can significantly impede comprehension. Merzenich's speculations about the way noise hinders brain connectivity, combined with the findings of this study, suggest that the rise in autism may be directly tied to our epidemic of excessive acoustical stimulation.

Whatever the source of my lingering hopefulness, it seemed impossible to deny that a crisis was at hand. Yet I kept feeling the problem had to do not just with noise but with how we've chosen to frame the problem. Turning off a white-noise device or an iPod is not like turning off a transportation system. If we wanted to, we could end this new noisiness nightmare in a split second. *Click.*

But if I was right and we were somehow focusing our efforts the wrong way, where *should* people be looking in order to break out of the noise/antinoise trap? I found myself thinking: Alright, the dragons have arrived. Now how do we go about trapping them?

There's a funny thing about dragons, though: once you set aside the Bible, they start taking on a very different appearance. In Buddhism, the dragon is a guardian of the enlightened teacher and Buddhist law. The dragon's presence is associated with the pursuit of silent illumination. It's also a shape-shifter, who can assume human form and even mate with our species. Almost all Japanese temples and Buddhist monasteries have dragons painted on their ceilings to protect the buildings and adjacent Zen gardens.

When it comes to dragons, apparently, just as with noise, it's all a matter of your point of view. Another way to trap the creature is by switching attention away from its monstrousness and beguiling the dragon over to your side. How, I wondered, might one do this with the beasts of loudness?

Since my efforts to look at the pursuit of silence through official channels of soundproofing and policy technocracies mostly ended up revealing new strains of noise, I thought to myself that perhaps I'd better go look at a dragon for inspiration. Or at least at one of the gardens that the swirly scaled beasts have been induced to watch over.

THE SILENCE GARDEN

On a cool spring morning I stood near the entrance of the splendid Portland Japanese Garden in Oregon, awaiting the arrival of Virginia Harmon, the director of grounds maintenance. I was looking up and down the road for a car, but Harmon rose abruptly over the crest of a steep hill beneath the garden on foot, accompanied by a petite woman of Asian descent who vanished after smiling at me, but whom we would glimpse occasionally gliding behind one or another screen of trees in the course of our ramble. "She's a chef. She's quite popular," Harmon rather cryptically observed.

Harmon herself is a tall woman of uncertain age with much elegance and wavy blond hair. She walks vigorously (when we met, she'd just strode for an hour up from the center of Portland) and maintains a brisk, articulate patter that seems intensely serious but is relieved by sudden, disarming smiles. I kept falling behind Harmon while we meandered the garden paths, but her description of the importance of silence in Japanese gardens and tea ceremonies captivated me. I've struggled to catch up ever since.

Harmon told me about the use of water as a purifying force in Japanese gardens, both with respect to ritual washing and for the way that its pleasant sound punctuates the silence. She talked about how, unlike in Western landscape design where a single structure serves as a focal point, a Japanese garden will present myriad centers of attention: stepping-stones, pines, a lantern. "All the elements are represented," she said, "the movement of branches, the sound of the wind in the branches, our own movement."

Eventually our walk led us to a garden of sand and stone, the "dry landscape" style developed by monks in Zen Buddhist monasteries. "The old feudal castles were taken over by monks who began raking the gravel—growing plants in the course of their meditation," Harmon said. The form evolved from Chinese ink drawings on scrolls with their cliffs and waterfalls, and vast empty spaces between the two, usually veiled in mist, suggesting the unknown beyond. The white gravel represents the void, *ma*, emptiness—which is also silence. The act of raking can be seen as a representation of man's aspiration to enlightenment. "Our visual focus," she continued, "is on the stone bridge in the distance, the place of actual transformation, man to spirit. The raking makes the focus on the emptiness ahead not so daunting—that giving of pattern. So by interruption, emptiness with pattern, we create a welcoming expanse."

In one of the earliest of such gardens, the fourteenth-century Moss Temple outside Kyoto, the Zen monk Musō Soseki gathered fifty large stones from an ancient necropolis to fashion a three-tiered dry waterfall. Although the only motion in this garden came from the shifting fall of sunlight through the trees, visitors who contemplated the rockfall described its almost total silence being interrupted periodically by the thunder of an imagined waterfall. These nearly plantless gardens, with their raked gravel swirls and irregularly positioned stones, are almost entirely creations of the viewer's mind. In reference to another such garden in Kyoto, the philosopher Eliot Deutsch describes how the garden creates a "multiplicity of perspectives *in potentia*." It stimulates meditation, but the meditation it occasions is not on the garden but on the deep stillness of being as such. This is a manifestation of *yūgen*, a notion akin to silence that Zeami, a fourteenth-century master of Japanese Noh theater, placed at the pinnacle of all human endeavors. The silence of *yūgen* connects to the aspiration for complete expression of being—pure presence.

From the Zen garden, we walked to a covered portico at the bottom of a winding path that led up to the teahouse. "This," Harmon said, "is the first point in the staging ground of the tea ceremony—a ceremony that could sometimes last for eight hours." She led me to a bench that gave a view uphill toward the teahouse. Sen Rikyu, Japan's preeminent tea master, who lived in the sixteenth century, went further than anyone in marrying the tea ceremony with ideas taken from Zen Buddhism, Harmon observed. He outlined an ideal for the architecture of teahouses based on rustic simplicity, restraint, and silence. "In Rikyu's era," Harmon said, "the Shogun finally lost control. People got more rights. Rikyu tried to show that you could find peace in a bowl of tea. The Samurai listened, and put away their swords for the chrysanthemum and the pen."

I liked the sound of it, but why had they listened?

"You are in the window seat," she went on. "This seat is for the guest who will excuse himself next to make the passage to the teahouse. It shows who is first, not who is higher in rank. Guests waiting on this bench would be silent, except to apologize at the moment of departure for going before the others."

We left the teahouse and started up the trail of broken stones, the "dewy path," to a spot where Harmon pointed out a low building to one side of the teahouse. "That's the changing arbor. The Samurai put aside their long swords in the arbor because they couldn't fit through the narrow crawl space of the teahouse entrance. This was intentional on Rikyu's part. Not a single blade of grass or iris leaf was allowed inside either because their shapes were reminiscent of the sword. Inside the teahouse, there was no differentiation among guests in gender or rank. No rich or poor. The only thing we carry into the tea ceremony is the fan, which represents peace, meaning: 'I've willingly set aside war and all my worries outside the teahouse.' "

We continued our ascent. The uneven pattern of the stones, Harmon said, forced guests to think about their passage from the crowded external world to a state of pastoral seclusion. The second guest would wait to leave the portico until the first guest was visible moving from the changing arbor to the teahouse. With each step, there was a peeling away of the outside world, an emptying and a clarifying. "I studied in Japan for six years," Harmon said, "and when I walked on the stepping-stones to the teahouse my teacher kept saying, 'There is something not right in how you walk!' He finally called his wife who trussed me up so tightly in a kimono that I could barely move—and then I understood the placement of the stones."

I asked her how she'd become involved with Japanese gardens. It was a long, winding path of its own, beginning in her childhood on her grandmother's Texas ranch that bordered the property of a family of Japanese farmers. At the age of seventeen, Harmon moved to New York City and became friends with a Japanese woman who introduced her to the world of Japanese language and thought. In the midst of many other pursuits, Harmon managed to complete a medical degree and become head of an endoscopy unit at St. Joseph Hospital in Houston. "And then one day," Harmon told me, "I just said to myself, 'I've done my last colonoscopy! I have to do something new.'"

※

As we entered the teahouse, Harmon remarked that once inside, every aspect of the experience was designed to harmonize with every other aspect. "Rikyu's idea," she said, "was that if we have harmony, respect, and purity, then tranquillity will surely follow."

She pointed out the different elements that made up the plain structure of the house—the long "sleeve gate" echoing the sleeves of a kimono, the tatami-mat seating area looking over the garden where the tea ceremony is performed. "Throughout the tea," she said, "there is no conversation. There might be moments of apology, but the well-trained guest knows when to perform the different actions without the host having to say anything. Everyone is seated on the floor. They are breathing in synchrony, so that even breath is not really heard. There's the whisper of the silk kimono on the mats as you move forward and back with the bowl of tea. And there are other small sounds. First, when the pot is on the coals, the hiss of the water. Then, as the kettle cools, the hiss stops, the guest takes a bamboo ladle for the water, making a clacking sound intentionally to accentuate the silence, to signal the depth of the solitude. There's the sound of the pouring water, and of sipping from the lip of the bowl."

Rikyu's era has been described by the historian Yuriko Saito as the flowering of an aesthetic of imperfection. Everything from the worn stepping-stones to the irregular water basins and tea utensils (Rikyu left detailed instructions as to how a host should handle a badly cracked tea bowl) was meant to emphasize usage and contingency. They tell stories without speaking. Part of what's being celebrated is the notion of transience itself. Yoshida Kenkō, a fourteenth-century Buddhist monk who inspired much of the aesthetic in which Rikyu's tea ceremony is grounded, wrote: "If man were never to fade away like the dews of Adashino, never to vanish like the smoke over Toribeyama, but lingered on forever in the world, how things would lose their power to move us! The most precious thing in life is its uncertainty." The chipped, worn implements of Rikyu's tea ceremony nurture, in Saito's words, the submission of one's ego to the natural process of change and mortality. Similarly, we might say that the intent quiet of the tea ceremony serves to spotlight individual sounds that arise from silence, then dissolve back into it.

At the end of the ceremony, Harmon said, the guests make a last bow to the single chrysanthemum blossom that gave its beauty for this one day. "They leave one by one, and will never speak of their experience with each other or anyone else. And if they are ever invited back to this teahouse, they will never be invited with the same group. Throughout the hours of the ceremony, the guests have watched the movement of sunlight and shadows through the screen. When we come out, the changed light shows us a different garden."

Rikyu seduced the Samurai to cast aside their swords for an experience of silence. The Samurai knew that they would get out of the tea ceremony exactly as much sensory revelation as they could make room for by quieting themselves. As Deutsch wrote, though one might initially be overpowered by a beautiful Zen garden, particularly when the experience of it takes the form of "a mere stepping away from the humdrum chaos of one's ordinary being and routine," one must learn to "become as the art-work itself is—in truth of being." Master Bashō, a seventeenth-century poet, described the practice of listening to the world as a way of coming to identify with it: "when we observe calmly we discover that all things have their fulfillment," he wrote. Thus, we are enjoined to "learn from a pine things about a pine, and from a bamboo things about a bamboo." In so doing, we allow a spontaneous, natural harmony to emerge—the same as the one evoked between guests at a tea ceremony.

In an essay written in 1929, a Western scholar of Oriental studies named A. L. Sadler characterized *Chanoyu*, the way of tea, as "an institution that made simplicity and restraint fashionable and at the same time kept itself accessible to all classes, providing a ground on which all could meet on terms of equality, thus combining the advantages of a Mohammadean Mosque and a cricket field, and, some may feel inclined to add, also those of a Freemasons' Lodge and a Quaker Meeting-House."

⁂

As we left, we came upon Harmon's friend in a small building at the back of the garden eating quietly from an enormous bowl of trail mix. Harmon smiled at me. And then it was time to leave the garden.

A WORLD OF SILENCE

I came back to New York in a buoyant mood—filled with admiration for the way that Rikyu had managed to carve out a space in which to quiet all visitors, even the Samurai. Yet I knew that my experience in the garden amounted to the study of a historical era that had passed. That didn't make it irrelevant. We ought to build more Zen gardens. But these enchanted oases won't recapture the devout attention they attracted in Japan some four hundred years ago. Harmon herself made the point to me that the only real way to appreciate a Japanese garden is in solitude. But the mandate of the Portland Japanese Garden is to be a public garden first, and only then a Japanese garden. Even in Japan, she added, there are almost no gardens left that limit the number of people who are admitted at any one time.

But what, then, can we do now? This much I felt I *had* learned from the Zen garden: if we want more silence—not just in our individual hearts but also in the public sphere—we have to build spaces that harbor silence just as we create structures to facilitate other pursuits. However otherworldly some of its associations might be, silence needs a home in the here and now. One might even say that our lack of silence today reflects a failure in architecture. The great American architect Louis Kahn believed that buildings could foster empathy, and the creation of spaces enfolding silence was at the center of his thinking. I wondered how one might begin to fashion such a space today. And then I had the fortune to meet Hansel Bauman.

DEAF SPACE

"I've resigned myself to the fact that this is going to be an adventure, and nobody knows what's going to happen." Hansel Bauman flicked open his cell phone to check the time. "We're running late—of course." He glanced up at the high-pitched Gothic Revival structure of Chapel Hall. "Boy, those Victorians knew what they were doing. Look at the way light passes through those long windows from one side of the building to the other. That transparency . . . inclusiveness to the whole campus—panes of glass on the south side half the size of those on the north— all the subtle connections they make to where the structure is relative to the sun . . . They really listened—heard the silence."

He flicked open his cell phone again. "I hope the community members will be sympathetic."

Bauman and I were standing in a parking lot at Gallaudet University, the foremost college for the Deaf in the world, awaiting the arrival of a group of his students for a daylong collaborative project with various groups from Washington, D.C.'s, troubled Fifth Ward. This event was one of the first to bring Gallaudet's students together with residents of the surrounding neighborhood. It was an icebreaker for a larger, more ambitious undertaking whereby the campus renovation that Bauman is spearheading will include the creation of a pedestrian thoroughfare (dubbed the "Sixth Street Corridor") linking the two communities. This is not just a typical campus upgrade linked to a vague gesture of community outreach. The redesign is being conceived as the launchpad for Deaf Architecture, which combines the perceptual experience of the Deaf with design. The Sixth Street Corridor plan is intended to show that the Deaf understanding of physical space has something vital to offer the larger world. What happens to your visual understanding of space if you look at it while receiving little or no auditory information? How might architecture designed to facilitate silent communication enlarge our relationship to the world whether or not we can hear? What would a building created for silence—a dynamic, sociable silence—look like?

Bauman is bright-eyed and fine-boned with short-cropped white hair. When his retro black glasses are pushed back on his head he resembles a Nordic ski instructor. Bauman has been given a signed nickname by his students that involves pinching the thumb and forefinger together, then sliding them down the left side of the chest. It means, "He's so cute you just want to put him in your pocket."

Deaf Architecture, which was first articulated in a series of workshops with Deaf faculty and students at Gallaudet, is in its infancy. Bauman, who is himself hearing, is gambling a great deal on the hope that the Gallaudet Deaf Space project can have lasting effects, but, as he told me in his gentle California twang, "Architecture is all I've ever known, and the unknown is a big part of that." When he was a small child, Bauman's mother deeded him their backyard. On Sundays, the two of them would go off to construction sites and steal scrap wood that he would then cobble into houses, which he would name after semi-mythical beasts and sell to his mother's friends. His last project before coming to Gallaudet was a building at Oakridge to house a proton accelerator. The scientists, he said, "definitely have their own language," and helped acclimate him to "working in cultures." If one had to sum up his diverse efforts, he told me, it would be about trying to humanize environments built for populations who've never been heard when it comes to designing their space. "A lot of Gallaudet was built by people who were incapable of hearing the Deaf," he told me.

※

Throughout the months I spent thinking about silence, I'd been more and more drawn to spend time with the Deaf. (The word is capitalized in recognition of the standing of the Deaf community as a distinct cultural group with its own language, traditions, and values.) I felt that the Deaf experience spanned the antipodes of my subject. On the one hand deafness is among the most marked and tragic consequences of excessive noise exposure. On the other hand, the Deaf often possess a special understanding of silence.

It's a tricky equation: the idea of silence has been imputed to the Deaf experience in a pejorative sense for centuries—as in the assertion that the Deaf are "locked in silence." Many Deaf people are also tormented by tinnitus, which can be maddeningly loud, and some suffer from other sounds produced within their own brains. "When the brain is cut off from sensory input, it hallucinates," the writer Michael Chorost told me. Chorost had been hearing impaired his whole life, but became profoundly Deaf in the summer of 2001. He explained how at that time he became subject to round-the-clock auditory hallucinations. "In the morning," he said, "it would be loud plane engines, chain saws—blasts of undetermined sounds. In the evenings, it was music—an endless jumble of melodies, with my brain ransacking its stores of auditory memory. The three months between when I lost the last of my hearing and when I got cochlear implants were the loudest three months of my life." As many people at Gallaudet reminded me, there is also such a thing as visual noise. If you go into the main cafeteria at Gallaudet, you will enter a space filled with many hands swirling and streaking through the air. I had one Deaf student tell me that the exhaustion from all this visual stimulation was such that when she left the cafeteria for the campus green she had a feeling of relief she imagined to be akin to walking out of a rock concert.

And yet, with all of these nuances to factor, the more conversations I had with members of the Deaf community, the more convinced I became that the Deaf have a great deal to teach the hearing about the meaning of silence. The Deaf generally have far less auditory overload from the outside world to contend with—and, commensurately, they have much more of what most people think of as quiet. Even today when many people at Gallaudet have cochlear implants—which bypass the ear's damaged receivers and amplifiers to directly stimulate the auditory nerve—many students prefer to keep their implants off most of the time. Several students told me that in the course of an ordinary day the amount of time during which they enjoy or desire sound is minimal. Why should this be the case? Now that more silence has become the goal for so many of us, it makes sense to turn to the Deaf as authorities on the pursuit of silence.

I know that I've never felt so acutely listened to as I have with some of my Deaf interlocutors. The words of Pierre Desloges, a Deaf man who lived in the late eighteenth century and composed the first known public defense of sign language, ring true: "The privation of hearing makes us more attentive in general. Our ideas concentrated in ourselves, so to speak, necessarily incline us toward reflectiveness and meditation." Louis-François-Joseph Alhoy, a Deaf educator who rose to become head teacher at the Institution Nationale, the most important facility for teaching the Deaf in the Napoleonic era, likened the hearing population to "children born to opulence"—numb to the wealth of sensory impressions lavished upon them. The singular vision that accompanies the silence of the Deaf has long been recognized. It's not coincidental that the Institution Nationale produced one of the richest legacies of gifted painters and sculptors in nineteenth-century France. Sometimes their visual capacity was also put to more mundane uses. In the 1920s, a Deaf school in Cape Province became renowned as a place to recruit people who could find any lost object.

UNHEARD OF

What would it be like to lose your hearing completely? I mentioned earlier the surprising finding that people who go suddenly Deaf often find themselves asking not *why* it is that they can't hear anything but *where* they are in space. My one experience of the state was when I took a float in a sensory deprivation tank. The tank was located in a small soundproof room.

After I got over my initial feelings of claustrophobia, I found that my tactile sense of the saline water wrinkling and smoothing in synchrony with my motion became more finely tuned. And then, about forty minutes into the float, I heard a strange raspy noise of water in plumbing. I thought someone must have turned on the tank's filtration device and was annoyed by the disturbance. The noise cut off, then came on again. The second time around, I realized that it was the sound of my own saliva. I wasn't hearing it through my ears but sensing the vibration of that liquid as it trickled down my throat, resonating along a channel of bone and soft tissue. People forget that the Deaf sense vibrations, but they do, often more intensely than their hearing counterparts because the feeling of sound waves on the skin is not scrambled up with auditory processing of sound. Floating in the tank, I began to understand what it would be like to hear the world through my whole body. This is also the state of all those creatures in the animal kingdom that don't have ears—not to mention our mammalian ancestors. Perceiving sound through the flesh has a way of returning us to the architecture of our own physical forms.

※

Ten years ago, Toni Lacolucci was training to run a half marathon by doing laps of the Central Park Reservoir. She did not consider herself to be an athlete, and the regimen of daily running gave her a new, unfamiliar feeling of strength. Her Walkman was pivotal to the training, since the hardest thing about the mileage she had to cover to maintain her fitness was the speed with which it became boring. One August day, she'd launched off with some of her favorite tunes streaming full blast into her ears—energizing her. But she started having trouble with the right side of her headset; it faded to almost complete silence with faint, intermittent static. This was the second day in a row that the headset had given her trouble. Then, all of a sudden, as she was flying along, despite the heat, a chill shot through her. What would happen if she reversed the headset so that the left side, which she knew was working, fed into her right ear? It took her a couple of minutes to work up the nerve to do so. Finally she turned the headset around—dead silence. She reversed the headset again, and finished her run. On returning home, she called an audiologist and scheduled an appointment for the next day.

The audiologist discovered that she had no hearing whatsoever in her right ear. She told Lacolucci that the deafness probably indicated just a faster than ordinary hearing loss associated with age and revealing damage to the inner ear or to nerve pathways leading from the inner ear to the brain. A CAT scan failed to identify anything wrong. A second experience of loud music a few years later at a musical performance was followed by abrupt deterioration of the hearing in her left ear. When she investigated getting a cochlear implant the doctors discovered an acoustic neuroma—a tumor on her auditory nerve. Though the evidence is not yet conclusive, studies are mounting that indicate a link between acoustic neuromas and prolonged noise exposure. (These tumors are also a concern for long-term cell-phone users.) Lacolucci herself is certain that the genetic condition underlying the formation of her acoustic neuroma was, at the least, aggravated by listening to loud music over many years. She believes she could have saved some of her hearing had she been more knowledgeable about the effects of noise. She might even, she thinks, have denied the tumor the acoustical stimulation that helped trigger its development.

Seated in the large, animated dining room of the Museum of Modern Art, Lacolucci, whom I met through the Helen Keller National Center for the Deaf-Blind on Long Island, told me the story of her deafness. (I wrote my questions on notepaper; she replied by speaking aloud.) The noise of scores of conversations competed with lounge music, the clatter of the bar behind us, and the banging of plates and glasses. "Right now," Lacolucci said, "this room is absolutely silent to me."

Today, a couple of years into the experience of profound deafness, Lacolucci told me that "95 to 97 percent of sound I don't miss. I don't feel badly at all that I'm sitting here and I can't hear the dishes clanking. It's very quiet, and that means I can concentrate more on everything visual. I can speech-read and eavesdrop if I want to. If I had a hearing aid, I'd be straining so hard to focus on what you're saying, but now I can look at the beautiful forsythia." My eyes followed her gaze and I saw a glorious crescent spray of sun-yellow blossoms, of which I'd been completely unaware. "I know this might sound strange," she continued, "but it's *nice* a lot of the time not having to deal with all the garbage that's thrown at you. It frees you."

Josh Swiller, a writer who became profoundly Deaf at four, and now has cochlear implants, spent five years living as a Buddhist monk. He views Buddhist meditation as "the study of silence," and sees parallels between his experiences of Buddhism and of deafness. Just as Buddhism teaches that it's a mistake to focus on one's identity as an individual, since in reality one is enmeshed with everything in the world, in Swiller's experience of deafness, "everything touches you in the same way, with the same volume." Where a hearing person might judge the significance of different events on the basis of loudness alone, the proverbial "squeaky axle" doesn't command the attention of the Deaf. For this reason, he believes, the Deaf are more likely to find the balance between detachment from particulars and attachment to the panorama of existence.

THE FABRIC OF BEING

While we waited for additional students to emerge from College Hall, Hansel Bauman reeled off some campus history. One of the central tenets behind Deaf Space is that along with all the new ideas informing the practice, it also represents a restoration of older elements in the campus plan that got woefully muddled in a 1970s renovation.

The first buildings at Gallaudet, mid-nineteenth-century

structures like Chapel Hall, were constructed to convey loftiness—some are literally elevated on unusually high plinths—with the aim of conferring dignity through architecture on a population that had hitherto been schooled in facilities modeled on asylums. In 1866, Frederick Law Olmsted, the ubiquitous nineteenth-century genius of landscape design, created the first campus master plan. Olmsted fought hard to ensure that what he called a "liberal appropriation of space" would be preserved as an "ornamental ground" or garden at Gallaudet. His argument was that an expansive green area would help to bring "the different elements of the composition into one harmonious whole."

Olmstead had a further reason for pushing his green space, however. He thought that architecture could serve as a tool to sensitize and educate the human senses themselves. As he wrote to Gallaudet's trustees, since "the inmates of your establishment" are "unable to hear or speak, any agreeable sensation or delicate perception must depend on the development of other faculties. In a well regulated garden, the senses of sight and smell are gratified in a most complete and innocent way, and there seems, indeed, to be no reason why the studies of horticulture, botany, ornamental gardening, and rural architecture should not be pursued to great advantage by your students if proper faculties are offered at the outset, and due importance is attached to that influential automatic education which depends entirely on habitual daily contemplation of good examples."

Though the next major wave of campus development, which took place in the 1940s, resulted in structures that were much more modest than those of the nineteenth century, Bauman believes they were equally successful. It was in this period that the campus mall, a new chapel, its library, new residences, and a student union were built close by an older gym. And the way they did it, Bauman said, involved bringing these different types of spaces into a kind of astronomical alignment. "All the buildings had wonderful wide windows so that you could actually see all the way through into the lives of each one. The chapel was the fulcrum. So think about it—you had mind, body, and spirit woven together. There were sidewalks connecting across the campus in zigzags. It was the whole ball of wax—the ideal of Thomas Jefferson's Academic Village. It had a natural tendency to become a collective space because you had all the different activities that make up our collective human enterprise." He looked up. "There's a movement in architecture now to create collective spaces, yet to a large extent they fail. They fail because architects think they can just assign that quality. But that's not how it happens. We're trying now to rethink what makes people want to congregate in a space. What draws us together if there's no loud music?"

The whole of this cosmos at Gallaudet was moated by a ring road. In the late 1970s, a fresh campus master plan was unveiled. For starters, the planners decreed that new dorms should be built on the far side of the ring road. That, says Bauman, was the beginning of the end. "They thought it would be a more efficient operational use of space if they maintained segregated blobs of functionality. People live way off apart from where they study. They pray and study way off from where they eat and exercise. This same thing happened both spatially and administratively. It was a profound misreading of the life of the Deaf on campus—

which was all about free-flowing circulation between different elements. But the authorities were truly not listening. What they did was to create islands that killed life on campus."

As Bauman spoke, I found myself thinking of the academic campus as a human brain. It's now well understood that different cortical regions absorb input from more than one area. This is especially so with respect to the auditory cortex, which has great sensitivity to visual stimuli. There are enhancements of overall perception taking place all the time as information from one sense is cross-referenced with information coming from another sense. These so-called "cross-modalities" pervade our sensory model of the world.

At Gallaudet in the 1970s, the "brain" of the campus had reverted to the older model of discrete brain regions delegated to perform separate tasks. I recalled the many experiences throughout my journey of the past year that were setups for this sort of unfruitful, noisy dissonance.

How, I asked Bauman, did you overcome this when Deaf Space was launched?

To a huge extent, he told me, it was a matter of listening. The first ideas about Deaf Space were created with Deaf faculty and students in a series of workshops. "There's a lot of lip service paid to ideas of inclusiveness today," he said, "but this really was about handing the pencil to the people who best understand the Deaf experience. Real inclusiveness can help make a collective space." He shrugged. "And I think this is one way Deaf Architecture could become an important influence. A lot of the global challenges we face today have spatial implications that need to be solved inclusively. In the Sixth Street Corridor phase of Deaf Space, the Fifth Ward community will be involved the same way that students and faculty were at the outset."

⚰

I took a stroll after our conversation to look at the Sorenson Language and Communication Center, the one building on Gallaudet's campus thus far that has been completed with the principles of Deaf Space in mind.

As I entered a doorway set in the expansive glass grid that dominates the building's façade, an abundance of sunlight played off different wood and metal surfaces, streaming through great chambers of open space. Putting the structure into historical context, one can identify traces of early modernism, a focus on what Le Corbusier called the "great primary (geometrical) forms," along with repetition, symmetry, and the expansive use of glass to maximize sight lines. The architecture also pays homage to the traditional Mediterranean courtyard in providing access to natural light as frequently and widely as possible. (Deaf people are acutely conscious of the passage of the sun over the course of a day because of how the angle of light can help or hinder communication by sign language.) Colonnades and porches create permeability between inside and outside spaces. The idea of nurturing unimpeded circulation and free-flowing curvilinear movement is apparent in exterior walls and interior corridors. All the emphasis on transparency and openness enables people to rely on visual cues where one would ordinarily depend on sound. There's a sense of being in multiple perspectives, multiple sight lines, simultaneously.

Bauman described the overall aspiration of the space to me as "cubist." The completed building and sketches for additional structures I saw also made me think again of Louis Kahn. Kahn was a zealous champion of natural light, arguing that, while artificial light could convey only one static moment of light, natural light, with its "endlessly changing qualities," made each room "a different room every second of the day." Kahn also believed in a mystical connection between the principles of light and silence, with silence representing the desire for expression, and light as that which bestows presence. Of the pyramids, he wrote that to look at them today, when all the cruel circumstances of their construction had faded, "when the dust is cleared, we see really silence again." And this silence in the guise of light sculpted by architecture links us to the "prevalence of spirit enveloping the Universe."

⁂

When I wandered back to find Bauman, the last of our students had arrived and we got into a van to drive to the Trinidad Recreation Center less than a mile away. Other student groups were meeting with community members at other locations. At the center, we met Wilhelmina Lawson, a regal, soft-spoken woman wearing a bright red cap and big black sunglasses, who heads up the Neighborhood Action Committee of the Fifth Ward. Unfortunately, she was the only community member to appear. "I gave out as many fliers as I could," Lawson said. She addressed the Gallaudet students for a few minutes, confirming Bauman's remarks about the challenges facing the community and saying that she wanted to strengthen the partnership with Gallaudet as a way of de-marginalizing them both. She herself had come to the District from a "concrete jungle" in New Jersey—against all the advice of her family and friends. But she'd fallen in love, she said, with the neighborhood's trees, flowers, and "above all, *children*." She had tried, she said, "to turn the Fifth Ward from a drug community into a garden community."

Bauman, putting a good face on the low turnout, spoke a little more about his excitement for the Sixth Street Corridor, the pedestrian walkways that would actively stitch the two communities together. Ideas for what will be housed in the buildings lining the corridor are still being developed, but part of what Gallaudet hopes to inspire through the development is a dialogue about silence itself. In addition to facilities like a child development center and community theaters, the university is considering more provocative venues, like a silent drinking establishment in which, whether one is hearing or Deaf, spoken communication will be prohibited.

Though this idea might sound hopelessly fanciful, one of my more delightful forays into silence was a Quiet Party, staged at a SoHo bar called Madame X. The brainchild of two city friends, Paul Rebhan and Tony Noe, who met up for drinks one night in 2002 but couldn't find a single bar that wasn't deafeningly loud, Quiet Parties are now held on a fairly regular basis in cities around the world. Guests meet in spaces separated from a larger bar. They're provided with pencils and notecards. All talk is forbidden and the room itself is kept quietish (very low or no music; subdued clatter from behind the bar).

The night I went to Madame X the red-lit room was crowded with people, and the loudest sound was the soft laughter sparked as guests read each other's written wit. It was mostly a singles scene, but one with a refreshing, unfamiliar note of gentleness. The young men and women hailed from all over the world (Korea, Tunisia, France, and Russia), and included chemists, accountants, students, and teachers. I kept my cards from that night. Several of my silent acquaintances wrote about the need to create more refuges like the Quiet Parties. ("Indeed—there are no silent zones anywhere!") Some were funny. ("I must be drunk—I'm blurring my letters.") And a few waxed lyrical.

Other ideas for the Sixth Street Corridor include plans for a space that will replicate aspects of Deaf experience. In a soundproof chamber, the designers plan to display an array of noisemaking technologies on which the hearing rely for entertainment and information—but without the sound. "We want to get people to talk about what that experience is, and about how they reorient to the space itself in complete silence," Fred Weiner, the special assistant to the president for planning at Gallaudet told me.

※

The project Bauman was organizing with the Gallaudet students and the Fifth Ward community members was a photography exercise intended to explore the different ways they each looked at the world. We were to pair up—one Deaf student with one Fifth Warder and a camera—and walk through the neighborhood up to the Capital City Market. The person holding the camera would be guided by the other to the shot they wanted to snap—whereupon the "eye" would tap the shoulder of the person holding the camera. I was paired with Erin, a gentle young blond woman with deep-set eyes. She's a business student at Gallaudet, and I was a bit disappointed not to have been partnered with someone working more directly on the architecture project so that I would get a sense of what it was like to see the world with that kind of special visual consciousness.

But the experience with Erin was revelatory. I consider myself a reasonably visually aware person, but she guided me to different viewpoints with unbelievable precision and got me to look at things from perspectives that would never have occurred to me. While sirens wailed and the wind gusted loudly, she led me to a brick façade with an inlaid pattern of white diamonds, a corner of a neo-Tudor building, four boarded-up windows in a brick wall that from the angle she chose looked classical. She kept moving my hands, changing the angle, changing the depth of field from wide angle to telephoto, making me kneel down very close or lean back to catch the sky. We took multiple, minutely varying shots of the red door at a child-care center. At a certain point, I realized that I'd completely lost track of time. I'd slipped into silence and had an awareness of the movement of sunlight on stone and grass, skin, paint, and cloud surface that was truly uncanny. When I ran into Bauman, I told him that now I thought I understood what he'd meant about cubism and Deaf Space. "Yeah," he said, "you see now! It's the way Erin is trying to take in everything—to show you the totality of a condition."

After the exercise had been completed, I got into conversation with another Gallaudet student majoring in business, a lightly goateed and heavily tattooed young man named Michael. He said he'd been partnered with several community members inside a church. "What they wanted me to snap," he said, "were objects that reflected the values of their community, but with no attention for the objects themselves. So they'd say, 'Flowers are important to my community'—and then they'd guide me anywhere where the flowers were in the frame. I'd encourage them to take the picture from different angles—bird's-eye view, from the right, the left, up, down, back and forth. I wanted to get them to take it from different perspectives—to see what it was and how it fit in with everything else in the church."

Michael's experience revealed the way that the community members were letting words and concepts blind them to the actual world they were standing in. The idea of "flowers" hid the blossoms themselves. The unassuming young man, because of his knowledge of silence, was able to show the hearing world how to see.

But how might this expanded perspective play out in architecture? Were there tangible gains a hearing person might receive from the Deaf knowledge of silence and space?

COLLECTIVE VISION

Robert Sirvage is a Deaf graduate student in architecture who has helped Bauman formulate some of the central tenets of Deaf Space. Sirvage has an auburn beard, sideburns razored close to his sharp cheekbones, and eyes that gleam with a striking pale-blue light.

He is writing his dissertation on proxemics—the study of how people move through space. When two Deaf people are walking together while signing, a complex choreography unfolds in which the person not actively signing is also watching over the other's steps to protect them from falling or colliding with something. This has implications for how close together two Deaf people will walk. Sirvage referred to the process of Deaf people walking together as a "package agreement." Bauman's brother Dirksen, who teaches Deaf studies at Gallaudet, described the emphasis in Deaf culture on engagement with others. He maintains that among the hearing, the ability to hear oneself speak is crucial to how we maintain our sense of being present in the world. But this kind of "auto-stimulation" is unavailable to the Deaf. Instead, he maintains, what the Deaf have is "the face of the other as you sign." This fact of always being held in the visual embrace of another person, he believes, creates the basis for a collectivist culture.

Sirvage has spent a great deal of time videoing the movement of Deaf and hearing people through the same space. When I watched some of these videos, I saw what he was talking about— it's as though an invisible tether links the steps of Deaf people in conversation, in a manner that simply has no equivalent in the motion of the hearing. Hansel Bauman believes there's an architectural corollary to this—space that helps people remain in each other's visual embrace.

I got a sense of how this might work when Sirvage took me on a tour of the campus. He wanted to show me two places, he said. One that students shunned, but which had been built as a gathering point, and another which they themselves had made their main gathering point.

The first place he took me was in front of one of the central campus buildings. He asked me to sit down on one of two facing benches. There were high brick walls at my back juxtaposed at different angles, and various shrubs configured around the seating areas. Sirvage watched me carefully, and broke into a laugh when I found myself irresistibly drawn to turn around—several times in the course of a few minutes. Then he pointed out how, because of the juxtaposition of wall lines and plantings, there was no way anyone sitting on one of the benches could see another person approaching. Every arrival was a surprise, and—especially in the absence of auditory signals—this made for an uncomfortable sense of vulnerability. Even with the ability to hear, I felt jittery because the space left me without a visual tether to the larger world.

Sirvage smiled when I said this and noted that in the Canadian state of Ottawa, where he is originally from, there is a museum built without a single straight line or hard corner. It was all curves he said, because the Native Americans believed that devils lurk in corners. (Zen gardens also incorporate the idea that demons can only travel in straight lines.) Another touchstone for Deaf Architecture is a notion developed by the psychologist Wolfgang Köhler. Köhler invented two nonsense words, "maluma" and "takete," to illustrate the spatial associations we bring to different sounds. While maluma evokes images of soft, curvilinear, maternal forms, takete conjures sharp, angular shapes. Surveys indicate that the Deaf overwhelmingly opt for design elements reflecting maluma-type patterns. Sirvage mentioned to me that there is no sign for a square shape.

The second location Sirvage took me to was an expanse of cement at the entrance to a dorm. The building itself was an unimpressive, drab, modern space. I gave Sirvage a questioning look and asked whether this was really the hot spot he'd meant to show me. He gave a mischievous grin. I turned back to the vista before me and when I made myself sink into the place for a few minutes, I did feel something calming. I became conscious that I was looking over an unusually open view—the exact opposite of the previous location. But Sirvage showed me something further, which had not factored into my conscious impressions. By a fortuitous alignment of buildings, landscaping, and roads, the peripheral sight lines where I was standing were as spacious and open as the center of the visual field. "To me," Sirvage said, "this place embodies ideas of silence, the peace we associate with quiet."

In fact, research has established that the Deaf have greater peripheral vision than the hearing. An architecture that embodies Deaf awareness of a wider peripheral field might help to conjure the mental state we yearn for in silence.

There's another possibility as well, one involving metaphysical sight lines. Sirvage told me how important the idea of showing the history of a building's use was to Deaf Space. "A scuffed floor communicates to us," he said, "because of what it says about how people interact with a space." Deaf people don't come to spaces because of the sounds emanating from them; they look for other points of attraction. "This can sound New Agey," Sirvage continued, "but maybe there really is a flow of energy—an electrical path—that we can become aware of that indicates that something significant happened here."

This is obviously a tenuous point, and Sirvage didn't push it too hard, but I came away from our conversation feeling that he may be right and that, at the least, the Deaf have an intense capacity to tune in to how people have navigated a given architectural setting over time. This deepens the pull of spaces they care about. Here as well, the layering of silent meaning onto physical space could enhance the experience for the hearing. It doesn't have to be thought of as mystical. The marks of usage that were so important to Sen Rikyu in the teahouse performed the same function—suggesting a story, creating negative space for the imaginative life of the participants to unfold in.

BREAK INTO SILENCE

I asked Bauman what he felt he'd learned from working with the Deaf. He scratched his shock of bright white hair and pushed his black glasses higher up his nose. "There was a moment," he said, "that I'll never forget. It was about a year and a half into working on Deaf Space. I was still living at the time in a small apartment in San Francisco that overlooked the city toward the East Bay—commuting back and forth to D.C.—working around the clock on trying to hammer out the initial concept for the plans." One day, he said, he was sitting before the window of his apartment, staring at the view. A deep silence filled the room. In the visual field closest to him, he looked over the architecture of rooftop elements belonging to other buildings; in the middle ground was the city of San Francisco itself; far off were the hills. As he gazed off through the glass, Bauman said, he suddenly felt "cold chills" go through him, "and the whole scene became totally different. Now I'm not looking out the window, the view was no longer a painting on the wall, *I'm in the picture. I'm part of the system.*" He made the motion of a wave with his hand. "The same soil underneath my building carries on beneath the other buildings before me and the city farther off, and then swells up to form the hills. It was a visceral understanding of being in the world."

Bauman's description of this moment made me remember an interview I'd seen with the Dalai Lama in which he recounted the process of contemplating the mandala, a diagram of the cosmos used to focus meditation. "The main thing is visualization," he said, "the reminder of our visualization contained in the actual mandala. First you meditate on *shunya*, emptiness, then that very mind which is completely absorbed in outward nature becomes transformed into the physical world."

As Bauman began working to implement the notion of a unifying substrate into campus design, he discovered something was missing. He devised architectural solutions to promote the flow of motion around campus—strategies like increasing transparency and eliminating sharp turnoffs in passageways. Yet the further he and his colleagues went in developing these principles, the more they found it necessary to break up the flow in ways that would give people a respite, "privacy, a degree of enfolding enclosure, opportunities for stationary conversation." As an example, he asked me to imagine "a garden wall that would provide a place to lean back against, providing a sense of safety, but also radiating heat. Maybe there's a tree nearby providing shade and dappled light." What he had discovered, he told me, was that for the design of the campus to work, it depended on the creation of "holes in the fabric." Holes were, he said, in fact, "the central element that ties the fabric together." The holes, he concluded, are the silences.

Bauman is aware of the fragility of the Deaf Space project in an atmosphere of general economic retrenchment. Between cochlear implants, improved hearing aids, advances in the ability to teach oral speech to Deaf children, and the ability of the Deaf to communicate via the Internet in a manner identical to their hearing counterparts, there are increasingly voices being raised questioning why the Deaf need to be educated in a setting where sign language is the principal mode of communication.

But whatever happens to Deaf Space, it's an extraordinary experiment, one we could all learn from. In all my experiences with sound, what I'd been most conscious of was overstimulation and our collective fear of the silent interval. Of course we cannot learn to replicate the singularity of Deaf vision, but that doesn't mean that more silence wouldn't enhance our ability to see. Even a very brief reduction in stimulus from one sense can trigger a heightened perceptual rush in another. On one occasion, I trooped around Columbus Circle in Manhattan with a peculiar group called PDM that promotes spontaneous group meditation. At a prearranged signal, our little band would all drop into a sitting position on a street corner and close our eyes. By the third time we did this, the sound around the circle—of which I'd frankly been oblivious—became overwhelmingly loud. The next time I stopped moving and shut my eyes, I instantly felt I was listening to the soundtrack of a terrifying horror movie. Try it. Go to some corner where you live. Stop where you are and shut your eyes for a few minutes. You'll be surprised by what you hear.

I had to leave Gallaudet to catch a flight, but as I stepped out-side, the drama of the sunlight stopped me in my tracks. I was alone on the campus mall. The moving clouds created patterns that arose and dissolved, casting into luminescence and shadow every leaf, stone, wall, and open space. I flashed back to the Quaker Meeting House where I'd been at the very beginning of my pursuit of silence.

Louis Kahn once proposed that the entire notion of a division between silence and light might, in fact, be artificial, since together they composed what he called "the ambient soul." It's common for mystics to speak of their experiences of the transcendent—experiences often precipitated by silence—in terms of intensifying illumination. But the link may not be only spiritual. Perhaps we really do see a brighter light when we are in silence.

In the essay "Nature," Ralph Waldo Emerson wrote of how the sun "illuminates only the eye of the man, but shines in the eye and the heart of the child." Yet in the quiet landscape of the natural world, the "spirit of infancy" could be recovered. In the hour of quiet contemplation "mean egotism vanishes," Emerson wrote: "I become a transparent eyeball—I am nothing; I see all." Instead of helping us feel ownership of space, an architecture of silence might bring home the fact that we are part of what we gaze upon.

CHAPTER TWELVE

Silent Finale

When I stepped out into the sunlight at Gallaudet, I finally grasped the deeper reason why my mounting frustrations with the battle against noise had not left me demoralized: all the while I'd been probing the psychological and sociological limits of our ability to stop the din, I'd been interspersing my investigations with experiences of silence. Many of these had been lovely; a few even approached the sublime. In the midst of all the doom and boom, breathtaking silences are still out there, awaiting our attention.

On top of this, I'd found that, with a few villainous exceptions, the people I encountered who were, so to speak, on the pro-noise side of the debate, were more complex and frankly just more likable than I'd expected them to be. To my happy surprise I even received an e-mail from Leanne Flask nine months after I visited the mall announcing that she'd resigned from DMX to start her own music-design business, which was to have a major philanthropic component aimed at enriching children's understanding of music so that they can become advocates for keeping music education in the school system.

By and large, the unabashed noise lovers I met seemed to me to be exactly as barbaric as was the greater society in which we mostly live today. That's to say, as barbaric as we choose to make them out to be, leaving aside aspects of their character we elect not to listen for because they squelch our caricature. If we use affinity for noise as a criterion for judging a person's degree of civilization, there's no great distinction between the erstwhile Boom THUG bumping down the streets of Bed-Stuy and the well-coutured young professional commuting to the gym with her personal sound device pumped to bump her own brain cells. The us-or-them divide doesn't hold. We may feel that all the noise of the age is simply too much and that we must either make an all-out assault against it or retreat into our own personal version of the monastery. Or we may determine that in the criss-crossing nuances of the dilemma there are unexpected opportunities.

My last lesson in the unpredictable interplay between noise and silence occurred in connection with worms. Inside a neurobiology laboratory, I saw how easy it was to reawaken our wonder at listening to what only becomes audible when the world quiets down.

⚹

In a famous passage from *The Origin of Species*, Darwin writes: "It may metaphorically be said that natural selection is daily and hourly scrutinising, throughout the world, the slightest variations; rejecting those that are bad, preserving and adding up all that are good; silently and insensibly working, whenever and wherever opportunity offers, at the improvement of each organic being in relation to its organic and inorganic conditions of life." Darwin makes the silent evolutionary process itself the supreme agent of differentiation and, in the action of distinguishing, of the amelioration of the world.

Darwin also had a keen ear for the contradictions that accompany noise and silence. While exploring the coast of Brazil, Darwin wrote of how "a most paradoxical mixture of sound and silence pervades the shady part of the wood. The noise from the insects is so loud, that it may be heard even in a vessel anchored several hundred yards from the shore; yet within the recesses of the forest a universal silence appears to reign." Darwin knew that these paradoxes are never more poignant than when they're manifest in human nature. In his autobiography, he recounts an amusing story of a dinner he had with Thomas Carlyle, of the not-so-soundproof study. Carlyle, Darwin wrote, "silenced every one by haranguing during the whole dinner on the advantages of silence."

One of Darwin's great heroes in the epic of natural selection is the worm. The supremely unprepossessing worm that turns the soil in silence, sifting and reconstituting the earth's composition as a by-product of its own digestive process, Darwin found emblematic of the way all work ought to be performed. The worm has neither the capacity nor need to make a noise about its achievement. And while its stature could not be more lowly, its accomplishment outstrips that of the most cultivated farmer. Darwin writes, "The agriculturist in ploughing the ground follows a method strictly natural; he only imitates in a rude manner . . .

the work which nature is daily performing by the agency of the earthworm."

⚎

The worms I chose to look at were members of the nematode species graced with a Latin name that means "ancient, elegant rod." At one millimeter in length, *Caenorhabditis elegans* is even tinier and lowlier than the earthworm. Yet when it was selected as genetic research subjects in the late 1960s, the dream was that this little creature would enable us to understand the entire nervous system. Scientists believed that if you could characterize its every neuron, discover their locations and the neurotransmitters they use, all the secrets of the human brains would be revealed. It hasn't quite worked out this way. But the revelations provided by the worms are still legion. The first complete genome of a multicellular organism to be sequenced belonged to *C. elegans*. And today some of the most important research into RNA transpires through their simple bodies. No less than the service of astronaut Suni Williams, whom I had sought out at the beginning of my research for her insights into the noiseless depths of outer space, the service of the nematodes struck me as worthy of a moment of silent observation.

I had another motive, as well, for visiting a laboratory. Based on a few remarks by a scientist friend about the long hours of ascetic observation in her lab, I'd conceived a notion of the laboratory as a contemporary version of the monastery. I pictured rows of people bent over their microscopes, scrutinizing the minutiae of life's genetic coding in an atmosphere of rapt concentration that evoked the silent Cistercians hunched over holy writ.

Thus, one summer afternoon, I traveled uptown to the brown monolith of the Hammer Building on West 168th Street, where I met a friend who used to work in a neurobiology lab there.

We entered a large, fluorescent-lit room lined with black counters and high white shelves crammed with orange-capped glass bottles, microscopes, stacks of petri dishes, sleek instruments, and fat dark files. A number of researchers were hard at work in the space.

They were not, however, all quietly bent over their microscopes. Rather, most were talking intently in pairs and trios. Claire Benard, the high-spirited principal lab assistant, told me right off that she would be *years* farther along in her research were it not for the noise-related distractions of the lab—if she'd been able to work in solitude instead of being constantly interrupted by colleagues, centrifuges, freezer mechanisms, fans, and the popping hiss of the giant worm sorter. When she needed to concentrate, she told me, she wore state-of-the-art noise-cancellation headphones.

I thought it actually seemed pretty quiet in the room. The people engaged in conversation were speaking softly. There was no background music; no big machines were running. But I'd been disabused of my laboratory-monastery analogy. And with a sense that I'd again gone off into the world in pursuit of silence only to find another strain of noise, I asked to be taken around the corner to the darkened room where I was to look through a high-power microscope at the worms, whose neurons, I learned, had been grafted with luminescent jellyfish genes to illuminate them.

I took my seat before a big white Zeiss. My friend adjusted the focus and turned to Benard to continue a conversation they'd begun in the corridor. I bowed my eyes to the stereoscopic viewfinder, and suddenly I was transported. The worms, inlaid with soft emerald glows, swirling microscopic cosmos, took my breath away. Inside their bodies floated nebulae of pale green (the neurons) and tiny, hard bright glitterings ("gut granules"), little accumulations of fat crucial for the worms' survival. I watched a pair of worms tie themselves into a sailor's manual of knots. The circle within my viewfinder became an upside-down planetarium, presenting constellations in motion—the birth and destruction of galaxies; hieroglyphics raveling and unraveling—pricked with fiery cat eyes.

I don't know how long it was before I realized that, while I hadn't given a thought to the silence of the worms' labors, I'd lost all consciousness of the ventilator above me, and even of the voices of my friends. They were just gone—vacuumed into the intensity of this vision. The composer John Cage wrote: "There is no such thing as an empty space, or an empty time . . . try as we may to make a silence, we cannot." Yet the reverse is also true. Sometimes, try as we may to make noise, we cannot. Just as the moment of quiet when ground control cut out enabled astronaut Williams to see the depths of space, the fathomless sight of these blurring emerald stars and filigrees of light had created silence everywhere.

I finally managed to lift my eyes, but words still failed me.

Benard smiled. "Yes . . . It's beautiful. *This* keeps me going—still."

⚹

We wandered back to the main room of the laboratory. And there, another extraordinary thing happened.

As we entered, one of the scientists lifted a petri dish, opened it, brought it down on the counter with a hard click, and slid it closer to her microscope.

"That sound!" my friend laughed, remarking how it brought back memories of her years at the lab. She picked up another dish—they resemble big round eyeglass lenses—and repeated the motion, unscrewing it and bringing it down: a hard *tick*, followed by a cool *crissing* scrape.

Another researcher was using a device that looked like a thick pen to lift tiny plastic vials, release drops of liquid from them onto a slide, then eject the vials into a bin.

"Do you hear that?" Benard smiled. "That sound of the tip releasing—it's like a camera shutter." I listened harder as she replicated the gentle, split-second whir. Benard added that one of her favorite sounds of the lab—though she felt awful admitting it—was the sound made when you burn a worm. The scientists have to do it, she explained. "If we pick up a larva, say, when we're trying to get a group of hermaphrodites . . ."

My friend turned up the flame on a small Bunsen burner. "I like the burner sound too," she said. She turned it high. It crackled like a bonsai fireplace. Benard lifted a long, thin needle and danced it in the flame until it glowed. Then she dipped it into the gel on a petri dish until she'd plucked a worm. She brought that over the flame and I heard a faint, fleeting, *kihh* amidst the fire noise. "I don't know why—I love that sound." Benard laughed.

Luisa Cochella, a woman at the counter behind us, abruptly remarked that she loved the sound of "chunking." Chunking involves cutting out a tiny slab of gel to replenish the food on a petri dish. She demonstrated the process, heating a tiny, thin silver spatula over a flame, then lowering its blade into the gel. As the hot spatula hit the gel, the two substances made a delicate squeezy-kiss. Cochella's eyes lit up and she laughed.

"And then of course there's this noise." My friend lifted a glass slide, then neatly tossed it into a red bin where it struck a mound of other discarded slides with a sharp *ting*. She did it again. This time the *ting* mixed with *crunnch*.

Suddenly different people at work around the room began entering into the play, pressing different sounds on me. I hadn't sought out this strange, enchanting hear-and-tell. It hadn't occurred to me to do so, but one after the next they came. And after each noise, the scientists would ask, "Hear that? Do you hear?," repeating the actions that made their favorite sounds with infectious delight.

The laboratory wasn't silent the way a monastery is silent. Yet it was quiet enough for the people working there to take the aural temperature of where they were. To hear and savor a great deal that might easily have been lost. These were the subtle sounds that picked out the hours for them—little noises that opened vast networks of association, like the constellations of neurons glowing through the bodies of the worms. Listening to these sounds was at once the recreation and reminder of the substance of their day.

All at once, I felt myself back by the side of my child as he floated in the bath and we fell quiet together, listening for the world of sounds surrounding our infinitesimal pocket of life. How many different sounds can you hear? What is that sound? One by one, the scientists presented the sonic fruits of their contemplative labors. The windows behind them glowed. Then, in sublime and unremarkable silence, the sun slipped from the sky.

THE RIGHT TO QUIET

None of the silences I've encountered provide the definitive answer. But all the silences I've explored have something rich to offer. I came to appreciate the idea of a variety of microclimates of quiet that need cultivating if we don't want the atmosphere to become sonic CO_2, an all-pervasive electroacoustical emission we cannot breathe in.

Throughout my pursuit of silence, a voice in my head kept repeating the refrain, "We have our sights aimed wrong." And I found myself returning to the writing of Theodor Lessing, another great turn-of-the-century noise activist, like Julia Barnett Rice.

⚄

Lessing's notion that people who lack economic and social power often strive to expand their physical impact on the world by making noise has a long philosophical lineage. We can trace it back to Nietzsche, who argued that people who are denied space for action will compensate with some imaginary form of revenge. And on through Schopenhauer, who identified noise as the most flagrant spoiler of the capacity for concentration on which all great minds depend. But Lessing, unlike his philosopher forebears, tried to put these ideas into action through the founding of a social movement.

Lessing was nothing if not versatile. In different phases of his career, his energies were channeled into philosophy, journalism, pedagogy, and activism on behalf of various progressive movements. Lessing was one of the first writers to analyze the idea of "the self-hating Jew"—the phenomenon whereby Jews came to internalize the libels directed against them by anti-Semites, and which he saw as a grave threat to the future of the Jewish people. The notion of internalizing stereotypes may also have informed his views on the problem of noise. He wrote in his book about Jewish self-hatred that "to change human beings into dogs, one only needs to shout at them long enough, 'You dog!'" Similarly, Lessing argued, the attraction of loud, unruly behavior for the working classes was symptomatic of both their lack of healthy outlets for instinctual drives and a form of vengeance exerted against those who stripped them of power and positive social value.

Lessing idolized Rice. He devoted a significant part of a book he wrote on noise to detailing the activities of her society. After visiting New York in 1908 to study the results of her work, Lessing immediately set about launching an antinoise society of his own. And he asked Rice to serve as the leader of this organization. She apparently declined the invitation.

But although Lessing adopted some of Rice's strategies, the principal motto of his society was "Quiet Is Distinguished." He championed classical associations between silence and profundity (Plutarch declared that "we learn silence from the gods, speech from men") and the Eastern ideal of the contemplative life. In Lessing's argument, silence served as an emblem of wisdom, against the egoistic Occidental value system. "Culture is evolution toward silence," he declared in his book *Der Lärm*. And he developed various quirky schemes to foster this evolution. One of them involved preparing a "blue list" of the names of hotels, apartments, and houses where members of his society could expect to find quiet. He also designated "houses of silence," in which, he said, it would be possible to hear a pin drop, and no pianos or parrots would be allowed to enter. Himself an idealistic teacher—his refusal to kowtow to German nationalism led to his being literally shouted out of the college where he taught—Lessing also fought to have schools built in gardens and forests in order that the silence of nature might catalyze learning. Another motto of his society was *"non clamor sed amor"*—roughly translated, make love not noise.

It's easy to see why Rice's campaign against unnecessary noise sparked popular support while Lessing's more ambitiously philosophical program did not. On the surface, her strategy seems a straightforward, practical solution to a highly complex problem. However, as we've seen, there was a flaw at the core of Rice's position, one that continues to hamper legal and political struggles against loud sounds today: When it comes to noise, how do we tell the necessary from the unnecessary?

Lessing's movement, lampooned in the press as elitist and hostile to modernity, failed to build momentum. Yet people may have been too quick to dismiss the implications of his position: that we need to dedicate less energy to reducing noise and more to increasing silence. His gripe with the age was not against tech-nology per se but with the way society organized itself around the machine in opposition to fundamental physiological and psycho-logical needs. And he was not given much opportunity to make his case. The noisy unrest that would make Hitler's loudspeaker heard around the globe was already amping up. (In 1933, Lessing himself became the first person assassinated by Nazi agents on foreign soil.) Ultimately Lessing's assertion that quiet is distin-guished was meant as a rallying cry to the classes that had en-joyed little opportunity for distinction, rather than as a call to close ranks among an already anointed silent elite. If you contin-ually scream at people that they're dogs, they may one day lash back with a loud snarl. By the same token, if you treat people as men and women of distinction, capable of appreciating the riches of their own higher nature, many of them may be drawn to cultivate silence of their own volition. Lessing's work implies that the deficit of silence in our civilization reflects a breakdown in education.

※

Perhaps we are misallocating our precious resources. Rather than dedicating so much money, energy, and time to measuring noises we already know to be loud and fighting policy battles that will never fully succeed, why not at least split our investment in two—putting half our capital into activities and spaces that pro-mote silence?

As Colin Grimwood, an adviser working with the Depart-ment for Environment, Food, and Rural Affairs in the United Kingdom to protect quiet spaces, put it to me, the problem with our current model is that we "spend all this money making noisy places a little less noisy. At the end of the day, we've managed to take a few dBs off, and they're still noisy. That's why we have to prioritize quiet."

Grimwood and others argue that because quiet spaces in cities tend to be small-scale, contained areas, they can be created at far less cost than the infrastructure changes in road, rail, building HVAC systems, etc., required to bring about even a tiny reduction in overall noise levels for a busy neighborhood.

And as it turns out, designers of quiet spaces have found that one of the root causes of the problem of noise—overcrowding—can also contribute to its solution. High-density development, in which building façades form a wall that follows traditional street blocks, can be enormously effective at blocking sound on the rear. An unbroken line of dwellings, or office buildings, gives each individual structure a "quiet side," and if there's an outdoor common area or courtyard in back, this immediately becomes a secluded quiet space. The city planner Max Dixon remarked to me that a mere 5 percent gap in a perimeter enclosure will let through 80 percent of the noise. Seal up the row entirely, and you've got something close to quiet. (Air traffic is the outstanding threat.) Dixon reminded me that antecedents of this design principle can be traced back, not only to the shared rear gardens of Georgian houses in many London neighborhoods but to cloisters and to the buildings framing courtyards in some of humanity's earliest cities. A recent Swedish study has indicated that, even when people live in a loud area, if residential buildings have a quiet side there's a 50 percent reduction in annoyance levels. Add to this barrier of façades some acoustic absorption, such as a thickly planted ground surface, and perhaps a small fountain—avoid the use of machines around the back area that produce negatively perceived sounds, like air conditioners—and one has carved out a haven against the loudening world. But only by adopting a fresh approach to educating people about sound can we hope that these simple yet effective quiet spaces will ever be treated as such.

❅

Though we have a tendency to romanticize the silence of the past, throughout history many cities have been incredibly loud. Not only were there traffic noises of carriages, coaches, and chariots on rough paving stones, as well as disparate animal sounds and all the commotion of fixed and itinerant vendors, there were also industrial workshops intermingled with private residences. In Pompeii, for example, the main entrance of the patrician House of the Fauns was adjacent to two clamorous blacksmith shops. Indeed it's been suggested that one reason why the ancient Greek city of Sybaris became as cultured and wealthy as it did, relative to other cities of the age, was because of the space for refinement of the sensibilities created when the authorities began zoning industry away from living areas. That said, there was also, as a rule, more acoustical contrast in cities of the past than can be found in today's cities. Except in the most crowded metropolises, areas of urban congestion were often interspersed with patches of undeveloped land, an open riverbank, commons, temple yards, and cemeteries. Many city dwellers fortunate enough to have their health and a little freedom did not have to travel the distance we do to leave the cacophony behind for a time.

We probably do not need a pervasive silence—desirable as this might seem to some. What we do need is more spaces in which we can interrupt our general experience of noise. What we must aspire to is a greater proportion of quiet in the course of everyday life.

SOUND DIET

In almost all my conversations with antinoise activists, the person wound up declaring, "We need to fight noise pollution in all its forms." But how many forms does noise pollution actually have? Supersonic jets produce noise pollution. So do many power generators, along with certain manufacturing processes. The most heinous form of noise pollution today may be that caused by naval sonar, which results in whales dying of disequilibrium by diving too deeply as they try to avoid this new wave of noise. But the majority of noises in our lives do not meet this definition of the extraordinarily loud.

Rather than conceiving of the noise surrounding most of us as a pollution issue, we might think of it as a dietary problem. Our aural diet is miserable. It's full of over-rich, non-nutritious sounds served in inflated portions—and we don't consume nearly enough silence. A poor diet kills; but it kills as much because of what it does not contain as from what it includes. For this reason, we approach the challenge of correcting unhealthy eating habits differently than we do that of plugging the chimney on a factory. When we educate children about diet, we talk not only about the hazards of fast food but also about the benefits of healthy nutriments. Why can't we do the same with quiet?

We talk a great deal about the terrible dangers of loud noise—so much so that the young tune out the din of the negative message. We are almost silent about the benefits of silence. Yet we already know a great deal about what these are from both a scientific and humanistic perspective. Why can't we begin introducing some of what we already know about silence into public education, while working to expand our knowledge of its desirable effects?

As I learned everywhere from rural Iowa to exurban Florida to England and New York, our schools are filled with an entire generation for whom, especially among those from difficult socioeconomic backgrounds, there is simply no positive experience of silence. I have a friend named Lyman Casey who teaches math in a public high school in Brooklyn. It's considered a good school in a tough stretch of town. Casey and I have had a number of conversations about the struggle he's undergone trying to cajole and discipline his students into being quiet for even a single moment. This is not an issue of authority. Casey is six foot five, a basketball player, and a natural leader. It is a matter, he told me, of kids literally not knowing what it means to be quiet.

Casey was fortunate to spend a good deal of his youth outside in nature. It troubles him no end that his students have nothing equivalent in their own lives to fall back on as a source of inner strength. After our conversations, he began trying, now and then, to impose a moment of silence on his classes. To begin with, it was tough going. The kids would last about twenty seconds before one of them made a crack, or cracked up, or simply forgot to be quiet and shot off a remark to someone, whereupon the whole class would explode back into noise. However, one day near the end of the school year Casey finally succeeded in coaxing a full two minutes of quiet out of a group of tenth graders. At the end of this time, he said to the class, "Now wasn't that nice? You see how it can be positive and meaningful to take a moment to enjoy silence." His students just stared at him. "Why?" one of them finally asked. "Why is it positive or meaningful?" "They had *no idea* what I was talking about," Casey told me. "And yet they were curious."

I confess that I found this story hard to believe. So I asked if he would help me conduct a little experiment. I requested that he ask his students to think of one moment of silence that had been meaningful in their lives. Then I went to the school to hear for myself what they had to say.

Five minutes into our discussion, I was overcome with emotion. But not for the reasons I'd anticipated. Out of the ten students who talked to me about experiences of silence, *nine* described situations in which they'd been unable or unwilling to speak because of overpowering anguish. One talked about the period after his mother died when he had to go and live with his father, whose attention he could never get. He didn't speak to anyone but his closest friends for months, he said, and was ultimately forced by the school into therapy. Another said that when he was six years old his stepfather hit his mother and that for several months thereafter he didn't talk to anyone because he didn't know how to verbalize the experience. Another described the silence he fell into after his older brother was killed in a gang fight and his father came home weeping. Another talked about how his mother became ill and had to undergo an operation, and how when that was happening he didn't want to speak to a single person in the world. For each of these young people, the idea of silence had one association: a tragic, or at least extremely disturbing, event that left them bereft of words. The sole exception was a young woman who described how when her beloved grandmother "passed," she stepped out of the funeral and suddenly everything became completely silent. People were all around her, but she couldn't hear anything. She thought there was something wrong with her. She turned back toward the church and saw her grandmother standing on the steps above her. Her grandmother smiled without saying anything. Then her grandmother disappeared and she could hear again.

Surely, as a society, we owe these young people a wider association with the idea of silence than the ones these painful memories convey.

After the initial round of comments, a few students acknowledged that silence could be good, that it could give one a chance to think and allow one to relax. But none of them had specific recollections of this sort of silence. When I asked them to describe a place they went to when they wanted quiet, several of them spoke about closing themselves inside their rooms and playing a computer game or turning on the television. As for their school environment, all of the students described it as "very loud." One young man, who said he talked all the time, declared, "I can't go quiet in a loud environment, so I fall into the habit of my environment!"

On the other side of Brooklyn is a private Quaker Friends School. From the time they are in preschool, right on through high school, students are made to take moments of silence as a part of their everyday learning experience. They learn how to be quiet from the start of their education, and to understand why that experience is enriching. Jonathan Edmonds, an elementary-school teacher who has taught at Friends for seven years, told me that what makes the silence work is "practice, and a lot of it." Although he is not himself a Quaker, Edmonds has found the silence "an important part of the school day and a huge part of what's missing from many classrooms. Just the stopping and slowing down. The simplicity of silence helps kids get the right ordering of things. It's the reflective element that's sadly missing from so much of what we do." He believes that the reflection that comes with silence helps children understand that "less is more" and builds their social conscience. He attributes the success of Friends at inculcating these values not to discipline per se but to the school's own priorities, which it is able to establish free from the oversight of the city's Department of Education. "I know from colleagues who've taught in the public schools about the insanity of public-school testing today," he said. "That leaves *no time* for deep, contemplative personal thought."

It's the old distraction of obsessive measurement at work once again.

᚛

When people speak of changing the way Americans eat, they understand that the transformation will depend on both education and the availability of healthier food options. As we know, in many poorer neighborhoods the options outside of the fast-food chains are minimal. Exactly the same dynamic holds sway in the

sonic realm. If we want more people to appreciate the importance of silence, we have to create more affordable environments
in which to enjoy it.

I cherish the memory of the time I spent on a silent retreat at
an ashram, gazing at a group of people scattered across a grassy
hillside like roosting birds—all of them concentrated on doing
nothing but being still and listening to the natural world. But the
people who go to ashrams, vipassana centers, and all the rich
variants of silent-meditation retreats are, for the most part, reasonably well off. Like me, they had the money, the time, or
simply the social context that enabled them to wake up one day
and say to themselves, "You know what? I'm going on a silent retreat." I'm worried about all the people who, for one reason or another, lack the resources to discover what silence can bring.

⬚

We must encourage the kinds of urban-design projects that nurture appreciation of silence. We need more pocket parks. And
bigger parks when the money can be found. But the quiet spaces
we make shouldn't be limited to the outdoors. Why can't we
show a little carnival bravado when it comes to creating silence?
Why not take some of the money seized from drug dealers, gun
runners, and financial crooks and use those funds to buy up a
few dozen fast-food franchises that can be turned into contemporary quiet houses? Not recreation centers or computer labs.
Places open late and early, filled with blank paper and pens,
furnished with a few chairs and tables, pillows, plants—with
no personal sound devices, cell phones, or conversation. Sort of
like secularized Christian Science reading rooms. I'm sure they

would be used and maybe in some cases become places not just of escape but of growth. How much could it cost to try?

Or, for starters, what about taking one evening a week in recreation centers and officially designating them quiet times? Or what about getting a coalition of philanthropists to purchase empty lots and have students build Zen gardens inside them? Or what about starting a foundation that gives scholarships to young people who write essays or create artworks that promote the place of silence and contemplation? What about hosting not just Quiet Parties but quiet walks through our neighborhoods, adventures in silence after dark, and quiet festivals of silent arts? Let's hold a moment of silence in memory of silence! We have to find some means of giving more young people the opportunity of experientially learning why quiet is distinguished, or there will be no distinction between noise and signal left.

THE PURSUIT BEYOND

When I made my pilgrimage to the monastery, I concluded that one value of silence was as a restorative of the unknown. In an age when many of us are searching for a way out of patterns of life we feel we know too well, the value of quiet as a channel to reflection and awe is immense. Yet I felt I had to go out into the world to gain a better sense of what *was* known in order to distinguish between the realm of the heard and the still unheard. So I spoke to scientists who study the evolution of hearing, along with hearing specialists, neuroscientists, and psychologists who look at what happens in the ear and the brain when we perceive sound. The more that I learned about the delicate sensitivity of our hearing and the degree to which survival in the wild has depended for most of history on an ability to remain silent in a world rife with predators, the more it seemed to me that the real mystery lay in why we ever began to be so loud. This brought me to researchers studying animal mating calls and the vocalizations used to scare off rivals. It seemed a natural segue from the noises animals make in sex and battle to that of the noise deriving from our commercial and entertainment sectors. It was this noise that interested me most because it seemed to be the form of clamor that, with all the sound mitigation and regulatory advances made in the past century, remains defiantly on the rise everywhere.

While it's true that traffic is currently the dominant global noise source, it's just possible that one day in the not too distant future the electric car really will dramatically quiet our highways. (Furthermore, the loud noise made by most cars is an unintended by-product of engine operation, not a sought-after effect in itself.) I visited different commercial environments, which many people today decry as being unconscionably loud, to try and grasp their owners' motivation in ratcheting up the volume. Stores and restaurants make noise to seduce us, overstimulate us, and prove they exist. Fear of disappearing, of the stillness of eternity lurking in the recesses of silence is, of course, also a reason that individuals like to hear themselves talk, and turn on a television the moment they walk into an empty room. The people I spent time with whose personal sound devices provide the soundtrack for most of their waking and sometimes their sleeping lives told me that the louder the sound, the more their minds and bodies literally throb to the beat—and the better job it does at blocking out the undesirable distractions both inside and outside of them. For me, the litmus case of noise for noise's sake was the realm of car-audio competition, where what seemed to drive the noise was twofold: a combination of sheer bass sensuality and the fact that most people driving boom cars have spent their lives immersed in the sound of loud traffic. There is a kind of sonic Stockholm syndrome at work in much of the noise of our contemporary world.

From the world of noise I stepped back to look at what people were doing to fight loudness. Soundproofing is more effective than ever before in history, but by and large the better it is, the more expensive it is; and when it's as good as it can get, it serves to isolate its users in a manner that has its own problematic social implications. On the policy front, though I admire the work of many activists fighting noise pollution today, I came away from their struggles feeling that they were fighting a war without winners. However enthusiastic different people I spoke to became about initiatives to quiet individual noise sources like leaf blowers, unmuffled motorcycles, and loud parties, nobody I talked with told me they thought the world in general was becoming a quieter place. Arline Bronzaft has been a dedicated antinoise activist for several decades—she conducted a pioneering study in the 1970s proving the deleterious effect of background subway noise on children's learning abilities, and has advised four New York City mayors on noise policy. When I asked Bronzaft about whether all the hard efforts were paying off in a quieter world, she responded with a question: "Are people getting nicer?" I was silent. "Then you have your answer. Forget planes. Trains. It's cell phones in restaurants. It's your neighbors who won't put some soft covering down on their floor. Noise is getting worse, even though policy gets better."

As I recognized the depth of this conundrum, I began to switch my focus from the battle against noise to the subject of how people succeed in making silence in the world. Here, at last, I found myself filled with excitement and hope. The best of the work being performed today by urbanists, architects, landscape designers, and soundscape experts draws extensively on both advanced techniques of acoustical engineering and the long, rich history of humanity's efforts to construct communal spaces of tranquillity. In the middle of some of the largest, most cacophonous cities in the world, people are managing to produce oases of quiet in which sounds that nurture our sense of peace, compassion, and imagination—like falling water, rustling foliage, and birdsong—become audible again.

In some countries, such as the United Kingdom, people now speak of a quiet-space movement. Nothing holds greater promise for rescuing us from the new noise nightmare. Bronzaft's remarks could be taken to imply that the increasing loudness of the world means that people are actually becoming less nice. They're certainly not going to become any friendlier if the only way they can be persuaded to turn down the sound is by humiliating and litigating them into sullen muteness. Which suggests, as one activist remarked to me, that the problem of forcibly silencing noisemakers will always resemble mole-whacking. When one source is silenced, the problem will morph into new forms as endlessly various as the parade of new gadgets we love to sound off.

The only way out of this bind is to make the pursuit of silence itself a more broadly inviting prospect. The more opportunity there is for people who are being increasingly excluded from silence to feel its influence, the more chance there is that silence will begin to confer its singular graces on society at large. Who knows, given enough quiet time, perhaps people may even find themselves tempted to become a little nicer.

☒

At the end of my journey, I realized that what I meant by the unknown when I sat in the New Melleray Abbey pervades the whole of creation. Before I set out, I would never have imagined that the mammalian middle ear evolved from the jawbone; that the sound of the big bang might resemble a gathering scream; that a tea ceremony could become a theater of silences; or that the Deaf perspective on silence could reveal the possibilities of a more attentive sensory awareness for everyone. I was blessed with the opportunity to go out and listen to a few dozen places, people, and stories that I never dreamed existed.

The French philosopher Maurice Merleau-Ponty writes in his last book that perception is differentiation, while forgetting is nondifferentiation. Earlier I took my stab at a definition of noise: sound that gets into your head and won't go away. It might be enjoyable or not enjoyable, but noise is sound that makes us, for the time it's there, cease to distinguish between the beings and objects outside us. Noise enables us to forget the larger world.

Conversely, if I were to hazard a definition of silence, I would describe it as the particular equilibrium of sound and quiet that catalyzes our powers of perception. Quiet is distinguished because it enables differentiation, and the more we observe the distinction between things, the less mental space we have for our isolate selves. It's not chance that even when we're talking about quieting our own voices, we speak of "observing silence," as though just by being silent we create something to behold beyond the self.

What's unknown, then, is the world around us; what's missing is our awareness that we do not know. Silence as a state of expectancy, a species of attention, is a key back into the garden of innocence. We may not stay. But God knows we listen for the sound of that opening.

Acknowledgments

So many people contributed to this book, both with regard to sharing specific ideas and to clarifying its larger argument, that the book became very much a mosaic of the voices I've had the good fortune to listen to while the work was in progress.

My agent, Scott Moyers, masterfully guided the book through every stage of its development, from helping to shape the initial concept to giving the complete manuscript the kind of exceptionally close scrutiny that enabled me to find its final form. I'm grateful to my editor, Phyllis Grann, whose passion for the subject helped inspire this book. Her singular expertise enabled me to think through many key passages to points of greater resonance. At Doubleday, I'd also like to thank, in particular, Karla Eoff, my admirable copyeditor, along with Jackie Montalvo and Rebecca Holland. On the editorial side, Kathy Robbins gave generously of her time and wisdom as an early supporter of the project. Linnea Covington assisted me with notes for the book with exemplary speed and accuracy.

I had most to learn in the realm of science and, in addition to providing her own manifold insights into different disciplines, Natalie deSouza deftly led me to many of the scientists and research environments that informed my approach to the interplay of noise and silence.

In terms of the mechanism of the ear, the biophysics of hearing, sensory neuroscience, and evolutionary psychology, a number of researchers and doctors helped me repeatedly and were inestimably important to the composition of the book. I'm especially indebted to Jim Hudspeth, Andy Niemiec, Thomas Roland, Mario Svirsky, and Rickye Heffner. Michael Merzenich, Kachar Bechara, Lucy Jane Miller, Yehoash Rafael, Andrew King, Barbara Shinn-Cunningham, Roberto Arrighi, Brian Fligor, Alan Gertner, and Robert W. Sweetow also provided me with valuable insights. Various researchers into animal hearing and vocalization further expanded my thinking about the relationship between noise and silence from a biological survival perspective. Gregory McDaniels, Karen Warkentin, Peter Narins, Albert Feng, Elisabetta Vannoni, Alan G. McElligott, and Heather Williams were particularly important sources in this regard.

With respect to the effects of silent meditation and silence on the brain, Lidia Glodzik-Sobanska helped me begin to understand the relevant neurological processes. The research findings of Vinod Menon were critical to the initial development of my argument. I'd also like to thank his colleague at Stanford Jonathan Berger. David Huron, Julie Brefczynski-Lewis, and Mony de Leon were additional important sources of insight. I'm grateful to Nadine Woloshin for having connected me with the Center for Brain Health at the New York City University School of Medicine. Mark Rosekind gave me grounding in the potential affinities between certain stages of sleep and silence from a neurological perspective.

My education into acoustics, the physics of sound, and the relationship of music to the ideas of noise and silence began with several compelling lessons from Daniel Gaydos. Tomlinson Holman, Nico Muhly, Roger Morgan, Christopher Jaffe, Otts Munderloh, Jim Holt, Gregory Stanford, David Sonneschein, Leanne Flask, Doug Manvell, Wade Bray, Karl Luttinger, Jim Weir, William Egan, and Richard Danielson also contributed to my thoughts in this area.

Many people in Florida and elsewhere around the country helped me fathom the logistics and lure of car audio competition. I want to thank in particular Buzz Thompson, Casey Sullivan, Robin Butler, Tommy McKinnie, Chris Hayes, and Jean Hayes. Amy Grace Loyd and Bryan Abrams helped me shape and fact check an earlier draft of my account of the Memorial Day competition at Explosive Sound and Video.

In exploring the world of noise policy, antinoise activism, and the new medical research that helps to fuel these initiatives, I'm thankful for the incisive help given me by Rokhu Kim, Colin Nugent, John Hinton, Arline Bronzaft, Catrice Jefferson, Val Wheedon, Irene van Kamp, and Christian Popp. Wolfgang Babisch, Michael Jasny, Michael Saucier, Dieter Schwela, and Ken Feith also broadened my understanding of core noise policy and noise health issues. I want to thank the organizers of Noise-Con 2008 (sponsored by INCE, the Institute of Noise Control Engineering), and ICBEN (the International Commission on the Biological Effects of Noise) 2008 Congress, for helping to facilitate my participation in these events. Thanks, as well, to Carol Hurley and Robert King.

In the realm of soundscaping and quiet space initiatives I benefited immeasurably from Max Dixon's depth of understanding and experience in the field. I'm also grateful to Colin Grimshaw, who first spoke to me about quiet space projects in England. Together with his very helpful colleague Claire Shepherd, Colin arranged an enlightening tour of London soundscapes, as well as a fascinating discussion under the auspices of the Greater London Authority with Max Dixon and others working to improve the soundscape in different London boroughs. I'm grateful to Yvette Bosworth for putting me in contact with Colin. Paul Jennings also gave me insights into the relationship between soundscaping and industry.

Andrew Pollack, Jason Everman, John Spencer, Suni Williams, and Robert Hayes Parton each kindly shared compelling stories of their own experiences with noise and silence that found their way into the book. I'm grateful to David Kaiser for having brought my interest in silence to the attention of Robert Hayes Parton.

Alfonse Borysewickz not only introduced me to many ideas of Christianity and silence, and shared personal stories with me, but was also my link to Father Alberic Farbolin and New Melleray. Father Alberic gave graciously of his time and insights into the theological significance of silence in general, and silence in the monastic experience in particular, while I was staying at New Melleray. I also want to thank at New Melleray, in particular, Father Brendan Freeman (Abbot), Father Neil Paquette, Father Paul Andrews Tanner, and Brother Felix Leja. Father David

Fleming and Brother Stephen Markham, both of whom work in the community beyond New Melleray, also gave me valuable insights.

Many thanks to Nancy Black and the other participants in the Brooklyn Monthly Meeting of the Religious Society of Friends whom I had the good fortune to meet. I also appreciate the hospitality extended me by the monks of Little Portion Friary, where I stayed early in my research.

Marco Roth was one of the first people to help me find a foothold in understanding the place of Zen Buddhism in contemporary American society. Gene Lushtak, Kris Bailey, Amber Vovola, Joan Suval, and the participants in the silent retreat she conducted at Ananda Ashram expanded my knowledge of the practice and potential of Zen and silent meditation. I'm deeply grateful to Virginia Harmon for introducing me to the place of silence in Zen gardens. David MacLaren helped me understand the creation of these gardens from a practical standpoint.

Hansel Bauman and Robert Sirvage gave me many critical insights into the Deaf experience of architecture in general and the aspirations of Deaf Space in particular. Also at Gallaudet, Dirk Bauman and Ben Bahan both expanded my knowledge of the rich context for ideas I was beginning to explore in relationship to the Deaf community and the cultural significance of Deaf visual acuity. I'm also thankful for the comments of Fred Weiner, Summer Crider, Josh Swiller, Michael Chorost, Erin Kelly, Adam Greenleaf, and Michael Hubbs. Nancy O'Donnell kindly arranged my initial visit to the Helen Keller National Center for Deaf-Blind Youths and Adults, which was my entry point into the world of Deaf experience. I'm grateful for the time and insights given me there by James Feldmann, Kathy Anello, Don Duvo, and Susan Shapiro. Susan put me in touch with Toni Lacolucci, whose inspiring strength of character and compelling thoughts on the experience of noise and silence, both when she was hearing and after she became Deaf, were vital to this book.

Claire Benard was the ideal guide to the world of noise and silence in the laboratory, and the quiet enthusiasm of her colleague, Luisa Cochella, for the sounds of their exacting work helped define this moment for me.

My education into the problem of noise in the education system and the potential of silence in the classroom was facilitated by the unstinting assistance of Lyman Casey. I'm also grateful to the many colleagues of Lyman who weighed in on their own experiences of the noise problem in the public schools. Jonathan Edmonds provided important viewpoints on this subject from the perspective of the Quaker education system. Above all I want to thank the students of Brooklyn Preparatory High School who shared their poignant stories with a candor and immediacy that brought home to me the imperative of extending the "right to silence" beyond those environments in which silence is customarily nurtured today.

In thinking about the relevance of Theodor Lessing's work to our contemporary noise dilemma, I was greatly helped by the generosity and scholarship of John Goodyear, who uncovered evidence that Lessing offered Rice the leadership of his organization. Paul Reitter also contributed to my understanding of Lessing's work.

Many friends told wonderful stories of their own experiences with noise and silence, in addition to giving me books to read and pointing me in important directions for further research. I'm especially grateful to Adam Cvijanovic, Frederick Kaufman, Elizabeth Berger, Lawrence Osborne, Paul Holdengraber, Barbara Wansbrough, Alexandra deSousa, Wayne Koestenbaum, Steve Marchetti, Shari Spiegel, Alan Berliner, Laura Kipnis, Richard Cohen, Anne LaFond, Tim Gilman, Arnon Grunberg, Inigo Thomas, Katherine Barrett, Benjamin Swett, Jonathan Nossiter, Michael Greenberg, Danielle McConnell, Christopher McConnell, Jenifer Nields, Nila Friedberg, Jim Holt, Raymond Teets, Wolfgang Schivelbusch, William Kolbrenner, Sina Najafi, Sandra Kogut, and Tom Levin. Thanks, also, to Julie Goldberg.

My family all gave me unflagging support throughout the long spells of silence and of noise in which the book was gestating. Ethan Prochnik, James Jodha-Prochnik, Samoa Jodha, and Elisabeth Prochnik each opened my eyes to pertinent subjects that deepened the book. Barbara and Brian Mead taught me much about the quiet refuge that can still be found in the English seaside. My parents, Marian and Martin Prochnik, offered the profound encouragement and love that nourishes all my writing. My children, Yona, Tzvi, Zach, and Rafael are an unremitting source of inspiration—and perspective. Watching them grow up concretizes my thoughts on the boundless possibility of the unknown.

My wife, Rebecca Mead, kept up a sustaining faith throughout the writing of this book that surpasses expression. Her editorial acumen sharpened and enriched the book throughout, just as her enthusiasm for the project made the writing of it possible. Her love gives pause to all the noise.

Notes

Introduction

4   *"The men whose labors"*: *Saia v. People of State of New York*, 334 U.S. 558 (1948), http://caselaw.lp.findlaw.com/cgi-bin/getcase.pl?court= US&vol=334&invol=558.

7   *"sometimes you feel everyone"*: Dr. Nancy Black and other members of the Brooklyn Friends Society at the Meeting House, interviews by author, spring 2008.

8   *"thin voice of silence"*: 1 Kings 19:11–12.

9   *"and when you have"*: Sunita L. Williams, interview by author, spring 2008.

10   *The night pass is*: Williams, e-mail to author.

10   *"the valleys echoed the sound"*: Henry David Thoreau, *A Week on the Concord and Merrimack Rivers*, Robert F. Sayer, ed. (New York: Literary Classics of America, Inc., 1985), 317–18.

11   *"Here, I can show you"*: Dr. Mario Svirsky, interview by author, summer 2008. I interviewed Svirsky on several occasions and he broadened my understanding both of how we process speech and of the complex history of cochlear implants.

12   *The roots of our English term*: John Ayto, *Dictionary of Word Origins* (New York: Arcade Publishing, 1990), 477.

13   *"Sound imposes a narrative"*: Adam Cvijanovic, interview by author, summer 2008.

13   *Recent studies using fMRI*: J. A. Brefczynski-Lewis et al., "Neural Correlates of Attentional Expertise in Long-term Meditation Practitioners," *Proceedings of the National Academy of Sciences* 104, 27 (July 3, 2007).

14   *Neuroscientists at Stanford*: Devarajan Sridharan et al., "Neural Dynamics of Event Segmentation in Music: Converging Evidence for Dissociable Ventral and Dorsal Networks," *Neuron* 55, 3 (August 2, 2007).

14   *affinities between certain stages*: Mark Rosekind, e-mail to author, winter 2009.

15   *45,000 fatal heart attacks*: Dieter Schwela, e-mail to author, fall 2009.

15   *A study released by the Johns Hopkins University*: Andrew Stern, "U.S. Facing Possible Hearing Loss Epidemic," *Reuters*, July 28, 2008.

16   *"Anytime you can hear"*: Tom Roland, interview by author, winter 2008. Roland met with me on several occasions and he vastly expanded my knowledge of the mechanism of human hearing, hearing loss, and cochlear implants.

16   *You can buy a Hannah Montana*: Today@UCI, "Greater Parental Guidance Suggested for Noisy Toy Use," http://archive.today.uci.edu/news/release_detail.asp?key=1702.

16   *one summer weekend*: John Spencer, interview by author, June 27, 2008.

20   *"Silence is not a function"*: Gene Lushtak, interviews by author, summer and fall 2008.

Chapter One: Listening for the Unknown

23   *"to be silent and listen"*: Saint Benedict, *The Rule of Saint Benedict*, Timothy Fry, ed. (New York: Vintage, 1998), 16.

25   *"entered the monastery to stay"*: Brother Alberic, interview by author. Alberic received permission from the abbot to speak with me over the course of my stay at the monastery in the winter of 2008—and

gave generously of his time. I also engaged in a lengthy e-mail exchange with him after I left New Melleray.

28   *at least one interfaith:* Integral Yoga Programs, "Ten-Day Silent Retreat: Awakening to the Inner Light," http://www.integralyogaprograms .org/ product_info.php?products_id=309.

28   *"Soothe the spirit":* Spa at the Cove, http://www.spaatthecove.com/.

28   *Gene Lushtak and:* Gene Lushtak, interview by author, summer 2008.

28   *in the Bay Area:* Patricia Leigh Brown, "In the Classroom, a New Focus on Quieting the Mind," *New York Times,* June 16, 2007.

29   *When I called her:* Kris Bailey, interview by author, winter 2009.

30   *"to place himself more intensely":* André Louf, *The Cistercian Way* (Kalamazoo, MI: Cistercian Publications, Inc., 1983), 60.

30   *"Just as, if you":* Peter France, *Hermits: The Insights of Solitude* (New York: St. Martin's Press, 1996), 29.

30   *spent three years:* Benedicta Ward, *The Desert Fathers: Sayings of the Early Christian Monks,* revised edition (New York: Penguin Classics, 2003), 2.

31   *"Go and sit in thy cell":* Ibid., 27.

31   *A sniper named Robert:* Robert Hayes Parton, e-mail to David Kaiser, winter 2009.

32   *doctrine of* tsimtsum: Gershom Scholem, *On the Kabbalah and Its Symbolism,* Ralph Manheim, trans. (New York: Schocken Books, 1965), 110–11.

32   *guardian angels used:* Avraham Yaakov Finkel, *Kabbalah: Selections from Classic Kabbalistic Works from Raziel HaMalach to the Present Day* (Southfield, MI: Targum Press, Inc., 2002), 203–7.

32   *"I can hardly open up my mouth":* Lawrence Fine, *Safed Spirituality: Rules of Mystical Piety, the Beginnings of Wisdom* (Mahwah, NJ: Paulist Press, 1984), 62.

33   *"How did He produce":* cited by Gershom Scholem in *Origins of the Kabbalah,* R. J. Zwi Werblowsky, ed., and Allan Arkush, trans. (Princeton, NJ: Princeton University Press, 1990), 450.

34   *"mazes of silence":* Arthur Green, *Tormented Master: The Life and Spiritual Quest of Rabbi Nahman of Bratslav* (Woodstock, VT: Jewish Lights Printing, 1992), 317.

34   *"Sometimes when I'm silent"*: Alfonse Borysewickz, interview by author, fall 2008. I had multiple interviews and e-mail exchanges with Borysewickz that were important to my understanding of the place of silence in Christian theology.

34   *"By the end"*: Amber Vovola, interview by author, winter 2008.

35   *"an enormous downstream"*: Lidia Glodzik-Sobanska, interview by author, winter 2008. In addition to several interviews with Glodzik-Sobanska, we carried on an e-mail exchange that was critical to my understanding of the neurological effects of silence.

37   *"allure her, and speak"*: Louf, 60.

37   *Silent Widows*: "Women Who Prefer Silence," *New York Times*, September 20, 1908.

38   *Rancé had been a dazzling*: Patrick Leigh Fermor, *A Time to Keep Silence* (New York: New York Review Books Classics, 2007), 52–59.

39   *copying the angels*: Scott G. Bruce, *Silence and Sign Language in Medieval Monasticism: The Cluniac Tradition. c. 900–1200* (Cambridge: Cambridge University Press, 2007), 25–28.

39   *"As the great clock of St. Mark"*: William S. Walsh, *Curiosities of Popular Customs and of Rites, Ceremonies, Observances, and Miscellaneous Antiquities* (Philadelphia: J. B. Lippincott Company, 1897), 190.

40   *"Glorious and Immortal"*: Dr. Adrian Gregory, "The Silence and the History," in Jonty Semper, *Kenotaphion* (Charm, 2001). This is an official recording of silent remembrances.

40   *"Its impressiveness is intensified"*: Ibid.

41   *But an oral history*: Benedict Julian Hussman, "Voices from the Cloister; Oral Perspectives on the Recent History of New Melleray Abbey," master's thesis (University of Northern Iowa, August 1989).

42   *75 percent of farmworkers*: "Listen to the Warnings," *Missouri Soybean Farmer* (January 2004).

45   *"Let us sacrifice"*: Pieter W. van der Horst, "Silent Prayer in Antiquity," *Numen* 4 (1994).

45   *"Whereof one cannot"*: Ludwig Wittgenstein, *Tractatus Logico-Philosophicus*, trans. C. K. Ogden (New York: Routledge and Kegan Paul Ltd., 1933), 189.

45   *"Above all, silence about"*: Martin Heidegger, *On the Way to Language*, Peter D. Hertz, trans. (San Francisco: HarperSanFrancisco, 1971), 52.

45   *"silence points to a state"*: Max Picard, *The World of Silence*, Stanley Godwin, trans. (Wichita, KS: Eighth Day Press, 2002), 20.

46   *The Apaches, among other:* Keith Basso, " 'To Give Up on Words': Silence in Western Apache Culture," in *A Cultural Approach to Interpersonal Communication: Essential Readings*, Leila Monaghan and Jane Goodman, eds. (Malden, MA: Blackwell Publishing, 2007), 77–87.

46   *tradition of the "dumb cake":* Walsh, 350–52.

46   *In the eighteenth-century:* Lucinda Lee Orr, *Journal of a Young Lady of Virginia* (Baltimore, MD: John Murphy and Company, 1871), 44.

46   *"Dumb Suppers":* Janice Van Cleve, "Traditions of the Dumb Supper," *Widdershins* 7, 5 (October 2007), http://www.widdershins.org/vol7 iss5/02.htm.

49   *Menon discovered that:* Angela Castellanos, "Mapping the Brain's Response to Music: fMRI Studies of Musical Expectations," *Stanford Scientific Magazine* (February 17, 2008).

49   *"Silence is golden":* Vinod Menon, interview by author at Third Annual Symposium on Music and the Brain, Stanford University, May 16–17, 2008. Interview on May 17.

Chapter Two: Why We Hear

51   *"You hear a snap":* Dr. Rickye Heffner, interview by author, spring 2008. I had several phone interviews and multiple e-mail exchanges with Heffner. Her assistance was vital to my understanding of the evolution of hearing in general and sound localization in particular.

53   *"The Evolution of Human Hearing":* Bruce Masterton, Henry Heffner, and Richard Ravizza, "The Evolution of Human Hearing," *Journal of the Acoustical Society of America* 45, 4 (1969): 966–85.

54   *"sound shadow":* S. S. Stevens and Fred Warshofsky, *Sound and Hearing* (New York: Time Incorporated, 1965), 102–3.

56   *The outer-ear channels:* Dr. Tom Roland, interview by author, winter 2009.

57   *huge "power gain":* Dr. Jim Hudspeth, interview by author, winter 2008.

59   *"become adjusted to"*: Morris Kaplan, "Surgeon to Study Noise-Free Tribe," *New York Times*, December 4, 1960.

59   *"Two Mabaans standing"*: Robert E. Tomasson, "Surgeon Suggests Hearing Tests May Help to Diagnose Heart Ills," *New York Times*, October 27, 1963.

60   *"totally tuned in"*: Jason Everman, interview by author, winter 2008.

65   *made a remarkable discovery*: Zhe-Xi Luo et al., "A New Eutricon-odont Mammal and Evolutionary Development in Early Mammals," *Nature* 446 (March 15, 2007), http://www.nature.com/nature/journal/v446/n7133/full/nature05627.html.

65   *"What was most revealing"*: Zhe-Xi Luo, interview by author, spring 2008.

65   *"I bite my teeth"*: Randall Stross, "Edison the Inventor, Edison the Showman," *New York Times*, March 11, 2007.

66   *"almost direct to my brain"*: George Bryan, *Edison: The Man and His Work* (Whitefish, MT: Kessinger Publishing, 2007), 102.

Chapter Three: Why We Are Noisy

69   *"Hitler sound waves"*: "Professor Says Hitler Hypnotizes Listeners with Voice at 228 Vibrations a Second," *New York Times*, December 29, 1938.

70   *had a voice double*: "The Voice of Hitler," *New York Times*, April 19, 1944.

70   *The American National Broadcasting Company*: "Adolf Hitler's Address on His War Aims Before the German Reichstag," *New York Times*, October 7, 1939. Charts reproduced with text.

70   *"The sexes of many animals"*: Charles Darwin, *The Expression of the Emotions in Man and Animals* (Chicago: University of Chicago Press, 1965), 84.

71   *"What are myna birds"*: Heather Williams, interview by author, summer 2008.

71   *has been constructing sonograms*: Eugene S. Morton, "Animal Communication: What Do Animals Say?" *The American Biology Teacher* 45, 6 (October 1983): 343–48; and Eugene S. Morton, "On the Oc-

currence and Significance of Motivation-Structural Rules in Some Bird and Mammal Sounds," *The American Naturalist* 111, 981 (September–October 1977): 855–69.

72 *"cat-and-dog squabble"*: Herbert N. Casson, *The History of the Telephone* (Chicago: A. C. McClurg & Co., 1910), 153–55.

73 *Researchers from the University of Zurich*: Elisabetta Vannoni and Alan G. McElligott, "Low Frequency Groans Indicate Larger and More Dominant Fallow Deer (*Dama dama*) Males," *PloS One* 3, 9 (September 2008): 1–8.

73 *At the peak of the rut*: Elisabetta Vannoni, e-mail to author, summer 2009.

73 *with significant traffic noise*: Kirsten M. Parris, Meah Velik-Lord, and Joanne M. A. North, "Frogs Call at a Higher Pitch in Traffic Noise," *Ecology and Society* 14, 1 (2009), http://www.ecologyandsociety.org/vol14/iss1/art25/.

74 *has tied the vulnerable submissiveness*: John J. Ohala, "The Acoustic Origin of the Smile," *Journal of the Acoustical Society of America* 68, S1 (November 1980): S33.

74 *"the more likely it is"*: John J. Ohala, "The Frequency Code Underlies the Sound-Symbolic use of Voice Pitch," in *Sound Symbolism*, Leanne Hinton, Johanna Nichols, and John J. Ohala, eds. (Cambridge: Cambridge University Press, 2006), 325–47.

74 *Since we are biologically*: Reuven Tsur, "Size-Sound Symbolism Revisited," *Journal of Pragmatics* 38 (2006): 905–24.

74 *object called a "bull-roarer"*: Mircea Eliade, *Patterns of Comparative Religion*, Rosemary Sheed, trans. (New York: Sheed & Ward, 1958), 41–42.

74 *"It's all about pecking order"*: David Huron, interview by author at the Third Annual Symposium on Music and the Brain, Stanford University, May 16–17, 2008.

75 *"Sound is a brute force"*: Daniel Gaydos, interview by author, summer 2008. Gaydos and I spoke on several occasions after my initial interview with him, and he was an immense help to me in understanding the physics of sound and human sound perception.

77 *the brains of many ADD*: Dr. Kenny Handelman, "White Noise Helps

with Concentration in ADD/ADHD," The ADD ADHD Blog, September 2007, http://www.addadhdblog.com/white-noise-helps-with-concentration-in-addadhd.

77   *already disordered cognitive*: Chris Chatham, "When Noise Helps: Stochastic Resonance and ADHD," Developing Intelligence Blog, September 21, 2007, http://scienceblogs.com/developingintelligence/2007/09/when_noise_helps_stochastic_re_1.php; and Lucy Jane Miller, interview by author, fall 2009.

78   *When you play two notes*: For example, see Jamie James, *The Music of the Spheres: Music, Science, and the Natural Order of the Universe* (New York: Springer-Verlag, 1995), 33–35.

79   *The Pythagorean moment*: M. F. Burnyeat, "Other Lives," *London Review of Books*, February 22, 2007.

79   *Pythagoras compared the entire*: Marc Lachièze-Rey and Jean-Pierre Luminet, *Celestial Treasury: From the Music of the Spheres to the Conquest of Space*, Joe Laredo, trans. (Cambridge: Cambridge University Press, 2001), 61.

79   *Apollo, the sun God*: Edith Wysse, *The Myth of Apollo and Marsyas in the Art of the Italian Renaissance* (Cranbury, NJ: Associated University Presses, 1996), 27–28.

79   *Augustine added a Christian framework*: Brian Brennan, "Augustine's 'De musica,'" *Vigilae Christianae* 42, 3 (September 1988): 267–81.

80   *In the summer of 2008*: David Ian Miller, "Move Over Madonna," *SF Gate*, July 28, 2008, http://www.sfgate.com/cgi-bin/article.cgi?f=/g/a/2008/ 07/28/findrelig.DTL.

80   *"the regular breathing"*: Aristotle A. Esguerra, "Gregorian Chanting Can Reduce Blood Pressure and Stress," *Daily Mail*, May 2, 2008.

81   *"We love similarity"*: Umberto Eco, *Art and Beauty in the Middle Ages* (New Haven, CT: Yale University Press, 1986), 31.

81   *A contemporary sound designer*: David Sonneschein, interview by author, spring 2009.

83   *"There's the base frequency"*: Andy Niemiec, interview by author, winter 2008. In addition to our initial interview, Niemiec and I had an e-mail exchange that was an inestimable help to me in under-

standing many aspects of how the brain maps sound waves. He also pointed me to many references that were vital to my research.

83 *Recently a few researchers*: Sukhbinder Kumar et al., "Mapping Un-pleasantness of Sounds to Their Auditory Representation," *Journal of Acoustical Society of America* 124, 6 (December 2008): 3810–17.

85 *"at all of his public"*: "Hitler at the Top of His Dizzy Path," *New York Times,* February 5, 1933.

86 *"almost apocalyptic vision"*: Leni Riefenstahl, *Leni Riefenstahl: A Memoir* (New York: Picador, 1992), 101.

86 *"no part catching up"*: Mark Whittle, "Primal Scream: Sounds from the Big Bang," http://www.astro.virginia.edu/~dmw8f/griffith05/griffith .html.

Chapter Four: Retail: The Soundtrack

89 *"It's so difficult getting"*: Michael Morrison, interview by author, spring 2008.

89 *"Right?" Leanne Flask*: Leanne Flask, interview by author, summer 2008. She was my guide to Barton Creek Square mall. She also gave generously of her time for several phone interviews and e-mail exchanges.

90 *"relax in the noise of familiars"*: Irving Howe, *World of Our Fathers* (New York: Galahad Books, 1994), 257.

91 *"unnecessary rackets"*: "Mrs. Rice Seeks Noise; And Finds It, Plenty of It, on the East Side," *New York Times*, November 7, 1908.

91 *"only a few sentimental"*: "East Side Pushcart Market About to Van-ish," *New York Times*, January 5, 1940.

95 *"feel its sounds"*: Ker Than, "Stone Age Art Caves May Have Been Concert Halls," *National Geographic News*, July 2, 2008.

96 *"even in a place unsuited"*: Iegor Reznikoff, "On the Sound Dimen-sion of Prehistoric Painted Caves and Rocks," in *Musical Signification: Essays on the Semiotic Theory and Analysis of Music*, Eero Tarasti, ed. (Berlin: Mouton de Gruyter, 1995), 547.

96 *his whole body vibrating*: Iegor Reznikoff, "On Primitive Elements of Musical Meaning," *JMM: The Journal of Music and Meaning* 3 (Fall

2004/Winter 2005), http://www.musicandmeaning.net/issues/show Article.php?artID=3.2.

97 *moving in synchrony*: Scott S. Wiltermuth and Chip Heath, "Synchrony and Cooperation," *Psychological Science* 3, 2 (2009): 3.

98 *from January 1939*: "Pier Equipped for Music Night and Day to Make Longshoremen Work Happily," *New York Times*, January 29, 1939.

98 *"riveting to rhythm"*: F. H. McConnell, "Riveting to Rhythm," *New York Times*, August 31, 1941.

99 *number-two complaint*: Nicholas Sampogna, of *Zagat Survey*, provided me with statistical data from Zagat indicating the prevalence of different complaints of restaurant patrons over multiple years.

99 *a "double bomb" rating*: Michael Bauer, "Is Noise Hazardous to Your Health," Between Meals blog, posted August 16, 2007, http://www.sfgate.com/cgi=bin/blogs/mbauer/detail?blogid=26&entry_id=19428.

100 *The first rigorous study*: Ronald E. Milliman, "The Influence of Background Music on the Behaviour of Restaurant Patrons," *Journal of Consumer Research* 13 (September 1986): 286–89.

100 *at Fairfield University*: Vincent Bozzi, "Eat to the Beat," *Psychology Today* 20 (February 1986): 16.

100 *Dick Clark's American Bandstand Grill*: Andrea Petersen, "Restaurants: Restaurants Bring In da Noise to Keep Out da Nerds," *The Wall Street Journal*, December 30, 1997.

100 *researchers at the Université de Bretagne-Sud*: Nicholas Guéguen et al., "Sound Level of Environmental Music and Drinking Behavior: A Field Experiment with Beer Drinkers," *Alcoholism: Clinical and Environmental Research* 32, 10 (October 2008).

101 *heightens the effect of MDMA*: Michelangelo Iannone et al., "Electrocortical Effects of MDMA Are Potentiated by Acoustic Stimulation in Rats," *BMC Neuroscience* 7, 13 (February 16, 2006).

101 *A group of men*: C. Ferber and M. Cabanac, "Influence of Noise on Gustatory Affective Ratings and Preference for Sweet or Salt," *Appetite* 8, 3 (June 1987): 229–35.

102 *eat potato chips*: Massimiliano Zampini and Charles Spence,

"The Role of Auditory Cues in Modulating the Perceived Crispness and Staleness of Potato Chips," *Journal of Sensory Studies* 19, 5 (October 2004): 347–63.

102 *"one of the loudest places"*: Marc Weizer, "Tiger Stadium One of Loudest Places in Nation," *Athens Banner-Herald*, October 23, 2008.

102 Sports Illustrated *put Arrowhead:* Wikipedia, Arrowhead Stadium, http://armchairgm.wikia.com/Arrowhead_Stadium

102 *"it scared the hell"*: Frank Schwab, "Visitors Not Welcome/Rowdy Fans in the 'Black Hole' Make Games," *The Gazette*, November 30, 2003.

103 *reached 127.2 decibels:* MCT News Service, "Autzen is a nightmare for opposing teams; can USC handle hostile Oregon crowd?" *Daily Press*, October 28, 2009.

103 *loudest roofed stadium: Sports Illustrated*, photo gallery, http://sports illustrated.cnn.com/vault/topic/video/Qwest_Field/1900-01-01/2100-12-31/8/376/index.htm.

103 *eleven false-start:* John Branch, "For N.F.L., Crowd Noise Is a Headache" *New York Times*, September 24, 2006.

103 *"That place had to be miked up"*: "In Seattle, 49ers Must Deal with Crowd Noise," *The Mercury News*, September 13, 2008.

104 *"The building doesn't make"*: Jack Wrightson, interview by author, fall 2008.

104 *It's also every electronic:* Doug Robinson, "Games Have Gotten Way Too Loud," *Deseret News*, May 27, 2008.

105 *"right in your ear"*: Judy Battista, "Colts' Crowd Noise Is 'Like a Loud Train That Never Stops,' " *New York Times*, January 15, 2006.

Chapter Five: Sounds Like Noise

107 *"We're pattern recognizers"*: Wade Bray, interview by author, spring 2008.

108 *affiliated with Boston University:* Karen M. Warkentin, "How Do Embryos Assess Risk? Vibrational Cues in Predator-Induced Hatching of Red-eyed Treefrogs," *Animal Behaviour* 70, 1 (July 2, 2005): 59–71.

109   *"The army told me"*: Dr. J. Gregory McDaniel, interview by author, spring 2009. McDaniel gave a compelling talk on his research on April 24, 2009 at the Waves and Signs conference at MIT and also provided me with a number of papers by him and his colleagues that gave me further insight into communication and sound perception among frogs and frog embryos.

109   *At a meeting*: "Roar of Cities Has Musical Undertone," *New York Times*, January 4, 1931.

113   *a series of extraordinary*: Warren Moscow, "Protests Cause End Tonight of Grand Central Broadcasts," *New York Times*, January 2, 1950.

Chapter Six: Silent Interlude

118   *the old Stork Club*: Ralph Blumenthal, "Paley Is Donating a Vest-Pocket Park to the City on Stork Club Site," *New York Times*, February 2, 1967.

118   *"a corner of quiet delights"*: Jack Manning, "Tiny Paley Park Opens with a Splash," *New York Times*, May 24, 1967.

118   *"acoustic perfume"*: "To Reduce City's Din," *New York Times*, June 5, 1967.

119   *Jacob Riis is credited*: Thomas P. F. Hoving, "Think Big About Small Parks," *New York Times*, April 10, 1966.

120   *"sit-ability"*: William H. Whyte, "Please Just a Nice Place to Sit," *New York Times*, December 3, 1972.

121   *John Evelyn, the seventeenth-century*: Gilbert Chinard, "The American Philosophical Society and the Early History of Forestry in America," *American Philosophical Society Proceedings* 89, 2 (July 1945).

122   *Deaf man watching*: Michael Fried, *Absorption and Theatricality* (Chicago: University of Chicago Press, 1980), 78.

122   *"an unbearable racket"*: Ibid., 41.

123   *"vision-for-action channel"*: Ladislav Kesner, "The Role of Cognitive Competence in the Art Museum Experience," *Museum Management and Curatorship* 21, 1 (March 2006): 1–16.

Chapter Seven: Soundkill

126 *"As we listened"*: F. T. Marinetti, *Futurist Manifesto,* Umbro Apollonio, ed., Robert Brain et al., trans. (New York: Viking Press, 1973), 19–24.

126 *"Today, noise is triumphant"*: Luigi Russolo, "The Art of Noises: A Futurist Manifesto (Mar. 1913)" in *Modernism: An Anthology,* Lawrence S. Rainey, ed. (Malden, MA: Blackwell Publishing, 2005), 23.

127 *800,000 pamphlets:* Marjorie Perloff, " 'Violence and Precision': The Manifesto as Art Form," *Chicago Review* 34, 2 (Spring 1984), http://humanities.uchicago.edu/orgs/review/60th/pdfs/56bperloff.pdf.

127 *"Enough! Stop whispering"*: Anne Bowler, "Politics as Art: Italian Futurism and Fascism," *Theory and Society* 20, 6 (December 1991): 763–94.

127 *"Burn the gondolas"*: F. T. Marinetti, "Futurist Venice," *New York Times,* July 24, 1910.

128 *"The everlasting sound"*: *Early Western Travels: 1748–1846,* Reuben Gold Thwaite, ed. (Cleveland, OH: Arthur H. Clark Company, 1905), 230.

128 "sound out idols": Friedrich Nietzsche, *Twilight of the Idols,* R. J. Hollingdale, trans. (London: Penguin Books, 1990), 31.

129 *"Cannons gutting space"*: Luigi Russolo, *The Art of Noises,* Barclay Brown, trans. (New York: Pendragon Press, 1986), 26.

129 *Rome was becoming:* "Rome Starts Drive to Suppress Noise," *New York Times,* October 17, 1925.

130 *"When hot-rodding"*: Bettina Boxall, "Sound of Music?," *Los Angeles Times,* July 16, 1989.

130 *"A coachman who"*: Lawrence Baron, "Noise and Degeneration: Theodor Lessing's Crusade for Quiet," *Journal of Contemporary History* 17, 1 (January 1982): 165–78.

131 *names like "Sound Quake"*: Katherine Bishop, "Laws Aim to Turn Off Ear-Splitting 'Boom' Cars," *New York Times,* January 17, 1990.

131 *America's urban traffic:* Texas Environmental Profiles, http://www.texasep.org/html/air/air_5mob_carred.html

131 *driving delays in twenty-six:* Tom Vanderbilt, *Traffic* (New York: Knopf, 2008), 131.

132 *"These criminals are"*: catdaddybaycali@yahoo, e-mail to Noise Free
America, Listserv posting, May 24, 2008, noisefreeamerica@yahoo
groups.com.

133 *CalusaCustomConcepts*: "Who Cares About Words?," Florida Car
Radio blog, posted December 14, 2007, http://www.floridacaraudio
.com/ category/rant/.

134 *MP3 Pimp*: Robin Butler, interview by author, spring 2008.

137 *If you are 3 feet away*: Quiet Solution Decibel Chart, http://www
.quietsolution.com/Noise_Levels.pdf.

148 *Casey Sullivan*: Casey Sullivan, interview by author, spring 2008.

148 *Buzz Thompson*: Buzz Thompson, interview by author, spring 2008.

Chapter Eight: Freeway to Noise

155 *A recent European Environment Agency*: European Environment
Agency, "Transport at a Crossroads: TERM 2008: Indicators Tracking Transport and Environment in the European Union," EEA Report
no. 3/2009 (Copenhagen, 2009).

156 *Howard Stapleton developed*: Compound Security, http://www
.compoundsecurity.co.uk/mosquito-products-0.

156 *"a demented alarm clock"*: "Teen-Repellent to Be Regulated," *Health24*
(April 2008), www.health24.com/news/Teens/1-950,45864.asp.

157 *Teen Buzz*: Melissa Block, "Teens Turn 'Repeller' into Adult-Proof
Ringtone," *NPR*, May 26, 2006. Web site for the ringtone can be
found at www.teenbuzz.org.

157 *"I didn't know whether"*: ProSoundWeb Life Chat, interview of
Tom Danley, moderated by Keith Clark, March 12, 2002, www1
.prosoundweb.com/chat_psw/ transcripts/danley.shtml.

157 *"the Guy"*: Michael Heddon, interview by author, fall 2008.

158 *as Hillel Pratt*: Dr. Amanda Harry, "Wind Turbines, Noise and
Health," February 2007, http://www.windturbinenoisehealthhuman
rights.com/wtnoise_health_2007_a_barry.pdf.

160 *"We've been punishing"*: Clive Stafford Smith, "Welcome to 'the
Disco,'" *The Guardian*, June 19, 2008.

160 *"masking sound"*: Cynthia Kellogg, "Music in Dentist's Chair Soothes

Child and Adults," *New York Times*, August 12, 1960. Also see Thomas E. Morosko and Fred F. Simmons, "The Effect of Audio-Analgesia on Pain Threshold and Pain Tolerance," *Journal of Dental Research* 45 (1966): 1608–17.

160 *for use in childbirth:* Stacy V. Jones, "New Device for Seeing in Dark," *New York Times*, June 3, 1961.

161 *mounted a hostile campaign:* Benjamin Schwaid, "Audio-Analgesia May Be Hazardous," *The Journal of the American Dental Society of Anesthesiology* 7, 10 (December 1960): 24–25.

161 *Sound Pain Relief:* Sound Pain Relief, http://www.soundpainrelief .com.

161 *"awful sounds of the city":* Ron Alexander, "Stereo-to-Go and Only You Can Hear It; For the Thinking Man," *New York Times*, July 7, 1980.

162 *"There are buses":* Georgia Harbison, J. D. Reed, and Nick Balberman, "A Great Way to Snub the World," *Time*, May 18, 1981.

162 *When Sony initially:* Steve Crandall, "Sony Walkman History," tingilinde blog, October 19, 2003, http://tingilinde.typepad.com/ starstuff/2003/10/sony_walkman_hi.html.

162 *One of the popular:* "Classic Sony Walkman Commercial," YouTube, June 8, 1985, http://www.youtube.com/watch?v=iO8FDPtN_8M.

163 *220 million had been sold:* Phil Schiller announced this figure at the Apple Rock and Roll Event, Yerba Buena Theater, San Francisco, September 9, 2009.

163 *a total of 150 million:* Priya Johnson, "Timeline and the History of the Walkman," Buzzle.com, April 30, 2009, http://www.buzzle.com/ articles/timeline-and-history-of-the-walkman.html.

163 *New York City population:* Census figures, http://www.nyc.gov/html/ dcp/pdf/census/1790-2000_nyc_total_foreign_birth.pdf

164 *the population of inner London:* http://www.demographia.com/ dm-lonarea.htm.

164 *Tokyo, which also saw:* Tokyo Statistical Yearbook 2005, http://www .toukei.metro.tokyo.jp/tnenkan/2005/tn05qyte0510b.htm.

165 *"filter out distractions":* Dawn Foster, "Why I Love My iPod (Yes, This Is Work-Related)," *Web Worker Daily*, January 2, 2009, http://

webworkerdaily.com/2009/01/02/why-i-love-my-ipod-yes-this-is-work-related/. See comments especially.

166   *one in ten:* Gina Hughes, "One in 10 Minor Traffic Accidents Caused by 'Podestrians,'" Yahoo Tech blog, October 9, 2008, http://tech.yahoo.com/blogs/hughes/34543.

166   *When Dirksen Bauman:* Dirksen Bauman, interview by author, winter 2009.

167   *nine states banned the use:* Joyce Purnick, "Council Bill Seeks Headphone Curbs," *New York Times,* August 19, 1982.

167   *Woodbridge, New Jersey, went further:* "Jersey Township Passes Curb on Headphones," *New York Times,* July 12, 1982.

167   *The most authoritative:* "New iPod Listening Study Shows Surprising Behavior of Teens," ScienceDaily, February 28, 2009, http://www.sciencedaily.com/releases/2009/02/090218135054.htm.

Chapter Nine: Home Front

170   *Noise-Con 2008:* Noise-Con 2008, Hyatt Regency, Dearborn, Michigan, July 28–31, 2008.

174   *when John Deere proudly:* Marlund Hale, "Noise Control Foundation Session One," panel discussion at Noise-Con 2008, July 29, 2008.

176   *"viscoelastic material":* Green Glue, http://www.greengluecompany.com.

177   *the giant theater of Epidaurus:* "Ancient Greek Amphitheater: Why You Can Hear from Back Row," ScienceDaily, April 6, 2007, http://www.sciencedaily.com/releases/2007/04/070404162237.htm.

178   *by way of "pugging":* Theodore H. M. Prudon, "Deafening: An Early Form of Sound Insulation," *Bulletin of the Association for Preservation Technology* 7, 4 (1975): 5–13.

178   *"SILENCE, SILENCE":* Thomas Carlyle to Geraldine E. Jewsbury, June 15, 1840, The Carlyle Letters Online: A Victorian Cultural Reference (Durham, NC: Duke University Press), http://carlyleletters.dukejournals.org/cgi/content/full/12/1/lt-18400615-TC-GEJ-01?maxtoshow=&HITS=10&hits=10&RESULTFORMAT=&fulltex

t=%22SILENCE+SILENCE%22&searchid=1&FIRSTINDEX=0&r
esourcetype=HWCIT.

178 *"vile yellow Italian"*: John M. Picker, "The Soundproof Study: Victorian Professionals, Work Space, and Urban Noise," *Victorian
Studies* 42, 3 (April 1, 1999): 427–53. The subsequent quotation
from the *City Press* is also taken from Picker's wonderful essay, which
helped shape my thoughts on the Victorian soundproofing enterprise.

179 *"We are again building"*: Thomas Carlyle to James Marshall, September 19, 1853, The Carlyle Letters Online, http://carlyleletters.duke
journals.org/cgi/content/full/28/1/lt-18530919-TC-JMA-
01?maxtoshow=&HITS=10&hits=10&RESULTFORMAT=&fulltext
=We+are+again+building &searchid=1&FIRSTINDEX=0&re
sourcetype=HWCIT.

180 *"Irish laborers fetching"*: Ibid., Jane Carlyle to Thomas Carlyle, December 19, 1853, under Sourcenote, http://carlyleletters.dukejournals
.org/cgi/content/full/28/1/lt-18531219-JWC-TC-
01?maxtoshow=&HITS=10&hits=10&RESULTFORMAT=&fulltex
t=%22our+house+once+more+a+mere+dust-cloud&searchid=1&
FIRSTINDEX=0&resourcetype=HWCIT.

180 *"Now that I feel"*: Ibid., Jane Carlyle to John A. Carlyle, July 27, 1852,
http://carlyleletters.dukejournals.org/cgi/content/full/27/1/lt-18
520727-JWC-JAC-01?maxtoshow=&HITS=10&hits
=10&RESULTFORMAT=&fulltext=%22Now+that+I+feel+
the+noise%22&searchid=1&FIRSTINDEX=0&resourcetype=
HWCIT.

180 *shut himself up*: "Carlyle's Soundproof Room," *New York Times*, February 24, 1886.

180 *"was a flattering delusion"*: Jane Carlyle to Thomas Carlyle, July 21,
1853, The Carlyle Letters Online, under Sourcenote, http://carlyle
letters.dukejournals.org/cgi/content/full/28/1/lt-18530721-JWC-TC-
01?maxtoshow=&HITS=10&hits=10&RESULTFORMAT=&fulltex
t=%22was+a+flattering+delusion%22&searchid=1&FIRSTINDEX
=0&resourcetype=HWCIT#FN6_REF.

181 *Franz Kafka grew reliant*: Franz Kafka, *Letters to Felice*, Erich Heller

and Jurgen Börn, eds., James Stern and Elizabeth Duckworth, trans. (New York: Schocken Books, 1973), 449.

181 *Floyd Watson, author of*: Floyd Watson, *Sound-proof Partitions: An Investigation of the Acoustic Properties of Various Building Materials with Practical Applications* (Urbana, IL: University of Illinois Bulletin, March 1922), http://www.archive.org/stream/soundproofpartit00wat suoft#page/n1/mode/2up.

182 *When Shepherd Ivory Franz*: Shepherd Ivory Franz, "A Noiseless Room for Sound Experiments," *Science* 26, 677 (December 20, 1977): 878–81.

183 *"There is always something"*: John Cage, *Silence* (Middletown, CT: Wesleyan University Press, 1961), 8.

183 *"thick, elastic cushion"*: advertisement, *Western Architect & Engineer* 52–53 (1918): 152.

183 *"If it isn't sound-proof"*: Ibid.

183 *A captain affiliated*: "Use Seaweed for Soundproofing," *New York Times*, February 17, 1929.

183 *At a London trade show*: "Silent House Shown: Doors of One at London Can Be Slammed Without Noise," *New York Times*, September 21, 1930.

184 *Even the stolid United States*: "Problem of Sound-Proof House Engages Bureau of Standards," *New York Times*, October 2, 1927.

184 *A new chapel at Sing Sing*: "Sing Sing Chapel Opened: Sound-Proof Partitions Permit Two Services There at One Time," *New York Times*, September 2, 1929.

185 *"We don't need any more"*: "Lighter Views of Life in New York City," *New York Times*, May 2, 1909.

185 *"Preventing noise"*: R. V. Parsons, *Station WJZ*, December 26, 1929. Transcript in *City Noise: The Report of the Commission Appointed by Dr. Shirley W. Wynne, Commission of Health, to Study Noise in New York City and to Develop Means of Abating It*, Edward F. Brown et al., eds. (New York: Department of Health, 1930), 238.

185 *"punctuated by the penetrating*: "Anti-Noise Experts Experiment in Secret: Find Their Sound-Proof Room a 'Torture Chamber' When City's Clamor Is Reproduced There," *New York Times*, April 24, 1930.

185 *scientists from the Tokyo Hygienic:* "Longer Life Amidst Noise but Bad Effects Noted Also," *The Science News-Letter* 30, 802 (August 22, 1936): 119.

188 *"You can make your own":* Super Soundproofing Community Forum, May 7, 2008, http://supersoundproofing.com/forum/index.php?topic =2262.0.

188 *already patented Silence Machine:* Marina Murphy, " 'Silence Machine' Zaps Unwanted Noise," *New Scientist* (March 28, 2002).

189 *"a very, very, very large":* Andy Pollack, interview by author, 2009.

195 *"the quietest products":* Jeff Szymanski, Noise Control Foundation, Session One, panel discussion at Noise-Con 2008, July 29, 2008.

Chapter Ten: This Is War!

200 *"Clamor Against Noise":* Gladwin Hill, "Clamor Against Noise Rises Around the Globe," *New York Times*, September 3, 1972.

201 *On October 1, 1935:* "Mayor La Guardia's Plea and Proclamation in War on Noise," *New York Times*, October 1, 1935.

201 *a total of 5,317 warnings:* "Whole City Joins in War on Noise," *New York Times*, October 6, 1935.

201 *ballooned to 20,546:* "It's Still Bedlam-on-the-Subway," *New York Times*, September 29, 1940.

202 *"Make Rome as Quiet":* Arnaldo Cortesi, "Rome a New City in Humbler Things," *New York Times*, September 10, 1933.

202 *my great-grandfather:* "Physicians Combine to Abolish Noise," *New York Times*, August 5, 1912.

202 *During the late 1960s:* Catrice Jefferson, e-mail to author, June 2009. Ken Feith's summary of the history of the Noise Control Act was redacted for me by Catrice Jefferson, his very helpful colleague.

203 *Russell Train, who served:* Russell Train, interview by author, spring 2008.

204 *Dr. Rokhu Kim:* Dr. Rokhu Kim, interview by author and e-mail to author, 2008–2009. Kim was immensely helpful in my research into the WHO's noise policy efforts and the place of those efforts in the larger configuration of European environmental agencies.

204   *"So I guess he"*: "Pacoima Man Shot to Death Over Loud Car Stereo,"
      CBS Broadcasting, Inc., August 13, 2008, http://current.com/items/
      89203218_pacoima-man-shot-to-death-over-loud-car-stereo.htm.

205   *"Currently we have been"*: Captain Stitler, interview by author, spring
      2009.

206   *using the Internet*: Catrice Jefferson, presentation at Noise-Con
      2008, Hyatt Regency, Dearborn, Michigan, July 29, 2008.

206   *"sounding within public"*: Henry Strauss, "The Law and Noise:
      Wartime Regulations," *Quiet* 2, no. 12 (March 1941): pp.13–14.

207   *completed an MD*: Mrs. John A. Logan, *The Part Taken by Women in
      American History* (Wilmington, DE: Perry-Nalle Publishing Co.,
      1912), 602. Additional background biographical material appears in
      the entry on Mrs. Isaac Rice.

207   *"the finest view"*: Christopher Gray, "A Fading Reminder of Turn-of-
      the-Century Elegance," *New York Times*, August 24, 1997.

207   *of solid rock*: batgirl, "Rice's Gambit," Chess.com, September 29,
      2008, http://blog.chess.com/batgirl/rices-gambit.

207   *In the summer of 1905*: Mrs. Isaac Rice, "An Effort to Suppress
      Noise," *Forum* 37, 4 (April 1906). This article by Rice recounts in de-
      tail the history of her fight against tugboat noise.

209   *"useless and indiscriminate"*: "River Craft Ordered to End Their
      Noise," *New York Times*, November 25, 1906.

209   *occasional churlish skipper*: "Two Skippers Up for Loud Tooting,"
      New York Times, May 9, 1907.

210   *Rice was voted*: "Mrs. Rice Put at Head of Anti-Noise Society," *New
      York Times*, January 15, 1907.

211   *reproduced the noises*: "Canned Din Phonograph," *New York Times*,
      October 31, 1908.

211   *hospital quiet zones*: "Makes Quiet Zones for City Hospitals," *New
      York Times*, June 24, 1907.

211   *"that deplorable craving"*: Mrs. Isaac Rice, "The Children's Hospital
      Branch of the Society for the Supression of Unnecessary Noise,"
      Forum 39, 4 (April 1908). The essay describes this campaign in
      detail.

213   *"efforts were baffled"*: Frank Parker, "The War," *The New McClure's*

(December 1928). I later discovered that the automobile was also identified as the source of the society's collapse in Mrs. Isaac Rice's *New York Times* obituary, published November 5, 1929.

213   *the first private:* batgirl, "Rice's Gambit."

213   *"high-handed outrage":* "Automobile Cars Barred: Jefferson Seligman and Isaac L. Rice Lose Park Permits," *New York Times*, December 16, 1899.

213   *Their daughter Dorothy:* Frank L. Valiant, "Motor Cycling Fad Strikes Fair Sex," *New York Times*, January 15, 1911.

213   *One madcap flight:* "From Her Sick Bed Plans New Flights," *New York Times*, November 28, 1916.

214   *"fifty-five sensation":* E. E. Free, "How Noisy Is New York?," *Forum* 75, 3 (February 1926): 21–24.

215   *"a strangely fitted":* Shirley H. Wynne, "Saving New York from Its Own Raucous Din," *New York Times*, August 3, 1930.

215   *"environmental noise monitoring":* Jim Weir, interview by author, spring 2008.

216   *"They order these things":* Mrs. Isaac Rice, "An Effort to Suppress Noise."

217   *Manvell told me:* Doug Manvell, interview by author, B&K plant and at Colin Nugent's EU office. I also carried on an e-mail correspondence with Manvell and I am grateful for the investment of time and energy he made to help me understand both B&K's business and the larger EU noise-mapping initiative.

217   *European Noise Directive:* European Commission/European Union, documents of European Union Noise Policy, http://ec.europa.eu/environment/noise/directive.htm.

218   *"The experienced Harley":* "Harley-Davidson: The Sound of a Legend," *Automotive Industries* (November 2002), http://findarticles.com/p/articles/mi_m3012/is_11_182/ai_95614097/?tag=content;col1.

218   *the noise of Jaguar:* Paul Jennings, interview by author, spring 2008.

221   *historical soundscaping:* Max Dixon, e-mail to author. My understanding of the potential of soundscaping was hugely assisted by e-mail exchanges with Max Dixon, who provided me with many key references and who also was instrumental in expanding my grasp of quiet

spaces. Colin Grimwood, who introduced me to Max Dixon, also provided me with important insights into these subjects, in particular the idea of iconic sounds.

221   *areas with sound barriers:* Jian Kang, Wei Yang, and Dr. Mei Zhang, "Sound Environment and Acoustic Comfort in Urban Spaces," in *Designing Open Spaces in the Urban Environment: A Bioclimatic Approach,* Dr. Marialena Nikopoulou, ed. (Center for Renewable Energy Sources, 2004), 32–37, http://alpha.cres.gr/ruros/dg_en.pdf.

222   *while falling water:* G. R. Watts et al., "Investigation of Water Generated Sounds for Masking Noise and Improving Tranquillity," presented at Inter-Noise 2008: From Silence to Harmony, Shanghai, China, October 26–29, 2008, http://tadn.net/blog/wp-content/uploads/2008/10/in08_0375.pdf.

222   *Honda recently paid:* The Gigdoggy blog, "Groove Encrusted Asphalt to Bring Musical Roads at the Top of the Charts," September 23, 2008, http://gigdoggy.wordpress.com/2008/09/23/groove-encrusted-asphalt-to-bring-musical-roads-at-the-top-of-the-charts/. The fate of this project was explained to me by Claire Shepherd of Bureau Veritas Acoustics and Vibration Group.

224   "Art of Cartography": "Jorge Luis Borges, "On Exactitude in Science," Andrew Hurtey, trans. in *Collector Fiction* (New York: Viking, 1998), 325.

227   *"All in all":* Colin Nugent, interviews by author, 2008–2009. In addition to interviewing Nugent in Copenhagen in 2008, we conducted a phone interview and e-mail exchange in 2009 in the course of which he helped me follow the progress of the END.

227   *In 2012, member states:* Europa: Summaries of EU Legislation, http://europa.eu/legislation_summaries/environment/noise_pollution/121180_en.htm.

228   *specific health hazards:* Dr. Wolfgang Babisch, *Transportation Noise and Cardiovascular Risk* (Berlin: Umweltbundesamt, January 2006).

229   *stringent set of noise: Noise Night Guidelines for Europe* (World Health Organization, 2007), http://ec.europa.eu/health/ph_projects/2003/action3/docs/2003_08_frep_en.pdf.

230   *The cost of noise mapping:* John Hinton, e-mail to author. Estimate

given me in e-mail exchange with Hinton, who created the pioneering Birmingham noise map.

230   *"Important as the measurement"*: Henry J. Spooner, "The Progress of Noise Abatement," in *City Noise II*, James Flexner, ed. (New York: Department of Health, 1932), 27–37.

232   *"How solemn it is"*: Søren Kierkegaard, "The Lily in the Field and the Bird of the Air," in *The Essential Kierkegaard*, Howard V. Hong and Edna H. Hong, eds. (Princeton, NJ: Princeton University Press, 1980), 335.

Chapter Eleven: The Dragon Trap

233   *"do away with unnecessary"*: City Noise: The Report of the Commission Appointed by Dr. Shirley W. Wynne, Commission of Health, to Study Noise in New York City and to Develop Means of Abating It, Edward F. Brown et al., eds. (New York: Department of Health, 1930), 273.

233   *"Behold the noise"*: *City Noise II*, James Flexner, ed. (New York: Department of Health, 1932).

234   *conversation with Michael Merzenich*: Michael Merzenich, interview by author, fall 2008.

234   *reportedly some 75 percent*: Marie Evans Schmidt et al., "The Effects of Background Television on the Toy Play Behavior of Very Young Children," www.srcd.org/journals/cdev/0-0/Schmidt.pdf.

235   *a study at the Children's*: "Brains of Autistic Children Slower at Processing Sound," *New Scientist* (December 1, 2008), http://www.newscientist.com/article/dn16174-brains-of-autistic-children-slower-at-processing-sound.html.

236   *guardian of the enlightened teacher*: Japanese Buddhist Statuary, http://www.onmarkproductions.com/html/dragon.shtml.

236   *the splendid Portland Japanese Garden*: Virginia Harmon, e-mail to author, winter 2009. I visited the Portland Japanese Garden early in 2009. I subsequently carried on an e-mail exchange with Harmon in which she elaborated on some of the ideas she presented during our tours and pointed me to various references.

238   *Musō Soseki gathered*: Graham Parkes, "Further Reflection on the

Rock Garden of Ryōanji: From Yūgen to Kire-tsuzuki," in *The Aesthetic Turn: Reading Eliot Deutsch on Comparative Philosophy*, Roger T. Ames, ed. (Peru, IL: Open Court Publishing Company, 2000), 15–17.

238 *"multiplicity of perspectives"*: Eliot Deutsch, *Studies in Comparative Aesthetics* (Honolulu: University of Hawaii Press, 1975), 25–32.

241 *aesthetic of imperfection*: Yuriko Saito, "The Japanese Aesthetics of Imperfection and Insufficiency," *The Journal of Aesthetics and Art Criticism* 55, 4 (Autumn 1997): 377–85.

241 *"If man were never to fade"*: Ibid., 382.

243 *"an institution that made"*: A. L. Sadler, "The Tea Philosophy of Japan, a Western Evaluation," *Pacific Affairs* 2, 10 (October 1929): 635–44.

244 *"I've resigned myself"*: Hansel Bauman, interview by author, 2009. I conducted multiple interviews with Bauman in 2009. It is impossible to overstate the importance of the insights he provided me in shaping my thoughts on Deaf Space and the architectural tradition that project engages with.

247 *"When the brain"*: Michael Chorost, interview by author, August 24, 2009.

248 *"The privation of hearing"*: *The Deaf Experience: Classics in Language and Education*, Harlan Lane, ed. (Washington, DC: Gallaudet University Press, 2006), 37.

248 *"children born to opulence"*: Jonathan Rée, *I See a Voice: Deafness, Language and the Senses—A Philosophical History* (New York: Metropolitan Books, 1999), 185–86.

248 *a Deaf school in*: M. Miles, "Deaf People Living and Communicating in African Histories, c. 960s–1960s," *Independent Living Institute* (2005), http://www.independentliving.org/docs7/miles2005a.html.

250 *Toni Lacolucci was training*: Toni Lacolucci, interview by author, 2008. She gave generously of her time and energy on numerous occasions to help me understand her experience of deafness. She also helped me form my initial contacts at Gallaudet University.

252 *"everything touches you"*: Josh Swiller, instant message to author, January 30, 2009.

253 *"liberal appropriation of space"*: Frederick Law Olmsted, "Report of

Olmsted, Vaux & Co., Architects," in Edward Miner Gallaudet, *History of the College for the Deaf 1857–1907* (Washington, DC: Gallaudet College Press, 1983), 236–38.

256   *"great primary (geometrical) forms"*: Le Corbusier, *Toward a New Architecture* (New York: Dover Publications, 1986), 29–30.

257   *"endlessly changing qualities"*: Louis Kahn, "Silence and Light II," in *Louis Kahn: Essential Texts,* Robert Twombly, ed. (New York: W. W. Norton & Company, 2003), 232.

257   *"when the dust is cleared"*: Ibid., 240.

257   *"prevalence of spirit"*: Louis Kahn, "Space and the Inspirations," in *Louis Kahn: Essential Texts,* 225.

258   *Quiet Party*: Rebfile.com, www.rebfile.com/quietpartyabout.htm.

259   *paired with Erin*: Erin Kelly, author's partner for Bauman's project.

260   *young man named Michael*: Michael Hubbs, interview by author, spring 2009.

261   *a Deaf graduate student*: Robert Sirvage, interview by author, winter 2009. Sirvage shared with me extremely important insights into the Deaf experience both at Gallaudet and during a conference we attended at MIT.

263   *"maluma" and "takete"*: V. S. Ramachandran and E. M. Hubbard, "Synaesthesia—A Window into Perception, Thought and Language," *Journal of Consciousness Studies* 8, 12 (2001): 3–34.

266   *with the Dalai Lama*: Dalai Lama, interview by Werner Herzog, *Wheel of Time* (Werner Herzog FilmProduktion, 2003).

267   *group called PDM*: Alex Cequea, "How to Conduct Your Own Public Meditations," Publication Meditation Project, http://alexcequea. type pad.com/my_weblog/files/Public_Meditation_Project_How-to.pdf.

268   *"the ambient soul"*: Louis Kahn, "Silence and Light II," 236.

Chapter Twelve: Silent Finale

270   *"It may metaphorically"*: Charles Darwin, *The Origin of Species* (New York: New American Library, 1958), 80.

271   *Darwin makes the silent*: Adam Phillips, *Darwin's Worms: On Life Stories and Death Stories* (New York: Basic Books, 2000).

271 *"a most paradoxical mixture"*: Charles Darwin, *The Voyage of the Beagle* (New York: Modern Library, 2001), 12.

271 *"silenced every one"*: Charles Darwin, *The Life and Letters of Charles Darwin: Including an Autobiographical Chapter, volume 1*, Francis Darwin, ed. (London: John Murray, 1887), 77.

271 *"The agriculturist in ploughing"*: Charles Darwin, "On the Formation of Mould," *Proceedings of the Geological Society of London* 2 (1838): 576.

273 *where I met a friend*: Natalie deSouza, interview by author, summer 2009. DeSouza did more to give me a grounding in a spectrum of scientific disciplines than I can say, along with providing me with many references that were vital to my research.

273 *she would be* years: Claire Benard, interview by author, summer 2009. In addition to the assistance provided me on that summer afternoon, Benard graciously invited me back to the lab on another occasion in the midst of a move to her own lab in Massachusetts. She also answered many of my questions about research at the lab in subsequent e-mail exchanges.

274 *"There is no such thing"*: John Cage, *Silence* (Middletown, CT: Wesleyan University Press, 1961), 8.

277 *trace it back to Nietzsche*: Lawrence Baron, "Noise and Degeneration: Theodor Lessing's Crusade for Quiet," *Journal of Contemporary History* 17, 1 (January 1982): 165–78.

278 *"to change human beings"*: Theodor Lessing, "Jewish Self-Hatred," in *The Weimar Sourcebook*, Anton Kaes, Martin Jay, and Edward Dimendberg, eds. (Berkeley and Los Angeles: University of California Press, 1994), 271.

278 *Lessing idolized Rice*: "Germans to War on Street Noises," *New York Times*, August 9, 1908.

280 *In 1933, Lessing himself*: "Lessing, German Refugee, Slain in Prague; Attacks on Others Abroad Are Feared," *New York Times*, August 31, 1933.

281 *"spend all this"*: Colin Grimwood, interview by author, spring 2009.

281 *High-density development*: *Sounder City: The Mayor's Ambient Noise Strategy* (London: Greater London Authority, 2004), 181–87.

281 *A recent Swedish study:* Mistra: The Foundation for Strategic Environmental Research, "The Right to a Good Soundscape," February 29, 2008, www.mistra-research.se/mistra/english/news/news/the righttoagoodsoundscape.5.61632b5e117dec92f47800028054 .html.

282 *In Pompeii, for example:* Mary Beard, *The Fires of Vesuvius: Pompeii Lost and Found* (Cambridge, MA: Belknap Press of Harvard University Press, 2008), 62.

282 *the ancient Greek city: City Noise: The Report of the Commission Appointed by Dr. Shirley W. Wynne, Commission of Health, to Study Noise in New York City and to Develop Means of Abating It,* Edward F. Brown et al., eds. (New York: Department of Health, 1930), 5–6.

284 *friend named Lyman:* Lyman Casey, interview by author, spring 2009. I'm grateful to Casey for the time he took out from his busy teaching schedule to help deepen my appreciation of the noise situation faced by teachers today. My thanks go out to all the students of Brooklyn Preparatory High School who shared with me their experiences of noise and silence with such candor and grace.

287 *"practice, and a lot of it":* Jonathan Edmonds, interview by author, spring 2009.

291 *"Are people getting":* Arline Bronzaft, interview by author, spring 2008. I later interviewed Bronzaft at her home and held additional phone interviews with her. She was instrumental in helping me understand the work of antinoise activists at the grassroots level around the country.

293 *perception is differentiation:* Maurice Merleau-Ponty, *The Visible and the Invisible,* Alphonso Lingis, trans. (Evanston, IL: Northwestern University Press, 1968), 197.

Author's Note

There were many works that helped me formulate the ideas in this book beyond those that contributed to specific passages and are listed in the notes.

I found myself returning in particular to R. Murray Schafer's remarkable book *The Soundscape: Our Sonic Environment and the Tuning of the World* (Rochester, VT: Destiny Books, 1977), as well as to various works of George Steiner, such as the T. S. Eliot Memorial Lectures of 1970, collected in *In Bluebeard's Castle: Some Notes Towards the Redefinition of Culture* (New Haven, CT: Yale University Press, 1971), along with his essays in *Language and Silence: Essays on Language. Literature, and the Inhuman* (New Haven, CT: Yale University Press, 1967). Susan Sontag's essay "The Aesthetics of Silence," in *Styles of Radical Will* (New York: Dell Publishing, 1967), was also a valuable source.

When I began shaping my thoughts about the relationship between Theodor Lessing and Julia Barnett Rice, two essays were of great significance: Lawrence Baron, "Noise and Degeneration: Theodor Lessing's Crusade for Quiet, *Journal of Contemporary History* 17, 1 (January 1982): 165–78; and Karin Bijsterveld, "The Diabolical Symphony of the Mechanical Age: Technology and Symbolism of Sound in European and North American Noise Abatement Campaigns, 1900–40, *Social Studies of Science* 31, 1 (February 2001): 37–70. I also benefited from reading Peter Payer, "The Age of Noise: Early Reactions in Vienna, 1870–1914," *Journal of Urban History* 33, 5 (July 2007): 773–93.

Many books by Thomas Merton were important references, especially *Mystics and Zen Masters* (New York: Dell Publishing, 1961); *The Sign of Jonas* (New York: Harcourt, 1981); and *The Silent Life* (New York: Farrar, Straus and Giroux, 1957).

Other books that contributed to my interpretation of the noise/silence problem and potential solutions include:

Jacques Attali, *Noise: The Political Economy of Music*, Brian Massumi, trans. (Minneapolis, MN: University of Minnesota Press, 1989)

H-Dirksen L. Bauman, ed., *Open Your Eyes: Deaf Studies Talking* (Minneapolis, MN: University of Minnesota Press, 2008)

Peter Burke, *The Art of Conversation* (Ithaca, NY: Cornell University Press, 1993)

Derwas J. Chitty, *The Desert a City* (Crestwood, NY: St. Vladimir's Seminary Press, 1966)

Harlan Lane, *When the Mind Hears: A History of the Deaf* (New York: Vintage Books, 1989)

Oliver Sacks, *Seeing Voices* (New York: Vintage Books, 2000)

William C. Stebbins, *The Acoustic Sense of Animals* (Cambridge: Harvard University Press, 1983)

Jun'chirō Tanizaki, *In Praise of Shadows*, Thomas J. Harper and Edward G. Seidensticker, trans. (Sedwick, ME: Leete's Island Books, Inc., 1977)

Emily Thompson, *The Soundscape of Modernity: Architectural Acoustics and the Culture of Listening in America, 1900–1933* (Cambridge, MA: MIT Press, 2002)

Helen Waddell, *The Desert Fathers* (Ann Arbor, MI: University of Michigan Press, 1957)

Index